PENGUIN BOOKS

THE TAKEOVER

Stephen Frey is Vice President of Corporate Finance at the Westdeutsche Landesbank in New York. He lives in Princeton, New Jersey. *The Takeover* is his first novel, and has already been sold for motion pictures. His new novel, *The Vulture Fund*, is published by Michael Joseph and forthcoming in Penguin.

The Takeover and *The Vulture Fund*, both read by Colin Stinton, are also available as Penguin Audiobooks.

STEPHEN FREY

THE TAKEOVER

PENGUIN BOOKS

PENGUIN BOOKS

Published by the Penguin Group
Penguin Books Ltd, 27 Wrights Lane, London W8 5TZ, England
Penguin Books USA Inc., 375 Hudson Street, New York, New York 10014, USA
Penguin Books Australia Ltd, Ringwood, Victoria, Australia
Penguin Books Canada Ltd, 10 Alcorn Avenue, Toronto, Ontario, Canada M4V 3B2
Penguin Books (NZ) Ltd, 182–190 Wairau Road, Auckland 10, New Zealand

Penguin Books Ltd, Registered Offices: Harmondsworth, Middlesex, England

First published by Michael Joseph 1995
Published in Penguin Books 1996
3 5 7 9 10 8 6 4 2

Printed in England by Clays Ltd, St Ives plc

For my wife, Lil,
and our daughters, Christina and Ashley.
You mean so much to me.

PROLOGUE

February 1992

Life was good. Andrew Falcon was about to come into a tremendous amount of money—he hoped. Only fifteen months before, he had become the youngest partner in the 142-year history of Winthrop, Hawkins & Company, Wall Street's oldest and most prestigious investment-banking firm. He inhaled deeply from the Macanudo cigar, leaned back in his wing chair, and blew thick smoke gently toward the high ceiling of the Racquet Club, the staid New York City gentlemen's establishment. Typically, he didn't smoke a cigar, but tonight it tasted good.

Falcon's head was spinning. The annual partners' dinner—his first, since last year had been his first as a partner—was four hours old. He had enjoyed several Glenlivet cocktails prior to the meal and a bottle of cabernet with his filet mignon. Now he noticed the white gloved waiters beginning to uncork magnum bottles of Dom Pérignon.

It would take several minutes for the waiters to serve all seventy-six partners, and Andrew needed to maintain his stone-calm composure. In a very short time the annual bonuses would be distributed, and the anticipation was gut-wrenching. This wasn't the corporate "ten thousand dollars and a pat on the back" bonus. This was real money, investment-banking money. Falcon reached for the snifter of cognac standing before him on the linen tablecloth.

The tables were arranged so that they formed a large U shape in the dimly lit, mahogany-panelled room. The chairman and most senior partner, E. Granville Winthrop IV, great-great-grandson of the firm's founder—and a direct descendant of the Massachusetts Bay Colony's first governor—sat at the head of the arrangement. The other partners were seated on either side of Winthrop according to their tenure with the firm. The most tenured of the partners sat immediately to Granville's left and right and so on away from him as the individual's length of service to the firm decreased.

Falcon sat at one end of the U, directly across the room from Roland Thompson. Thompson was a thin, Waspish-looking man of thirty-eight who, even though his eyesight was 20/20, wore tortoiseshell glasses. Thompson had made partner two years ago. Almost overnight he had guided Winthrop, Hawkins to the top of the convertible-debt league tables. This year, however, it was rumored among the partners that Thompson had made some very bad trades and lost the firm a great deal of money. But only Granville, the four other members of the Management Committee, and Thompson knew for certain. Losses in specific groups of Winthrop, Hawkins were not disclosed to the partners. Of course, that did not stop them from speculating among one another. Andrew noted that Thompson had become drunk early in the evening. He also noted that no one seemed eager to speak with Thompson during cocktails. Now the man was so intoxicated his head was almost resting on the table.

Thompson's group was not the only area of the firm rumored to be bleeding. Revenues for the Fixed Income and Equity Underwriting divisions, two of the firm's flagship units, were supposed to be below the healthy numbers of previous years. Origination, underwriting, and trading figures in those groups were all off. Off as a result of what the President of the United States termed economic stability—slow but steady growth. And what the investment bankers called anemia. They didn't like slow and steady. They needed volatility to generate their huge profits. And there hadn't been much of that lately. Andrew puffed on the cigar. Perhaps he should not expect so much from this dinner.

Falcon glanced toward the head of the table. Granville was smiling in his restrained, guarded way at something one of the other senior partners was saying. It was the same way Granville smiled at any piece of information, be it good, bad, or indifferent. Andrew scrutinized Winthrop's face, but there was no way to determine anything about the bonuses from that visage. Granville was the consummate "I" banker, as investment bankers were called in Street parlance. His face never revealed his feelings. Because you could lose a deal that way.

Andrew relaxed into the comfortable chair, grinning. Granville acted differently away from Wall Street. As a rule, he didn't become overly friendly with others at the firm, but he had made an exception in Falcon's case. In the past four years, Andrew had become an increasingly frequent weekend guest at Winthrop's sprawling, oceanfront East Hampton estate—weekends Falcon wasn't putting together another multimillion-dollar deal. There Andrew had learned of Granville's personal side. He had learned of Granville's love of Thoroughbred racehorses—of which he kept four at the grounds' stables; of his prized antique gun collection; and of his huge yacht. They would sail all day with a crew of ten, then return at sunset to a delicious dinner prepared and served by the estate's staff. After dinner Andrew and Granville would retire to the mansion's venerable study to break open a bottle of hundred-year-old Scotch and discuss business and politics. They would talk for hours, and Falcon would commit to memory any shred of advice Granville imparted.

"What's so goddamn funny?"

Falcon turned. The speaker was Jim Kunkowski, the partner who headed Winthrop, Hawkins' interest-rate swaps desk. The smile faded from Falcon's face. "Nothing." It was the first word Falcon had said to Kunkowski despite sitting next to him for the past two hours. But that was investment banking. There were stories of men sharing offices for years and saying nothing to each other. They were there to make money. That was all.

Kunkowski was not a pleasant man. His temper was legendary, and it was no secret that people in his group despised him. But until this past year he had earned a great deal of money for the firm, so no one could complain about him openly. Making money was the bottom line at Winthrop, Hawkins, and he had been producing. But this year Kunkowski had lost a great deal of money, and the sharks were circling. "Nothing." Andrew said the word again quietly and turned away.

Falcon relaxed into the chair and closed his eyes. The Mergers & Acquisitions Group, the most profitable area of Winthrop, Hawkins, and the one in which he labored fourteen hours a day, was also seeing a decline in income. But Falcon was not worried about his position, even though other investment-banking firms were laying off M&A specialists in droves. The senior people at Winthrop, Hawkins loved him.

Granville Winthrop had made that clear just yesterday when they met in the senior partner's ornate office on the tenth floor of the firm's headquarters at 72 Wall Street. The two had laughed about the fact that Granville's office was on the tenth floor and not higher in the skyscraper, because the tenth floor was as high as New York City's fire-engine ladders could reach. And in the next breath Granville had showered Falcon with compliments. "Despite the difficult times," Granville had said, "you doubled your fee generation this year. You originated several important and visible transactions and brought a number of new, high-profile clients into the firm. We are all proud of you. Keep up the good work." Andrew could still hear the words.

There should be no need for Falcon to worry about his bonus. It ought to be at least fifty thousand dollars more than the two-hundred-and-fifty-thousand-dollar bonus he had earned last year as a vice president. But with the firm potentially performing poorly, Falcon realized that the compliments in Granville's office might have been intended to take the place of a good deal of this year's bonus. And he needed the money terribly. Somehow last year's two hundred and fifty thousand dollars was gone, despite being supplemented by his hundred-thousand-dollar annual salary.

Falcon opened his eyes and took another sip of the cognac. Did he have the fortitude to pull off what he was planning? Would he follow through on his convictions? Perhaps, even if the bonus was not what he hoped, he should remain conservative.

As the last glass of champagne was poured, Granville Winthrop rose slowly from his chair. Andrew watched the senior partner through the rivulets of cognac streaming down the sides of the snifter. Perhaps it was the distortion of the glass, but Granville seemed much older than the man with whom he had visited yesterday.

He moved stiffly toward a slightly raised podium in one corner of the room, pausing several times to bend down and whisper to some of the older partners seated near him. They treated him like royalty, several of them standing as he approached, nodding nervously at everything he said.

Falcon glanced about the room. The all-male partnership—there had never been a female partner at Winthrop, Hawkins—continued to speak to one another, but the noise level of the room subsided significantly as the men pretended not to notice Granville approach the podium.

The partnership was about to learn just how poorly the firm had performed this year, and they were nervous. A tremendous tension pervaded the large room, a tension Falcon could not sense, this being his first partners' dinner. Normally the men would be in a raucous mood by now, intoxicated not only by the liquor but also by the prospect of the money they knew they were about to receive. But this was the first time in many years that profits were rumored to be down. And though the majority of the partnership was unaware of the extent to which earnings had declined, they were certain, as a result of hushed, private conversations in the firm's rest rooms, in lonely conference rooms, and at secluded lunches away from Wall Street, that profits were definitely down.

Now each man was to find out how the Management Committee—the ruling body of the world's premier investment bank—truly perceived him as an individual. Those who were in favor would probably still receive strong bonuses even if they or their areas had not performed well, because for whatever reason they were liked. Because they had the correct last name, or the right country club membership, or a trophy wife who had been subtly made available to one of the Management Committee this past year.

Those who weren't in favor would likely receive nothing. It was called the "Sanction" at Winthrop, Hawkins. No bonus whatsoever. It meant that the Management Committee had determined you to be undesirable and wanted you gone. They waited until the economy was down to clean house. That way they could blame the denial of bonus on difficult times. But in reality, they did it because they didn't like you. They did it to send a message. And the message was: Get out. There was always enough money to go around at Winthrop, Hawkins.

The Sanction had last been delivered in 1981, over a decade ago. And while it was true that no bonus would be distributed to a man receiving the Sanction, the firm would buy back his partnership interest immediately, at full value—which meant millions, even on an after-tax basis. The pain of the Sanction was not so much financial as psychological. It meant the world's elite no longer wanted to associate with you; that for whatever reason, you did not measure up. And everyone in Wall Street's exclusive club would know.

Granville reached the podium. Andrew leaned forward and watched as the silver-haired senior partner painfully lifted himself to the lectern. Granville always struggled when he walked. His right leg had been torn apart by a sniper's bullet in Korea and had never healed properly, or so the story went.

He adjusted the small, gold-plated spotlight on the podium, then extracted a pair of half-lens reading glasses from his tuxedo jacket pocket and balanced them on his thin, patrician nose. As if on cue, the room fell silent. Conversations were abandoned in midsentence.

Suddenly, Granville thrust his champagne glass into the air. "Gentlemen, I bid you a prosperous new year!"

As one, the men slammed their shoes on the floor and champagne glasses in hand, rose from their seats. "Here, here!" The voices rose in unison, filling the great room.

Several of the partners glanced at Falcon to see if he had been caught unaware of the tradition. But he had risen exactly at the proper moment. The tradition was not to be revealed outside the room, but Andrew hadn't missed a beat. It was a good sign. It meant that their newest partner was adept at obtaining inside information, which in the long run could only mean greater profits for the partnership. To these men, inside information was only illegal at the SEC. It was an essential part of the business. A risk you ran. Andrew would never tell anyone that Granville Winthrop himself had disclosed the protocol yesterday in his office, because one never disclosed his source of inside information. That was the law.

"Mr. President, would you please give the partnership a synopsis of the financial results of Winthrop, Hawkins & Company for the fiscal year ended December thirty-first?"

"Yes, Mr. Chairman," Ben Weingarten answered from his position to the right of the chair Granville had vacated.

The partnership, resplendent in identical black tuxedos and studded white dress shirts, still thrusting champagne glasses aloft, held its collective breath. Falcon could almost hear the men's hearts pounding.

Weingarten read from an ancient leather-bound notebook. His voice was full and clear. "Mr. Chairman, for the year ended December thirty-first the partnership earned, before any employee incentive distributions, five hundred seventy-four million dollars, a six-percent decrease from last year."

Five hundred seventy-four million dollars! Falcon could not believe it. He performed several quick calculations. The figure worked out to well over seven million dollars per partner. And this was a down year. Even if the five members of the Management Committee appropriated twenty percent of the profits for themselves and set aside another fifteen percent for all of the other nonpartner employee bonuses, almost three hundred and seventy-five million remained. That was still close to five million dollars for each of the non–Management Committee partners.

Income figures were never released to anyone but the men in this room, Winthrop, Hawkins's accountants, and the Internal Revenue Service. It was one of Wall Street's last great secrets. Despite all his efforts, Falcon had been unable to access this information in his years as a nonpartner. Now that he knew, he was astounded. Perhaps he needed to rethink his decision.

The partnership seemed to exhale a collective sigh of relief. Profits were down but not as significantly as they had anticipated. Perhaps there would be no bloodshed after all.

"Thank you, Mr. President." Winthrop paused as he surveyed the men before him. "To your good health, gentlemen." The senior partner brought the glass to his lips and continued to drink until the pale golden liquid was completely consumed.

The rest of the partnership followed suit, every man standing until the last glass was empty. Then the men sat and waited as the white-gloved attendants refilled the glasses.

"Fellow partners, I will not take a great deal of your time tonight. I know that you are much more interested in the contents of what lies beside me than in what I have to say"—Winthrop gestured toward the seventy-six sealed envelopes stacked neatly on a sterling silver tray atop a stand next to the podium—"but I feel compelled to say a few words before I distribute the envelopes."

The partnership shifted uncomfortably in its seats. There was an ominous tone to Granville's voice.

"As you all have just heard, profits were down this year. And remember"—Winthrop paused for effect—"your personal cash flow will be cut significantly because of the high tax rates on the so-called wealthy the new administration has been able to ramrod through Congress."

The appropriate grumble rippled through the room at the mention of high taxes.

Winthrop continued. "Still, the profit decrease is an unacceptable development, even in the face of a difficult economy. A completely unacceptable development."

Here it came. The partners were suddenly on the edge of their seats again, particularly the middle-aged men who had experienced the last cleansing in 1981. Six men had received the Sanction that year.

"In addition to the decline in profits, we had other extraordinary cash needs. We completed the renovation of our offices. We installed several state-of-the-art computer systems. And we purchased the money-management firm of Bates, Hilger in July. And since we decided, as a firm, not to allow any of Bates, Hilger's senior managers to become partners here at Winthrop, Hawkins, we were forced to pay the purchase price completely in cash. In the long run that acquisition will pay off handsomely for us. We should thank our newest partner, Mr. Falcon, for initiating and negotiating the purchase on our behalf." Granville nodded in Andrew's direction.

Immediately Falcon's gaze dropped to the tablecloth. He sensed the eyes of the partnership upon him. He knew that not all of the men approved of the transaction, primarily because it took money out of their pockets in the current year.

"All of these developments have used cash. Therefore, gentlemen, do not be surprised if your bonuses are lower than last year. We on the Management Committee have been extremely discriminating, and we have rewarded your efforts based solely upon performance—something we have drifted away from in the past because of our robust earnings."

It was as if a strong riptide had suddenly swept through the room. The men held tightly to the meat-stained tablecloths, their clenched knuckles turning white. Their faces became grave, giving away the great strain each felt.

Granville nodded to the waiters, who quickly picked up predetermined sets of the envelopes and distributed them with speed and precision to the appropriate recipients.

Falcon stared at the plain cream-colored envelope set before him on the tablecloth. Neatly typed on the front of the envelope was simply his name—at least the name he had given to Winthrop, Hawkins seven years ago, the one he had given to Harvard Business School two years prior to that, and the one he had given to the University of Pennsylvania four years before that. Andrew William Falcon. Not his name by birth.

Life, as everyone on Wall Street knew, came down to a few vitally important seconds. Moments when all of the research and preparation either paid off or didn't. When the deal was won or lost. This was one of those moments.

Falcon inhaled deeply, terribly conscious of his breathing. Despite the alcohol's effect, his senses were suddenly aroused, and he was aware of every movement in the room. The adrenaline coursed through his body.

Light-blue Tiffany boxes had been positioned next to each partner's place setting since the beginning of dinner. In the box was a sterling silver letter opener engraved with the partner's name and the date—a date which would live in each man's memory forever, positively or negatively. Some of these men could barely remember their wedding days, but these dinners remained vivid in their memories.

Falcon reached for the box next to his unused dessert fork, removed the letter opener, and slid its protective blue felt covering from the polished silver. He stared at the opener for a moment. Then, deliberately, he turned the envelope onto its face, positioned the sharp point of the instrument into the slightly lifted back flap, and sliced open the small package. The paper tore neatly, and he was vaguely aware that seventy-five other envelopes were tearing just as neatly at exactly the same moment. Falcon swallowed and removed the contents—nothing more than a small piece of paper upon which again was typed his name, and just beneath, a number. His eyesight blurred slightly as he attempted to focus on the figures. Blood pounded in his brain. Suddenly his senses numbed. One million dollars. He blinked and stared at the figure again. A million dollars!

It was more money than some people earned in a lifetime. More money than his father, a foundry worker still living in a dingy row house of west Philadelphia—the same row house in which Falcon had been raised—could possibly imagine. It was not the five million he had calculated as each non–Management Committee partner's share of the firm's net income, but after all, he was only a first-year partner, the firm had incurred other cash flow requirements this past year, and some capital had to remain with the partnership to support future growth. There were senior partners at New York's most prestigious law firms not earning bonuses as grotesque as this—men and women who had been working at the law for decades. It was a huge amount of money for a man barely thirty-one. It was a huge amount of money for any human being.

But he felt no guilt over the amount of the bonus. It was deserved. The Management Committee had paid him this much because he was good. No, not just good. Very good. They paid him this much because he could instantly captivate a room of corporate executives with the burning stare, the smooth voice, and the tremendous knowledge of finance, tax law, and accounting he possessed. Because he had an innate, uncanny ability to sense value where others did not. And because he made the firm a tremendous amount of money—forty times the bonus amount. They had paid him this much because they wanted to keep him. There had been no reason to think he might not receive the huge bonus, especially given his relationship with Granville.

Falcon became suddenly calm. The calm for which he had already become famous at Winthrop, Hawkins. The elation subsided. A million dollars was acceptable, but he wanted more. Much more. And he wanted it quickly.

"You goddamn bastards!" Kunkowski roared to his feet. The wing back chair crashed loudly against the panelled wall as the man rose.

Falcon turned his head quickly as Kunkowski yelled, index finger extended toward the head of the table. By now Winthrop had returned from the podium to his seat at the head of the table.

"You sons of bitches!" Kunkowski screamed. He was obviously drunk.

Falcon shot a quick glance at the paper before Kunkowski's seat. There was no number beneath the man's name. He had received the Sanction. So the sharks had attacked after all.

"You think you can do this to me? You think you can play with me like some toy?" The room was deathly still. Through glazed eyes Kunkowski stared at Granville.

Granville motioned to the headwaiter. He seemed to be smiling slightly as he did so, as if he were amused. Or perhaps the smile was simply Andrew's imagination.

Kunkowski stumbled around the end of the table where Falcon sat and moved toward Granville. Several of the other senior partners stood as Kunkowski approached, but Granville remained seated, serene as he smoked a huge cigar.

Kunkowski stopped ten feet short of the head of the table. He was a big man, almost six-five and solidly built. He used his size to intimidate people—Falcon had seen him do it many times before. Falcon disliked people who behaved this way, and he watched with fascination, sensing that this time Kunkowski's display would not matter.

"You people have always hated me because I'm Polish and I'm Catholic." Kunkowski's voice was suddenly hushed. "You detest minorities."

"That is absurd." Granville continued to suck on the cigar. "You know very well that this gentleman on my right, Ben Weingarten, president of our firm, is Jewish."

"Half Jerish." Kunkowski slurred the word.

"You are very drunk, Mr. Kunkowski. Sit down." For the first time there was a hint of anger in Winthrop's voice.

It was good advice, Falcon thought. He scanned the faces in the partnership quickly and identified three others, including Roland Thompson, who had clearly received the Sanction also. Their dazed expressions revealed what they desperately tried to hide. But these three did not have Kunkowski's courage—or his stupidity. They sat riveted to their seats. It was foolhardy to confront the Management Committee. Once the Sanction had been decreed, the decision was never altered. You could continue working at Winthrop, Hawkins for as many years as you wished, drawing the same one hundred-thousand-dollar salary every partner drew, but you would never again receive a bonus. And one hundred thousand dollars wouldn't keep most of the partners' wives in clothes for a year, let alone meet debt service on the houses, cars, boats, and jewelry which had been purchased on margin. And if you complained or insulted the Management Committee, they could make repurchase of the partnership interest very difficult, stretching out the repurchase period over many years and negotiating and renegotiating the purchase price downward as you needed the cash. It was better to go quietly, collect the cash for your partnership interest quickly, and catch on with another, less prestigious investment bank.

"No, I'm not going to sit down. I'm not going to go quietly as you want me to do!" Kunkowski turned to the rank-and-file partners. "Come on. Who else just had a red-hot poker stuffed up his ass? I know I'm not the only one."

The three men with the ashen faces whom Falcon had identified moments before could not meet Kunkowski's gaze. Everyone else in the room stared straight back at him. Falcon congratulated himself on his ability to read a man's expression, but he was not surprised by this ability. After all, he had funded a great deal of his undergraduate living expenses with poker winnings.

"Please, you have to be with me. If we stick together, we can fight these bastards."

There was no response.

"Please . . ."

Still nothing.

Suddenly Kunkowski realized that he had made a critical error in judgment with his emotional, knee-jerk reaction. The shoulders of the large man slowly slumped as he turned back toward the senior partners. They stared back and Falcon could sense the hatred. No one addressed the Management Committee as Kunkowski had. They were gods. And they were not forgiving gods.

For a moment Kunkowski gazed at Granville through bloodshot eyes and then brought both hands to his face. The room was deafeningly silent except for Kunkowski's sobs, and the faint sound of Granville exhaling cigar smoke.

Four large security guards, there as a result of Granville's motion to the headwaiter several minutes before, broke the silence as they moved into the room. But they were unnecessary. Kunkowski was a beaten man.

And Falcon watched him completely disintegrate.

* * *

Granville Winthrop sat alone in a small private room on the fourth floor of the Racquet Club overlooking Park Avenue. He watched the headlights of the cars passing beneath the window as he smoked his third cigar of the evening. New York City seemed so peaceful at this time of night, especially under the light snow that was beginning to fall.

Falcon hesitated at the doorway. This wasn't going to be easy. Perhaps it should wait until Monday. He took a step away from the door.

"Come in, Andrew," Winthrop said quietly. "Close the door behind you."

Too late. At seventy-one Winthrop's senses remained sharp. Even after the immense amount of alcohol, the old man didn't miss a trick. Falcon took a deep breath and stepped into the room. The bonus envelope was safely stored in the inside pocket of his tuxedo jacket.

"So what did you think of your first partners' dinner?"

"Interesting. Ah, a rather difficult evening for Mr. Kunkowski and a few others." The door clicked shut.

"Yes, but necessary." Granville's tone became measured. He did not want to discuss Kunkowski. As far as he was concerned, Kunkowski might as well be dead. "Satisfied with your bonus, Andrew?" Granville's voice was subdued, but his eyes danced.

Falcon's eyes dropped to the deep blue carpet of the room. That was Granville, direct as hell. "Of course. My God, it's more money than some people earn in a lifetime." He thought of his father in the old two-story row house. He was probably sitting in front of the black-and-white television set at this very moment, watching an old movie, covered in blankets because he did not have the money to keep the heat in the drafty house above sixty degrees in the winter.

"There's more where that came from. Lots more." Granville waved his hand as if a million dollars were pocket change. "I tried to get you another five hundred thousand, but the other members of the Management Committee wouldn't go along. The firm bears my name, but I have to play politics sometimes." He paused and snorted as if this was the worst part of his job. "It's almost double what any first-year partner at Winthrop, Hawkins has ever received." Granville paused again. "But you deserve it. Every cent." His voice hissed, as if recalling the unpleasantness of the argument with his fellow Management Committee members over the amount.

"I can't tell you how much I appreciate it." Falcon shifted uncomfortably as he stood before Winthrop.

The old man stared at his young star. "I shouldn't tell you this, Andrew." Granville glanced out the window at Park Avenue and then back. "You remind me a great deal of myself when I was young. Brilliant, aggressive, intimidating, and, of course, undeniably a lady's man." Winthrop smiled widely, the lines of his face creating perfectly defined grids on either side of his mouth. "In all the weekends you have come to the estate, I don't think you've ever brought the same woman."

They laughed together, more loudly than was necessary. Not at Winthrop's attempt at humor, but because both men were suddenly uncomfortable with Winthrop's admission of his affection for Falcon. Men like Winthrop rarely made such admissions.

He drew in a deep breath. "You could become senior partner here someday, Andrew. Not too far in the future either. It might upset the old guard, but investment banking is a young man's game these days. The technology is passing us old men by. We're still feeding off of the relationships with clients this firm has had for a hundred years. That will continue to pay dividends for a while, but at some point we'll need more. We'll need you."

Again Falcon glanced at the floor.

"I'm making you uncomfortable, Andrew. I know that. It's the liquor talking—and the evening in general. It's pretty heady stuff for the firm to make almost six hundred million dollars in one year. Especially when just under half of that is mine."

Falcon's eyes rose immediately from the carpet. So Granville still owned that much of the partnership. Incredible.

The two men stared at each other for several moments, stone-faced. Then Granville's visage again broke into a wide, unguarded smile. "Anyone left downstairs, Andrew my boy?"

Falcon shook his head. He appreciated the fact that Granville always addressed him by his first name. Everyone else at the firm called him Falcon. Instinctively, it seemed. "No. They're all gone. It's three o'clock."

"Which of course leads me to my next question. What are you doing here?"

"I don't know. Just felt like hanging around, I guess. Didn't want to leave."

"Andrew, I've never known you to simply hang around. You are not one to waste time. You are too driven. It will be your undoing someday. I sensed your aggressiveness during the first three minutes of our interview at Harvard Business School, which is, of course, why I hired you. Every one of your actions has purpose. There is a reason for everything you do. There is a reason that you are the last person here."

Falcon eyed the older man. For the past four years Granville had been his mentor and friend, the closest thing to a father Falcon had experienced in a long time. And suddenly, despite the fact that Falcon was far from sentimental, he realized that he would miss Granville Winthrop. But Granville would understand. They would always be good friends.

"I am going to leave this firm." Falcon knew no other way than to be direct. It was his nature, just as it was Granville's. He searched Winthrop's face for a reaction, but there was none. He continued, uncomfortable at Winthrop's initial indifference. "I have an opportunity. An entrepreneurial opportunity. My partner and I have developed a software we believe will have widespread application in the health-care field. It's a potential economic windfall."

The guarded smile suddenly overtook Winthrop's face. "A million dollars in one night is not enough?" he asked quietly.

Falcon ignored Granville's remark and began to speak more quickly. The guarded smile was not a good sign. "It's a chance for me to run something myself. It's a chance for me to earn the kind of money you don't consider trivial. If it does as we believe it will, the company could be worth fifty to sixty million dollars in two to three years. Conservatively fifty to sixty million. Maybe much more. And of course I would select Winthrop, Hawkins to take the company public."

Granville turned back toward the window.

"I appreciate everything you have done for me, Granville. I've repaid my student loans for both college and business school, bought some nice things, and funded the start-up of this venture. All through the generosity of Winthrop, Hawkins. And tonight. Well, I still can't believe the amount of money the firm—that you gave me. But I have to try this. I would always wonder if I didn't at least try. I know it's risky, but hell, I don't have any family at this point. I don't have anyone depending on me. It's a perfect time for me to do this. And I don't want to wait ten or fifteen years to be senior partner here at Winthrop, Hawkins. It might never happen. I know you're behind me, but some of the others aren't. If you weren't around . . ." Falcon didn't finish the sentence.

His heart was pounding in his chest. "There is a very good chance, as you well know, that this won't work. Nine out of ten new businesses fail in the first year. And if that happens—the business fails, I mean—I will come crawling back, and I hope there will be a place . . ."

"Don't even think about coming back to Winthrop, Hawkins, Falcon." Winthrop's voice was inhumanly cold. As if the past four years had been immediately erased from his memory. He turned back away from the window and stared Falcon directly in the eyes.

Falcon stepped back slightly, as if he had actually felt a frigid wind cross his face. He sensed the sudden hatred. "Excuse—"

"Leave this establishment immediately." Winthrop's voice was perfectly calm, just as it had been with Kunkowski. "And do not attempt to enter our offices Monday morning because you will be denied access. I will contact the security guards myself. Your belongings will be boxed and sent to you. Because you have been a partner for only one year, you are not entitled, under the bylaws of the partnership, to receive any money for your partnership interest. If you don't believe me, check the documents. Good luck with your endeavor. Good-bye, Mr. Falcon."

Falcon considered an attempt to reconcile, to reach out to the old man. But he knew it was useless. He was suddenly in the same category as Kunkowski as far as Winthrop was concerned. Dead.

1

February 1996

Falcon stared at the numbers on the spreadsheet. It did not take a financial genius to analyze these figures. MD Link Limited Partnership, the computer software firm he and Reid Bernstein had founded only four years before, now had only ten thousand dollars remaining in cash—not even enough for Friday's payroll. There would be no more revenue checks for at least two weeks, and those would be meager at best, certainly not enough to cover interim operating expenses or another payroll.

He leaned back in his comfortably padded desk chair and began to count the tiny holes in the dropped tile ceiling. Unless something spectacular happened quickly, MD Link was going down. As they said on Wall Street, "Crash and burn, baby. Crash and burn."

Falcon counted fifty holes in one tile, realized the idiocy of the endeavor, and swivelled in his chair to gaze out the large window behind his desk toward the town of Princeton. From his fourth-floor office on Route 1 he could see the spire of Princeton University's chapel. It rose majestically into the cloudless, azure sky of a crisp late-winter afternoon. It was a beautiful day in central New Jersey.

He let out a long breath. MD Link should have gone public by now, and his five-hundred-thousand-dollar investment ought to be worth multimillions. But the young Mr. Bernstein, God's supposed gift to the computer world and the designer of the firm's primary product, had been unable to fix the catastrophic bug in the software. And his inability to resurrect the system was crushing Falcon's plans into a pipe dream and turning his five-hundred-thousand-dollar investment into what most considered worthless stock.

Slowly Andrew turned back to his desk. Through the office door he watched his new executive assistant finish word processing a letter. Jenny Cagle was pretty. Very pretty. Her long auburn hair fell loosely to her shoulders, framing her delicate face. The lashes surrounding Jenny's deep blue eyes were long and dark, her lips soft and full, and her skin smooth. He took a deep breath.

But there were problems too. Jenny had three earring holes in her left lobe, and a necklace with her name on it. Sometimes she wore too much blush on her cheeks and screaming shades of lipstick. And her mascara was much too thick. It was not the sleek model look with which he had become so familiar in New York. But most of the imperfections could be taken care of quickly with a trip to a Fifth Avenue salon. And he shouldn't expect so much anyway. After all, she was just a working-class Jersey girl. And though he had just come to meet her, he had known her all of his life.

His gaze strayed to the plunging neckline of her light sweater. The V ran deeply into her full chest, a style of dress Falcon would have to speak to Jenny about at some point. It was rendering the software engineers at MD Link helpless.

He looked down quickly as she rose from her workstation and entered his office with a stack of letters.

"Andrew?"

Falcon pretended to be immersed in paperwork.

"Andrew," she said again, not altering the intensity of her tone.

He glanced up from the numbers. "Yes, Jenny."

"Here are those letters you wanted."

"Sure, give them to me. I'll sign them right now."

Jenny watched him closely as he whipped off signatures on the paper. She had never known a man like Andrew Falcon. He was tall, over six-two, with long jet black hair, chiseled facial features, and broad shoulders. But it wasn't simply the physical attributes that made Falcon so attractive. He had what she termed "the edge"—an understated but certain confidence that manifested itself in his voice, his walk, his slightly crooked smile, and the way he constantly and methodically flexed his left hand. As she stood watching him sign the letters, Jenny suddenly realized how strongly she was attracted to him. But that was foolish, and she knew it.

"Do you want some coffee?" she asked as she retrieved the letters.

"Yes, I would. Thank you."

Jenny hesitated for a moment. Andrew's response was so formal, so distant. "Everything all right?"

Falcon nodded without looking up from the spreadsheet. In his peripheral vision he watched her short skirt swinging easily from side to side around those thighs as she moved toward the office door. "Oh, Jenny?"

She stopped at the door. "Yes?"

Falcon resisted the temptation to stare at her legs again. "Have you been able to find Reid?"

Jenny seemed slightly disappointed at the question, as if she had anticipated something else. She shook her head, causing the long auburn hair to fall down about her face. "No. I've tried him several times at home. I've tried his car phone. I even tried him at Professor Bryant's office at the university. No luck."

"Okay. Keep trying, will you? It is extremely important that he get here for our four-thirty meeting with Lord Froworth."

"Sure." Again Jenny hesitated at the doorway, as if she wanted to ask him a question. But she thought better of the idea and disappeared.

Andrew returned to the gloomy financial prognosis. MD Link

was well behind its financial projections, and the money, though not gone, was cascading out of the corporate checkbook. The concept had been pretty simple: connect physicians' offices directly with insurance companies via a computer system so that medical claims could be processed immediately—before the patient left the office. Doctors would receive their payments in days versus months and cut down significantly on paperwork. Insurance companies would slash multiple layers of overhead and therefore save lots of salary costs. MD Link would produce the computer software for the system, sell it to the insurance companies and the doctors, and make a good bit of money not only selling the software, but also servicing and upgrading it down the road.

It sounded like a win-win situation for everyone except the poor bastards who would be laid off at the insurance companies. And of course the patients who could no longer bluff their way into free medical service. But the hell with the freeloaders and the insurance company employees. Cost cutting and downsizing were the business buzzwords of the nineties. Excess jobs represented opportunity for entrepreneurs who could replace people with software—software, which didn't push for outrageous labor contracts, amass sick days, or develop emotional problems that translated into downtime and inefficiency. Tiny software companies had become wildly profitable overnight as bloated manufacturing firms paid hundreds of million of dollars for "solutions." Then the software firms went public, making the entrepreneurs wealthy beyond imagination.

Hundreds of millions of dollars of revenue. That was what MD Link was supposed to have generated so far. But it hadn't. Last fall the software had developed a bug. Initially, Reid Bernstein, the engineer with whom Falcon had partnered to found MD Link, had described the problem as a minor glitch that would be corrected quickly. But October had become December, and now February, and still the problem remained, embedded somewhere in the logic of the huge program. In fact, the problem had worsened, even with the assistance of several Princeton University professors with whom Falcon was acquainted. Bernstein resented the academic aid, but it was Falcon's money funneling down the toilet, not Bernstein's, so Bernstein was forced to accept the help.

Last week, the firm's largest customer, two huge insurance companies, had discontinued the system as a result of the problem. These two customers accounted for seventy-five percent of MD Link's annual revenues, and their discontinued use of the product made sales to other firms all but impossible. Both companies were willing to reinstitute the product once the problem was fixed, but soon there wouldn't be an MD Link Limited Partnership, much less a product, unless he could find more money to keep the company afloat while they continued to try to solve the problem.

Falcon shifted uncomfortably in the chair. By nature he was calm, inhumanly calm, in the face of pressure. But the walls were closing in as they never had before. His eyes moved slowly to the spreadsheets lying across the oak desktop. His life was falling apart, and he felt the pangs of panic, an emotion which until now had been foreign to him.

"Here's your coffee, Andrew." Jenny moved slowly back into Falcon's spacious office, the steaming mug held out away from her body.

"Thanks." He did not look up from the figures.

Jenny put the mug down on a coaster. She gazed at him momentarily, hoping he would look up from the stupid numbers. But she knew he was under immense strain and had no time for that. Suddenly, Jenny realized that she was staring directly into the steel-blue eyes.

"Is there something I can do for you?" Falcon raised one eyebrow.

"Um, ah, no. No, I was just wondering, um, if we should have this Sir Frothwith picked up at the Princeton Junction train station by limousine."

"It's Lord Fro*worth*, and no we don't need to do that, but thanks for asking. He will be flying down from New York by helicopter, and I've asked one of the technicians to pick him up."

This time Falcon didn't watch her go, but gazed out the window instead. After the partners' dinner, so long ago it seemed now, Falcon had over seven hundred thousand dollars in the bank, even after paying taxes on the huge bonus. Now he had next to nothing, except for twenty-five thousand dollars in a numbered Citibank squirrel account—an account he had managed to keep secret from Bernstein. But twenty-five thousand dollars wouldn't keep him afloat for more than six months. Hell, the mortgage payment alone was three thousand dollars, and the monthly nut for the Porsche was another six hundred dollars.

Falcon rubbed his chin slowly. MD Link could survive. All it needed was one more round of seed capital. He was convinced of that. One more investment would see them through this difficult period, and then things would get better. For the last several months Falcon had attempted to raise that money from outside investors to keep the firm going while the software program was being debugged. However, the problems at the company had made raising money from outside sources extremely difficult. Only one potential investor remained out of all of the people Falcon had approached. This was Lord Froworth, who ran a stuffy British venture capital firm. Froworth had been considering the investment for some time but as yet had not committed the five-hundred-thousand-dollar infusion Falcon was seeking. MD Link needed Froworth's decision quickly if anything was to be salvaged, because the wolves were at the door.

Arms folded across his chest, Falcon watched the sleek navy-blue chopper touch down gently atop the giant X of the heliport on the far side of Route 1. "Jenny!" He turned his head slightly without taking his eyes from the helicopter.

"Yes, I'll be there in a second." Her voice came from the outer-office workstation.

Two figures emerged from the helicopter and walked quickly toward a waiting Buick sedan. They stooped as they moved out from beneath the rotating blades toward the car.

Falcon grasped his elbows as he watched their progress. Here was another one of those precious moments that determined life's direction. This meeting with Lord Froworth was going to decide if his five-hundred-thousand-dollar investment in MD Link would ultimately be worth anything, or if he would have to head back to New York into another finance job with nothing to show for his huge risk but a very few dollars and an aging wardrobe. Everything hinged upon this meeting—and Bernstein was still nowhere to be found.

He followed the sedan and its precious cargo as it reached the traffic light at Route 1. The car paused for a moment, then proceeded across the main road into MD Link's office park. Froworth would be in the office momentarily. "Jen."

"I'm right here, Andrew." Jenny stood just a few feet behind Falcon. His voice seemed strained, a tone she had not heard before.

"When was the last time you tried Bernstein?"

"Five minutes ago."

Falcon picked up the receiver from the desk phone and punched the engineer's home number. He fixed his gaze upon Jenny as he listened to the maddening rings continue at Bernstein's home. "Reid is going to blow this whole thing. He's known about this meeting for three weeks. I've reminded him every day. I can't answer the technical questions."

"Maybe one of the other engineers could answer those questions."

Falcon shook his head. "Lord Froworth wants to talk to

Bernstein." He replaced the receiver. "Go greet Froworth. And, Jenny, smile at him very sweetly. You know what I mean."

Jenny did not respond as she walked away.

Five minutes later Jenny returned with the two figures who had emerged from the helicopter.

Lord Froworth was tall and thin. He was about sixty-five years old, Andrew judged, but well kept for his age. His long gray hair was perfectly styled, as was his mustache. His expensive-looking, three-button charcoal suit was exactingly tailored, and his black wingtip shoes were spit-shined.

Falcon met the man at the office doorway. "Hello, Lord Froworth. It certainly is a pleasure to finally meet you after talking so many times by telephone." He spoke in a somewhat insincere tone as he shook the Brit's hand. If you were too friendly or too aggressive, venture capitalists, like all shrewd investors, sensed panic. And if they sensed even the slightest hint of panic, you would never hear from them again. Somehow they liked you better if you seemed disinterested. It meant you didn't need the money that badly, and that made them mad to invest. "We appreciate your taking time away from your meetings in New York to see us," he continued, leading Froworth into the office.

"I had to come to Princeton anyway," Froworth said with an aristocratic English accent. His tone was even more insincere than Falcon's. "My sister is at Princeton University on some sort of professorial exchange program with Oxford, though for the life of me I can't understand why she would want to leave England for four years in the United States." Froworth moved to the office window and looked out over Route 1.

Falcon shook hands quickly with Froworth's assistant, a small, mousy woman with short brown hair. The petite woman smiled meekly at Falcon, but his attention did not remain with her for long. She was not the decision maker.

"Why don't you have a seat, Lord Froworth?"

"Yes, why don't I."

Falcon could hardly bear the accent, but he needed Froworth's money—badly. "Would you care for some coffee?"

"Tea. Hot tea," said Froworth as he and his assistant settled into chairs in front of Falcon's desk. "You Americans seem to think tea means iced tea, you know." Froworth and his mousy assistant cackled at each other over the inane observation.

Falcon nodded at Jenny, who rolled her eyes and walked from the room, exaggerating the swing in her hips. He sat down in the desk chair, and as he did, noticed Froworth's longing gaze. Froworth was watching the short skirt move to and fro.

"Is that chair leather, Mr. Falcon?" Froworth asked, turning back toward Andrew.

"It is."

"Expensive, I'm sure."

"I really couldn't tell you." Falcon knew where this line of questioning was headed. Venture capitalists didn't like to see a dime wasted on anything superfluous—at least not until just before the initial public offering. Then they spent lavishly to spruce up the company so as to make it more attractive to public investors. "It was a gift from a friend," Falcon continued, careful to avoid the word girlfriend so that he would not appear to have any serious interests outside MD Link.

"I see." Froworth paused. "Where is this man Bernstein? The brains of the organization."

Falcon allowed the backhanded insult to deflect away. Then his demeanor became quite serious. "Unfortunately, a relative of Mr. Bernstein's died very suddenly, this morning, and he went to Philadelphia to be with his family. He is going to try to make it back by five-thirty." Falcon shook his head slowly, as if the death had affected him also. He could lie convincingly when he had to.

"A terrible shame, Mr. Falcon, but you see I brought Ms. Mullins with me for the express purpose of having her discuss the logic behind the software and, of course, the defect directly with

Mr. Bernstein." Froworth nodded at the mousy woman. "Is he Jewish, by the way?" His upper lip lifted slightly to one side.

"I believe he is."

Froworth sniffed.

"Is that a problem?" Falcon could feel his pulse quicken ever so slightly. He was not particularly religious or particularly close to Bernstein, despite the fact that they had cofounded MD Link. But Falcon had never lost his working-class hatred of snobbery.

"Of course not. Mr. Bernstein's denomination is none of my concern."

Froworth was not nearly as good a liar, a fact Falcon noted.

Jenny returned with tea for Lord Froworth and his assistant, and gently placed the saucers onto the front of Falcon's desk. "Hot tea. American style." Jenny smiled effusively at Froworth as she waited for him to taste the tea.

Froworth took a small sip.

"Is that all right?" she asked seductively.

"Oh, yes, quite." Froworth was suddenly flustered.

Falcon suppressed a smile. Jenny was doing all she could to help.

She winked once at Falcon as she walked from the office.

Froworth watched her go with an old man's longing, but once she had gone his demeanor changed rapidly. "What kind of car do you drive, Mr. Falcon?"

This guy is incredible, Falcon thought. He wants to make sure I am living a pauper's life so that I will be motivated. So I'll do anything to make the company a success. What a prick. But Falcon's expression did not betray his emotion. "Toyota Corolla. It has over one hundred thousand miles on it." He was going to kill Bernstein for making him go through this alone.

"Really?" Froworth sounded surprised.

Falcon nodded.

Since Froworth had entered the office, Falcon had been aware that the mousy assistant had not taken her eyes from him. Suddenly, out of the corner of his eye, he thought he noticed her look away.

"And in what kind of dwelling do you live?"

"I'm not sure what you mean." Falcon knew exactly what Froworth meant.

"Do you live in a house or a flat?"

"I rent a two-bedroom town house. I use one bedroom as a study."

Again Falcon thought he noticed the mousy woman look away.

"Tell me about your family."

Falcon took a long breath. "My father lives in a very small house in a lower-middle-class section of Philadelphia. My mother died twenty-four years ago. I have no siblings."

Froworth took a long sip from the teacup, replaced it on the saucer, then stared directly at Falcon. "Well, we finally receive a truthful answer from you. Did you inherit your ability to lie from your father?"

Falcon did not hesitate. "No, from my mother." Falcon thought he noticed the small hint of a smile cross the older man's face.

"I'll give you one more chance, Mr. Falcon. How much money do you have in the bank?"

There was no reason to attempt further deception. Lord Froworth, or more likely his obnoxious assistant, had done the homework. They probably knew more about his house and his Porsche than he did. "Just over four thousand dollars in a local checking account and twenty-five thousand in a numbered Citibank account."

"Very good, Mr. Falcon. Now we're getting somewhere." Froworth leaned back in his chair. "So you want me to take five hundred thousand of my good money and throw it in after five hundred thousand of yours. Is that correct?"

Falcon was suddenly very tired of the pompous Lord Froworth and his wordless assistant. He had been down this road many times before in the last three months with various investors, most of whom weren't nearly as bombastic as the snide individual sitting before him now. But they were all basically the same. They asked a lot of questions to make themselves feel intelligent and then ultimately decided against putting money into MD Link: "Too risky. A good opportunity but not for us. We just can't get our hands around the industry." Falcon had heard all of the excuses. Froworth would be no different. So it would be back to a job on Wall Street. He might as well resign himself to this fact now.

"Yes, Lord Froworth, that is exactly what I want you to do."

Froworth appeared ready to ask another question but hesitated. For a few moments he stared out the window behind Falcon, then slowly shook his head. "Mr. Falcon, I was going to ask you a lot of questions, you know, really begin the due diligence process. But I must tell you, after reviewing the numbers and the problems with the software, I just don't think it's worth wasting my time or yours. I mean, you can't even make your partner available . . ."

Falcon did not hear the remainder of Froworth's sentence. He was distracted by the growing commotion outside the closed office door. He could hear voices increasing in intensity; a banging noise; and then a door slamming wildly. Froworth stopped speaking and stared at the door. The mousy woman huddled near the wall.

Just then Jenny screamed. Falcon rose instinctively from the desk chair. At the same time the office door burst open, and Jenny tumbled into the room, falling onto her knees. She was crying hysterically. Calmly, Reid Bernstein stepped into the office and closed the door. He carried a large shotgun. Falcon instantly recognized it as the one he had loaned Bernstein for a supposed duck-hunting trip several weeks before.

"Reid, what in God's name . . ." Falcon began to move toward Jenny to see if she was all right.

"Shut up, Falcon. I'm tired of all your bullshit. Just shut the hell up!" Bernstein waved the gun menacingly at Falcon, who instinctively took a step back toward the window.

Jenny sobbed, hands covering her eyes.

"Shut up, you stupid tramp. I've been so nice to you and you've never even noticed me. But of course you could never do enough for Falcon. I hate you!" Bernstein kicked her in the ribs, and she crumpled to the floor. Again Falcon moved toward Jenny. Again Bernstein angled the shotgun in Falcon's general direction. But this time he pulled the trigger. The blast destroyed the window behind Falcon's desk.

"Jesus Christ, you idiot!" Falcon had felt the heat of the shot pass by him. He rose and started toward Bernstein.

"Falcon, stay where you are!" Bernstein hissed. He brought the barrel of the gun down so that it was pointed directly at Falcon's chest. "Is that clear?"

Falcon stopped and stared at the end of the gun barrel. It occurred to him at that moment that he had always wondered how he would react to being held at gunpoint. Now he wished he had never had to find out.

Bernstein turned slowly toward Lord Froworth. "So you must be the British venture capitalist who was going to be our savior. Stand up." Bernstein sneered at the elderly man. He was smiling a crazy smile.

Falcon could see that the pressure of the last few months and his failure to correct the software problem had driven Reid over the edge. Falcon glanced quickly at Froworth. Clearly he had never been held at gunpoint before either.

The older man rose slowly. "I am Lord Froworth." His stuffy voice shook noticeably. "I am the managing—"

"I don't care if you're Mahatma Gandhi." Bernstein grinned at Falcon. "I wonder why I thought of Gandhi at this moment. I'll have to reflect on that sometime." His voice became suddenly serious. Then he burst into laughter.

"Reid."

"I told you to shut up, Falcon." Bernstein glanced around the room. "Speak only when spoken to. That's what my mother always told me. Children were made to be seen, not heard. What a wonderful old broad she was."

Falcon saw the beads of perspiration pouring down Bernstein's face from beneath the dirty Boston Red Sox baseball cap that covered most of his curly dark hair.

"So did the limey come through, Andrew, or is he just like all of the others? Is he going to invest money into MD Link, or tell us to go screw ourselves?"

Falcon could feel Froworth's glance, but he did not return it. "Why don't you ask him yourself, Reid?"

"Well, hell. Why didn't I think of that?" Bernstein waved the gun at Froworth. "So, are you going to put some money into my little invention despite its itsy-bitsy problem? Well . . . are you?" Bernstein's voice became chillingly serious.

"I . . . I don't know yet."

"Do better than that, old man," Bernstein sneered.

"I am certain we can come to some sort of accommodation." Froworth's voice shook uncontrollably. Ms. Mullins suddenly let out an audible sob.

"You're lying!" Without hesitation Bernstein aimed at Froworth and fired. Steel shot burst through Froworth's chest and out his back, spraying the wall with blood. The older man was thrust backward over the chair and onto the floor.

Falcon pressed himself against the wall. The two women screamed loudly, panic-stricken.

"Shut up, shut up!" Bernstein's eyes darted around the room. In turn he pointed the gun quickly at Jenny, Falcon, and the mousy woman. "Just shut up!"

"Put the gun down, Reid." Falcon's voice sliced through the room. He could hear Froworth gasping for his last few breaths on the other side of the desk.

"Hey, what the heck's going on in there?" The unidentified voice came from outside the closed door.

Before Falcon could respond, Bernstein turned and fired another blast, this time through the door toward the voice. The door disintegrated under the hail of steel. Again the women screamed.

Immediately Bernstein turned back toward Falcon and leveled the barrel of the shotgun at him. Bernstein ignored the women's screams. His eyes were set in a death stare.

Slowly, Falcon began to move toward Bernstein, staring straight down the barrel into the crazed man's burning eyes.

"Don't come any closer, Andrew!"

"Are you going to kill me too?" Falcon inched toward Bernstein. He could see the body of Troy Hudson, a technician—the unfortunate voice on the other side of the door—lying facedown in a pool of blood in the outer office.

"I ought to. If you hadn't convinced me to leave my job at Microsoft, I'd probably be a sane and happy man right now."

"Give me the gun, Reid," Falcon whispered. He could hear sirens coming up Route 1. "It's over, and you know it."

"Oh, I do?"

"Yes, you do. That's the shotgun I loaned you for the duck-hunting trip. Three shots, Reid. That's all that gun will fire." The sirens were growing louder. "And you have fired all three already."

"This gun fires five rounds, Andrew."

"It would if it didn't have a plug in it, Reid. But it does. New Jersey law. Three shots. That's it."

Bernstein glanced quickly at the two women on the floor. They were staring at him, not daring to breathe. He looked back at Falcon. The gun dropped slightly, and Bernstein's expression became suddenly sad. His eyes dropped to the floor.

Falcon relaxed. "It's over, Reid." His voice was gentle. "Give me the gun."

Bernstein nodded. "Yes, it is over." His voice was barely audible. He raised his eyes to meet Falcon's. "You see, I may not know as much about software as I thought I knew. But I know everything there is to know about guns. I pulled the plug, Andrew."

With one motion Bernstein smashed the butt of the shotgun into the side of Falcon's head, then lifted the barrel. And fired.

2

Granville Winthrop stood next to the ceiling-high window of his Plaza Hotel suite, hands clasped firmly behind his back, gazing out at the sunshine that drenched Central Park. How many times had he stood at this same window searching for solutions: thinking about how best to structure a hostile acquisition, plotting the strategy of the deal? Hundreds of times? And here he was again. Except that this time the plotting had nothing to do with business. Not directly anyway.

He glanced at the rich, floor-length drapes covering the sides of the window. It was expensive keeping the suite, but it was easier than buying something on Park Avenue. The suite wasn't an asset that had to be maintained for sale someday, not a situation where he had to worry whether he was buying cheap and selling dear. And that was its attraction. It *wasn't* an asset. He had plenty of those. The suite was just something there for him when he needed it. He could extricate himself from the lease every year when it expired. But he never did.

Granville did not spend many nights in the city anymore. He preferred to take the forty-minute flight from the lower Manhattan helipad to his estate. He had come to care for New York City less and less as he had aged. But it was convenient to have this place on those late nights when he entertained.

He watched as thousands of people below milled through Sunday in Central Park. He watched them feed the ducks, buy hot dogs from sidewalk vendors, and stroll arm in arm—the typical things people did in the oasis of this cement jungle. They were so unaware. So completely unaware. For the most part, Winthrop believed, Americans were a terribly naive lot. They thought that as long as the country remained the most powerful military force in the world, it would be forever free. They did not realize that the greatest threat to any group or nation's security came from within. America was no different.

Granville unclasped his hands and turned toward the other man in the room. William Rutherford sat ramrod straight in a plush chair facing the window, his bearing military crisp. The others were not certain of Rutherford's talents. Not certain of his ability to execute orders. Of the necessity of his involvement at all. But Winthrop was absolutely certain, and that was all that mattered. Winthrop was the leader.

Winthrop reclined slowly into the leather chair beside the window. Rutherford was different from the others. Granville had to admit that. Rutherford was ex-army and ex-CIA. Afraid of nothing. The others were businessmen who knew nothing of killing. Rutherford knew how to accomplish a mission, any mission, and he would use any means at his disposal to do so—which was what the plan required and what intimidated the others. This wasn't some chickenshit thing they were trying to accomplish. This was serious. Things might get nasty. And sometimes, if you were going to come out of a nasty situation victorious, you had to have some tough people in your corner.

"How are you this morning, Bill?" Winthrop began.

"Fine, sir!" Rutherford answered emphatically in his raspy military voice.

Winthrop smiled at Rutherford. Just under six feet tall and at least two hundred pounds, he was a rock of a man. His hair was clipped so short he appeared blond, but his eyebrows were dark, giving away his true coloring. "Good, Bill. Good." Winthrop said the words soothingly, hoping Rutherford would relax. Knowing he wouldn't. "You will take care of that detail for me, the donation."

"I will. I'll move the money tomorrow."

"Thank you." Granville removed the reading glasses from the bridge of his nose and put them in his suit coat pocket. "And you will attend the function?"

"I will."

"Good." He watched Rutherford methodically, slowly cross his legs. It seemed that Rutherford did everything methodically, that every movement of his body, every plan he executed, every part of his life was calculated and had purpose. There was nothing spontaneous to this man. Once chosen, he did not veer from a path, and he allowed nothing to stop him from reaching the end of that path. He was absolutely and perfectly rational. Winthrop respected that most about Rutherford. Nothing was left to chance. Nothing was personal. It was all about accomplishing the mission. The rest of them could take lessons from this man. And to think, they had questioned Rutherford's initiation. Ridiculous.

Rutherford redirected the conversation. "Granville, how much of the company have we purchased so far?"

"About seven percent."

Rutherford pressed both forefingers against his nostrils. The air made a whistling sound as he inhaled. "Doesn't that mean we have to file something with a government agency somewhere? I thought I had read that."

Winthrop shook his head. Rutherford and his photographic memory. Of course all the best CIA operatives had photographic memories. And Rutherford had been a top man in Europe before joining them. "Yes. Once any entity or group of related entities owns more than five percent of a public company's stock, that entity is supposed to file a Form 13-D with the Securities and Exchange Commission. Its purpose is to alert the subject company's management to the fact that someone might be taking a run at them."

"It sounds, Granville, from the tone of your voice, as if we haven't filed our 13-D."

"No, we haven't."

"But the SEC will figure that out sooner or later. Won't they?"

"No. Trust me. I've been doing this for forty years. We have twenty different entities buying shares out of ten different countries. They couldn't figure it out unless they had someone on the inside. Only the seven of us know what's going on. If we can't trust ourselves, who can we trust?"

"What has the stock price done since we started buying?"

"Our first purchase six months ago was at twenty-four dollars a share. The stock closed Friday at twenty-five and an eighth. That's an increase of about five percent. In that same time frame, the Dow Jones industrial average has increased just over four percent. Average daily trading volume of the target's shares is not dramatically different than it was before we started buying because our brokers are using working orders—percentages of other, unrelated buy orders. So we're buying only when others are buying. Bottom line, our purchase activity shouldn't catch anyone's attention. And it hasn't."

"How do you know?"

"The New York Stock Exchange has an internal watchdog unit called Stockwatch, which is set up to track any unusual trading patterns in specific stocks. We know someone on the inside who is in that group. He reports that our stock has not aroused their interest."

"But our contact has no idea why we would be interested. Is that correct?" Rutherford was naturally security-conscious.

"None. He is simply reporting to us the names of stocks being scrutinized. He doesn't know of our specific interest."

"How much have we spent so far on the purchase of shares?"

"Roughly a billion."

"Jesus Christ, Granville! I didn't know we had that much."

"Yes. Actually we have another billion left, but that will be used as part of the equity for the leveraged buyout when we publicly announce our offer to purchase."

"So there will be no further share purchases?"

"Not much, if at all."

"At what price will we announce the public tender?"

"Hard to say for certain. Probably around seventy-five dollars a share."

"So we'd make about fifty dollars a share on what we've bought so far."

"Yes. About two billion in total, and we get back the billion we have already invested to buy the shares. But remember, that two-billion-dollar gain will be offset by the one billion we'll lose in the leveraged buyout."

"We still come out of it with three billion, which is a billion more than we started with."

"Making money on the deal isn't the primary objective, Bill."

"Understood. But it's a nice side benefit. Besides, we'll need a good bit of money to take care of our people after this is over."

Winthrop folded his hands on his lap and glanced out the window. "I hope tonight's mission goes well."

"It will. Phoenix Grey has never failed me." Rutherford's right foot twitched involuntarily.

The movement was subtle, but Winthrop noticed it.

"What about Falcon?" Rutherford asked. He did not want to talk about the mission.

Winthrop glanced into Rutherford's cold, black, sharp eyes. "What about him?"

"Has he joined NASO yet?"

"No, he hasn't. All in good time."

"How do you know he'll accept NASO's offer?"

"I know." Winthrop's voice became ice cold. "He'll join us, though he won't know he has."

Rutherford hesitated before asking his next question. Typically he never hesitated before asking anyone a question—not even the director of the CIA. But then the director was not in Winthrop's league. Very few were. Rutherford had checked. "This isn't personal between you and Falcon, is it?"

Winthrop searched Rutherford's eyes. "No. That would be irrational."

Rutherford tapped a finger against one of his large front teeth. "When is the next meeting?" Rutherford did not want to dwell on the question—or the answer. He simply wanted to let Winthrop know what he was thinking.

"Three weeks. It will be the next-to-last meeting before the Pleiade Project goes live."

Anwar Ali leaned back against the brick wall and pulled a long, settling breath from his Camel cigarette. Killing was the easiest profession in the world, provided you knew what you were doing. Ali slowly blew smoke into the cold night air. The key to the profession was not to kill anyone important. A very simple rule. The international assassins who killed politicians, judges, and filthy rich tycoons were insane. Sure, they made millions for each hit, but then they had world-class intelligence agents tracking them down for the rest of their lives, agents equipped with the latest technology and the latest weapons and, worse still, the ability to use the weapons and the technology without asking questions. Ali ticked off the agencies quickly: the Israeli Mossad, the CIA, what was left of the old KGB, and a new cooperative unit out of the consolidated Europe. Government-sanctioned killers who loved their jobs. A dangerous combination.

Ali preferred to murder low-profile, middle-class drones. Instead of high-tech agencies, he was pursued by inept local authorities who often did not find the victim's body until weeks after the kill. By then the body was cold and the clues were scant. His clients were primarily small-time hoods, small business owners, and jilted lovers. As a result of his clientele's composition, Ali was paid less than his high-profile counterparts—much less, in fact. Generally not more than twenty thousand dollars per kill. But he had a large home in Carmel with no mortgage and a substantial cash hoard in the bank. He had been killing people for nineteen years and only once had he come close to being caught.

This contract had brought him to Temperance, Michigan, a suburb of Toledo, Ohio. Ali had been here since Sunday, and already he was sick of the place. The early spring weather had been cold and raw since he arrived, and as a result he had developed a head cold. But the worst part about the place was that it was boring. The prostitutes were ugly and vulgar, and there was no gambling anywhere. At least none that he could find.

Ali shivered in the night air and pulled the down coat tightly around himself. He wanted to return to the warmth of California and his familiar stable of hookers. It was wonderful sleeping with a different woman every night. Men weren't supposed to be monogamous. And he wasn't about to interrupt the natural order.

Ali took one more puff from the cigarette, allowed the butt to fall to the pavement, and then snuffed it out with his shoe. He checked his watch in the dim glow of the all-night lights of the dry-cleaning store at the north end of the strip mall. Just after one in the morning. The mark was late.

Ali wanted to get on the road back to Carmel. If he could only fly, he would be in his own bed by daybreak. But he had to drive, of course, because he was carrying weapons. He groaned at the prospect. The drive to Toledo from California had been brutal.

He glanced around the mall again. Small-time hoods. They were the best clients. They never felt remorse for the killing. They didn't try to cut the fee. They paid in small bills, and then they never wanted to see you again. Small-time hoods maintained their silence no matter what.

Small-business owners were almost as reliable in terms of maintaining their silence. And you could count on the fact that no one would ever be able to trace the payment. Small-business owners took the sum out of petty cash, bit by bit, over several months so that there was no trail. Sometimes they tried to renegotiate the fee, but Ali did not renegotiate.

Jilted lovers were the worst and riskiest clients. Their rage was steeped in passion, making them irrational. Even if they appeared rational on the surface, Ali had come to understand over the years that they were only seconds from exploding at any time. Jilted lovers, especially the men, could never erase the mental picture of their mate with another lover. Ultimately, after the execution, the odds were good that the jilted lover would feel remorse. When that happened, it put Ali in a vulnerable position because it could drag him into the situation. In the worst case, the jilted lover might feel such guilt that he or she would confess to the authorities.

That had happened only once. Fortunately, in that instance the female client had not actually seen him. The woman's brother had arranged the murder and would have been able to identify Ali easily, but Ali murdered the man before the police got to him. He would have never worked for a jilted lover again except for one thing. Ali liked money, and there were lots of jilted lovers in the world.

Ali stared out over the small parking lot. It was illuminated by just two streetlamps and devoid of cars at this hour. Ali's car was parked a mile and a half away at an apartment complex. The trip back would be a brisk run through fairly dense woods, but he had practiced the route several times each of the last two nights and there would be no problem. Ali considered another cigarette but decided against it. In a few minutes he would be making his mark, and he wanted no distractions. Distractions could lead to jail, and Ali would commit suicide before going to jail. He had made that pact with himself long ago.

Unfortunately, tonight's client was a jilted lover, a wealthy old man whose young trophy wife was running around. Her lover did nothing but work out at a gym and steal other men's wives—or so the husband claimed. A muscle head. But there was a twist. Apparently the muscle head was aware that the old man was wealthy and somewhat a pillar of the community. He had communicated to the old man that he had managed to take pictures of himself and the trophy wife in various sexual contortions without exposing his own identity. The muscle head was prepared to distribute these pictures to various indiscreet organizations unless he received a fairly substantial monetary compensation. Specifically, a million dollars. The muscle head believed he was meeting Ali tonight to exchange pictures for cash.

A pair of headlights moved slowly into the strip-mall parking lot. Ali moved behind the corner of the dry-cleaning establishment and peered around the brick wall. As the car passed under the first streetlamp, he could see that it was not a marked police cruiser. But Ali would be careful. The police checked the mall at least three times a night—at least they had in each of the previous two evenings—and once the car had been an unmarked cruiser.

Ali glanced quickly over his shoulder at the trees and bushes at the edge of the parking lot toward which he would run after the execution. For a split second Ali thought he noticed something unusual, a movement which seemed somehow unnatural, as if it did not belong. He squinted into the gloom, but there was nothing. Just branches moving in the breeze.

The car rolled slowly across the lot to the covered walkway in front of the row of stores. It came to a halt before the Sicilian pizza parlor three stores down from the dry cleaner. The driver's side door opened, and a man stepped out onto the blacktop. He shut the door gently and whistled once. Ali relaxed. It was the mark. The whistle was the signal. Ali pressed his left arm against his side, feeling for the .22 pistol hanging from the shoulder holster. It gave him comfort to feel the gun there, like an old friend. He had chosen the .22 because the silencer attached more easily than to his .38 or his .44 Magnum. And the .22-caliber hollow-point bullets would be just as deadly from close range.

Ali's heart began to pump more quickly. Even after nineteen years and so many marks, the adrenaline still flowed just before a kill. It was a good sign. When the excitement was gone, he would know it was time to get out.

The mark stepped into the soft glow of the ultraviolet rays emanating from the card shop one store away from the dry cleaner and stopped. Ali pressed the .22 against his side once again for comfort, then whistled twice.

The mark's head turned quickly in the direction of the sound.

"Move this way," Ali whispered loudly, his Iranian accent still thick even after many years in the United States. He peered through the faint light, attempting to see the man's face, but the light was not strong enough. It was always better to see a man's face before you killed him.

The mark moved five steps toward Ali.

"Stop there."

The mark did exactly as he was told.

Ali stepped partially out from behind the corner of the building. The other man was less than ten feet away now. Ali's heart pumped furiously. "Do you have the pictures?"

"What?" The mark's voice cracked. He was terribly nervous.

"The package."

"Yes, yes, I have the package. Do you have the money?"

"Sure. Slide the package to me first." Ali glanced around the parking lot.

The mark reached into his coat pocket.

"Slowly." Ali melted behind the brick wall for protection in case the mark tried to pull a gun. He removed the .22 from his shoulder holster and quickly attached the silencer, twisting it onto the end of the barrel.

The mark produced an envelope, bent to his knees, and slid it across the pavement toward Ali. With practiced timing the Iranian moved out from behind the corner of the building, knelt, scooped up the package, stood, trained the revolver on the mark's chest and fired. The crack of the gun was muffled by the silence. Ali fired twice more into the mark's chest as the man fell backward onto the pavement.

Like a cat Ali was on the man. The mark moaned as he clutched his chest and stomach. Ali reached for the man's wrist and noticed immediately that it was not as thick as it should have been if this man pumped iron. There was little life remaining in the pulse. Ali stepped mercilessly on the man's neck, careful not to look into the pleading eyes, bent down, and fired once more, this time directly into the mark's heart. He was careful to aim in such a way that the bullet would not ricochet back at him. The mark's fingers twitched involuntarily for several moments, and then his eyes rolled far back in his head and his fingers lay still.

Quickly, Ali began to stuff the envelope into his coat pocket. He rose, and as he stood, he came face to face with a 9-mm pistol. Ali attempted to raise his own weapon in defense, but he didn't have a chance. The gun exploded into his face. For a brief moment there was searing pain, and then only darkness.

The Iranian tumbled sideways onto the body of Jeremy Case. Phoenix Grey hesitated for a moment to see if either man moved again, but there was no reason to wait. Both were corpses.

Phoenix reached into the pocket of his windbreaker for the Polaroids. He sprinkled pictures of the prostitute in various stages of undress over the two bodies. Grey had taken the pictures two days earlier in a remote Kansas field, promising five thousand dollars to the woman in return. Then he had shot her and dumped her body in a swamp. He hadn't even considered letting her go. He wasn't one to leave transactions open-ended.

Grey bent down to the .22-caliber pistol that had fallen from the Iranian's hand, removed the silencer, and stuffed it into his windbreaker. Then he placed the gun back down on the pavement. The silencer would smack of professionalism, and he did not want that. Grey moved to the other man's body and carefully pressed the 9-mm pistol into his dead, outstretched right hand. Jeremy Case was right-handed. He knew that. He knew everything about Jeremy Case.

A double murder over a woman. The police would find holes in the story but would have no other explanation and in the end would be satisfied. Grey stripped off the latex gloves, shoved them into his pocket, and walked to where the envelope had fallen onto the pavement. He picked it up, careful to avoid Ali's blood, which spattered the outside.

Grey stared at the fallen Iranian for a moment. Ali had bought the jilted-lover story so easily. He had had no idea what was actually in that package or what was at stake. He hadn't known who the other man really was or who the old man was and hadn't even tried to find out. Chump hit men were so gullible and so stupid.

Grey slipped around the corner of the dry-cleaning shop and moved quickly toward the woods. It had gone so smoothly. They would be appreciative.

3

The hospital reeked of disinfectant. Down the hallway, several nurses and doctors, clad in green surgical scrubs, rushed a supine figure atop a chrome stretcher into the emergency room. Their heads were covered with tight caps, and they screamed as they sprinted and banged between the double doors. Jenny shivered as she moved out of the hallway and into the private room. She hated hospitals. They reminded her too much of the weeks she had spent watching her mother fade slowly to nothing.

Falcon lay asleep on the sterile bed. His head remained heavily bandaged, but despite the gauze and the week he had already spent at the Princeton Medical Center, he still seemed vibrant to Jenny, still tremendously charismatic. She stared at his face as she moved across the room. Fortunately the butt of the shotgun had smashed into his scalp and not his face. The cut had required twenty-three stitches, and Falcon had lost a great deal of blood, but there would be no permanent damage.

Jenny stood by the bed for several minutes, watching him breathe. She had witnessed him fall to the floor from the blow of the gun stock and seen the blood begin pouring from the wound. It was bad—that was obvious immediately. But she could do nothing to help him because Bernstein had pointed the shotgun straight at her after smashing Falcon's head. For several seconds, what seemed like an eternity, he had simply stared at her. Then his eyes had begun to flicker into the tops of his sockets. Slowly at first, then rapidly, then furiously. Never had she been so scared. But suddenly her emotion had changed from terror to horror as Bernstein shoved the barrel of the shotgun into his own mouth and committed suicide, spraying particles of skull and gray matter across the ceiling.

Even as the bloody spray from Bernstein's brain began to mist down onto her and Froworth's assistant, she had crawled to Falcon and covered the gaping wound with her own hand, screaming at the other woman to call 911. Falcon had remained conscious for a few moments, and as she pressed firmly against the wound, he had stared into her eyes, unable to speak. Then his eyes closed. She thought he was dead, but she did not release her hand, nor did she cry—until the paramedics had loaded him into the ambulance.

Falcon's eyes opened. "Well, hello there. Are you an angel?" His voice was strong.

"Yes. You've died and gone to heaven." She turned and moved to the room's lone window.

Falcon looked around. "Hmm. This isn't exactly what I had in mind as heavenly decor. Perhaps you could speak to the chief angel and have things spiced up a little. Like, perhaps we could move a wet bar in here for starters."

So he was beginning to feel better again. "Oh, stop it!" Her tone was too reproachful, but Jenny couldn't help it. She didn't want him to hear her relief. That would have made her vulnerable.

"What's wrong with you?" Falcon groaned as he pulled himself to a sitting position.

"Nothing! And is there really any need to groan, Andrew? Aren't you overdoing it a little bit? I mean, it's not as if you were hurt that badly." She raised the window blind. It was sleeting. Spring was late in coming to the East this year. "You're just a big baby," she continued, "no different from any other man. Somebody gives you a little tap on the head, and you moan and groan and have to spend a week in the hospital."

Falcon grinned. He watched her closely as she gazed outside. She had followed the ambulance to the hospital after he was wounded. The nurses had insisted that she leave at midnight, but she had paid no attention, continuing to dab a damp cloth about his face until morning. And she had come to visit him each day since, because she knew there was no one else to come. He had halfheartedly told her that she didn't have to, but she would simply nod and be back the following morning. And he was glad. He was beginning to understand that the flashy looks were just one side of her. She also seemed a genuinely kind person. "Well, if you don't like my moaning and groaning, you can leave." Falcon thrust a third pillow behind his back so that he could sit up straighter.

Jenny turned slowly from the window, raised one eyebrow, and then began to move toward the door.

"Hey, come on. I'm just kidding. Hey!"

Jenny stopped at the end of the bed and stared down at him.

"I'm sorry, Jenny."

"Ask me to stay."

"Stay." Falcon said the word immediately. He tried to say it casually, but the look in his eyes belied his tone. He broke into a wide grin. "Please."

Jenny smiled back. She could not resist him.

Falcon cocked his head to one side. "It occurs to me that I don't even know where you have to come from when you make these Mother Teresa visits. Do you live around here?"

"No. I live in New Brunswick. It's about fifteen miles north of here." She paused. "I've lived there all my life. I like it there. It's a working-class town." She said the last few words matter-of-factly. "Not like Princeton."

So she didn't have a complex about her working-class town or about making it out, though she clearly could with her looks and her brain, Falcon thought. "Do you want to be a secretary, I'm sorry, executive assistant, for the rest of your life?"

"You don't beat around the bush, do you, Andrew Falcon?" Jenny asked.

He raised his hands in mock apology.

"I'm trying to save some money so I can go back to college and get my degree. I finished two years at Montclair State."

"Why did you quit? I know, too many parties."

Jenny shook her head. "Dad couldn't take care of my younger sister by himself when he got sick. So, I had to take care of her. One thing led to another, and I just sort of never went back."

"But your mom . . ." Immediately he wished he hadn't said it. How could he have been so stupid?

Jenny did not answer right away. "She died of lung cancer when I was very young."

"I'm sorry."

"It's okay, Andrew. Dad told me that Mom smoked two packs of cigarettes a day."

"You don't smoke, do you?"

Jenny shook her head. "Do you?"

"No."

They were silent for a few moments.

"What about you, Andrew? Tell me about yourself." Jenny attempted to get him to open up.

"Oh, I'm pretty boring. I like to work. That's about it."

Jenny waited a few moments, but he said nothing more. She played with the clipboard hanging from the end of the bed for a few seconds, then spoke again. "Andrew, I know this is difficult to have to face, but what will you do now that MD Link is . . ." She did not finish the sentence.

"Bankrupt. Kaput. Gonzo. Is that what you were trying to say?"

She nodded hesitantly, searching his face for emotion. But there was none.

Falcon stared at the ceiling for a moment and then grinned. "You don't suppose Froworth's assistant might invest in MD Link despite the little sideshow?"

Jenny shook her head. "Be serious, Andrew."

"Serious, you want me to be serious?" He exhaled loudly. "Well, I've always thought about moving to Vermont. It's a beautiful state, and I love to ski. Maybe I'll buy a house up there with some land and ski my life away. Of course, they'd probably want money for the house and the lift tickets."

"Do you have any money left?"

"A little." Falcon grimaced and touched his head again. "Funny how just the thought of money can induce physical pain." He glanced at her. "Do you like Vermont?"

"I've never been." Jenny smiled. "I've never been anywhere really."

"Would you like to go sometime?"

Jenny glanced up into Falcon's eyes immediately, wondering if he had meant what she so wanted him to mean by those words.

Falcon stared back. So she cared about him. He sensed it in her face immediately.

"Yes, I would. Of course I would."

He didn't respond to her answer right away. He simply continued to stare. She was so beautiful. And caring. Falcon bit his lip. But she was a Jersey girl. And he had dated lots of those in high school. "Great." He smiled. "You should get a bunch of your girlfriends together and go sometime. I could tell you all the right places to go. Out-of-the-way places the typical tourists wouldn't find."

Jenny's mouth opened slightly, and then she glanced down at the bed.

"Mr. Falcon!" There was a heavy knock at the door. "Time to take your vitals."

"I've got to go anyway." Jenny's voice was hoarse.

The door opened. An intern, stethoscope hanging from his neck, entered the room. He saw Jenny and stopped. "Oh, sorry."

"No, it's okay." Jenny turned and picked up her purse from the dresser and moved past the young man toward the door.

"Jenny! Wait! Jesus, you just got here." But she was gone. Falcon glanced at the intern, who shrugged his shoulders. "Sorry, Andrew."

Falcon shook his head. "It's okay." He stared at the door, still slowly swinging shut. "Sometimes I can be a real horse's ass," he muttered.

"Ladies and gentlemen, I have just been handed a special announcement!" The public-address announcer's voice boomed out over halftime at the Harvard-Penn basketball game. "Several moments ago, this letter was found in the press box. I will read it."

The crowd exchanged knowing glances. They had a good idea of what was about to transpire. It had happened every year at an important Harvard event since before the turn of the century.

"It says, 'Good afternoon. Will the person sitting in section seven, row seven, seat seven of the arena please remove the envelope taped to the underside of your seat and deliver it to Harvard officials.' The letter is signed only, 'The Sevens.' "

A bald man in a checkered sports jacket reached beneath his seat as the crowd began to cheer. He found the envelope immediately, ripped it from its hiding place, and held it aloft. The arena burst into thunderous applause. Quickly, the envelope was passed hand to hand up the crowd to the press box. The arena hushed as the envelope made its way to the public-address announcer.

"Ladies and gentlemen, in my hand I have a check made out to Harvard University. The instructions attached indicate only that the Board of Visitors use the money as they see fit. The amount of the check is seven million, seven hundred seventy-seven thousand, seven hundred seventy-seven dollars, and seven cents!"

The crowd exploded again, and by the time the great outpouring of appreciation had subsided, William Rutherford was gone.

4

Devon Chambers shook his head. "He's going to destroy us, Granville. He's already raised income tax rates on people like us to eighty percent and the inheritance tax rate on all estates over six hundred thousand dollars in value to seventy percent. And my sources inside the administration tell me that now he's talking privately about raising the estate tax rate to ninety percent and lowering the threshold amount at which the tax begins from six hundred thousand dollars to three hundred thousand. And you know what? With the kind of populist mandate he has garnered, he might just pull it off." Chambers paused. "It would be the end of the capitalist system as we know it. That kind of estate tax rate would effectively put everyone back to square one after two generations. It would kill any kind of incentive to achieve. It would be the end of the upper class."

Winthrop nodded slowly. "Rutherford suggests a scorched-earth policy." He smiled evilly.

Chambers shuddered, folded his arms across his chest, and shook his head again. He knew what Winthrop meant. "I told you that having Rutherford initiated into the Sevens was a mistake." Chambers' voice was barely more than a whisper—something he passed off as the result of a chronic sore throat. "He's just one of those military types who believes everything can be accomplished through force."

Granville Winthrop sipped on the Scotch mist and then replaced it atop the mahogany table in front of the low chair. "Do I need to remind you of your oath never to criticize another member of the society?"

Chambers' thin face settled into a superior expression. As if he would abide by what Winthrop had said only out of respect for the tradition—not Rutherford or Winthrop. He shook his head and coughed a deep phlegmy cough. "No, you don't need to remind me."

Winthrop glanced around the small, private card room of the Harvard Club. It was a nice place to come when you needed to have a private conversation away from Wall Street. The walls were painted a dark red and the molding a gloss white. On the walls were prints of foxhunting scenes: beautiful prints of horses, riders, and hounds churning through fields and over fences in search of the prey. It wasn't good to be the fox in life. But if there were no foxes, then there could be no horses, hounds, or riders—and no chase. And life would be awfully boring without the chase, Winthrop thought to himself.

He inhaled. The room smelled faintly of smoke as the oak logs burned slowly in the fireplace. The orange flames licked the blackened screen around the hearth. Outside it was cold and gray. In here it was warm and comfortable. Winthrop reflected briefly on the homeless man he had passed lying on Forty-fourth Street as he walked to the club from Park Avenue. A frigid night ahead for the indigent. Then he picked up his glass and forgot about the man. "Rutherford said we might have to kill you too if you can't keep up your end." Winthrop had noticed Chambers' superior expression.

Chambers glanced up quickly, his small brown eyes darting to Winthrop's. The superior expression melted from his face.

Winthrop stared at Chambers over the glass as he drank. "Not really, Devon." Winthrop replaced the glass on the table.

Chambers sank back into his chair, relieved. For a moment he had actually thought Winthrop was serious. A small man and reed thin, he had no physical courage at all. His power in life had come only from his corporate authority. His skin was pallid, almost devoid of pigmentation, and his hair, what little was left, was jet black. Combed to one side, it contrasted sharply with the pale forehead.

How did a man like this, a very ordinary man indeed, become chairman of the board of DuPont? Winthrop wondered idly. Of course he already had the answer. Chambers knew everything and everyone there was to know in the chemical industry. And he was a political animal. Which only made sense. He had been bullied as a child because of his lack of physical stature, and he had been forced to survive using his brain. "I would treat Bill with a little more respect, especially in front of me, Devon. I have a great deal of admiration for what he has accomplished in his life, and I happen to believe that there is a place in the world for physical intimidation. An important place. He has one of the most difficult assignments of all of us with regard to the project. Let's remember that."

Chambers recognized the serious tone and nodded meekly. He had made a grave error and would not make it again, no matter how much he despised Rutherford. Winthrop was not to be irritated.

Granville snorted. Chambers might be a powerful man in the industrial world, but Winthrop was the powerful man in the investment-banking arena. And to Winthrop, investment banking was many times more important than any other industry on earth.

"I'm sorry, Granville," Chambers whispered.

Now he was groveling. Winthrop finished the Scotch mist. Chambers was old and weak, and it had been years since he had really been a powerful figure in the chemical industry—he had retired six years ago from DuPont at the mandatory age of sixty-five. Although he hoped all of these things wouldn't infringe on Chambers' ability to hold up his end of the deal, Winthrop was becoming less and less confident each time they talked; but there was nothing that could be done now. Everything was already in motion, and Chambers was the front man. "I'm going to stay for a while, and we shouldn't be seen leaving together."

At first Chambers did not understand.

"Devon, don't let the door hit you in the ass on the way out."

Chambers rose immediately and left the room, closing the door behind him without a word.

Granville smiled at the elderly man in the coatroom of the Harvard Club as the man handed Winthrop his camel-hair overcoat. Granville slipped the man a twenty-dollar bill. Here was a person at least trying to earn an honest day's pay, unlike the indigent man, who was probably still lying facedown on the Forty-fourth Street sidewalk. Winthrop turned as he began to don the overcoat, and as he did, he came face to face with Falcon.

"Hello, Granville." Andrew's voice betrayed no emotion.

"Mr. Falcon." Winthrop stopped putting on his coat for a moment and then continued cautiously, not removing his eyes from the younger man. He was suspicious of Falcon's motives.

"How is the Mergers & Acquisitions Department at Winthrop, Hawkins?"

"Fine. Thank you for asking." Winthrop buttoned the coat.

A chilly gust tore through the small lobby as two men entered the club. They paused to say hello, as was the custom, but sensed that the scene was not altogether friendly and hurriedly passed Winthrop and Falcon into the trophy-lined great room beyond.

"I read a story in the *Wall Street Journal* a week ago pointing out that the firm's M&A business was off forty percent this year." Falcon touched his scalp lightly as he spoke. He was still experiencing slight headaches from the blow to his head.

Winthrop followed Andrew's fingers as they felt for the scar hidden beneath his hair, which had grown back in around the wound now. Then he smiled guardedly. "You can't always believe what you read in the press. You should know that, Mr. Falcon. Now if you'll excuse me . . ." Winthrop began to make his way down the steps toward the glass doors.

"I can bring five deals to the table tomorrow."

Winthrop stopped and turned. He looked at Falcon for a moment and then moved slowly back to where Falcon stood, until their faces were just inches apart. "Then why don't you call Merrill Lynch?"

Falcon showed no emotion. He had prepared himself for this reaction. "I guess this means we won't be seeing each other again."

Winthrop glared at Falcon, and then his visage slowly turned into a sinister smile. Without a word he wheeled around and left the club. Everything was proceeding as expected. Falcon had come begging. Now he was exactly where Winthrop wanted him.

5

For a senior vice president, Glen Malley's office was not terribly impressive, Falcon thought. It was expansive, but the furniture was dated and somewhat dusty. Nowhere in the office was there a Bloomberg terminal flashing updated stock and bond quotes. How in the hell did this guy keep in touch with what was going on in the world? So far the National Southern Bank hadn't impressed Falcon, and this was his fourth round of interviews. But what other choice did he have? The money was all but gone, even the squirrel account the bankruptcy judge hadn't found.

Falcon watched as Malley jawed on the phone. He was on the wrong side of forty, completely gray and fighting a weight problem with baggy suits. At lunch Malley had consumed a sixteen-ounce steak, a large, sour-cream-covered baked potato, several pieces of generously buttered bread, and a huge chocolate tort—in addition to the two martinis. His face was bright red, and it wasn't because he was Irish. Falcon wondered how soon it would be before Malley was killed by a massive heart attack.

Malley hung up the phone. "Sorry, Andrew. That was the call I was waiting for. My secretary won't allow us to be interrupted again."

"It's really not a problem, Glen."

"Thanks." Malley smiled. "Now, do you have any more questions about the National Southern Bank? NASO's evolution?

More about the direction of the bank in the future? That kind of stuff."

Falcon had read and reread the annual report. The National Southern Bank, or NASO, as it was known on the Street, was the fourth largest commercial bank headquartered in the United States, with over one hundred and seventy-five billion dollars in assets and almost fifteen billion in capital. It had been formed in 1991 by the merger of two of the largest commercial banks in the Southeast, First Atlanta and the Trust Company of Alabama. Subsequent to the merger, the combined entity acquired the Bank of Manhattan, or the BOM, as it was affectionately known in finance circles. The BOM was a substandard performer in the banking industry but had a nice headquarters building and a presence in New York State, which allowed NASO to move its executive offices to New York City. They were sitting there now, on the fourteenth floor of 350 Park Avenue. "Glen, I don't think I have any other questions."

Malley nodded. "Okay."

Falcon laughed. "It's funny how things come full circle sometimes."

Malley looked up. "What do you mean?"

"Winthrop, Hawkins represented the Bank of Manhattan when NASO acquired it."

"Really?" The other man seemed genuinely interested. "Tell me about it. I wasn't with NASO at that point."

"Well, the transaction was hostile, so the senior executives of the Bank of Manhattan knew they would be out on their asses if NASO was successful in acquiring the BOM. They fought it—at least until Winthrop, Hawkins negotiated some very nice severance packages for the top five executives. It may interest you to know, Glen, that they received a combined severance agreement of thirty million dollars, which of course came right out of the shareholders' pockets." Falcon related this tidbit to show Malley just how privy to sensitive information he had been at one time.

Malley was impressed. He was no longer smiling.

"The amount was never explicitly stated anywhere. It was buried in several different fees supposedly paid to us—I mean Winthrop, Hawkins—and several law firms. And it was to be paid out over four years. But Winthrop, Hawkins and the law firms simply took the money they received and sent it to the five executives."

"You're kidding." Malley was incredulous. "But that's ill . . ."

"Illegal? No, not really. Unethical maybe. But not illegal. I checked out the strategy with the attorneys myself. We had to be careful about taxes, but it was all very legal. Though, of course, it certainly came close to the edge. But that was what it was all about in those days. Coming as close to the edge as possible. Winthrop, Hawkins made ten million dollars as our standard advisory fee. We were also to receive another ten million if we were able to keep Bank of Manhattan independent for at least a year after NASO filed its 13-D. You see, the BOM's senior executives would be able to significantly increase their pensions if we were able to string it out over a year. Do you remember how long it took NASO to acquire the BOM from start to finish?"

Malley shook his head slowly.

"Fifty-three weeks. Winthrop, Hawkins made its extra ten million, and the BOM's senior executives pushed up their pensions by about fifty thousand dollars a year."

Malley laughed. "You were the partner responsible for the deal at Winthrop, Hawkins?"

Falcon nodded.

"Must have been pretty exciting at that time. Christ, there were takeovers and mergers popping up all over the place. Every day it seemed like. You couldn't pick up the *Wall Street Journal* without reading about another one."

"It was an interesting time, although at that point, in 1991, merger activity was already far below its high point."

Malley stared at a painting of colonial New York Harbor hanging on the far wall. "The late eighties really were incredible. Even for commercial bankers." Malley seemed wistful, as if he were recalling a tender moment with a child. "God, there was so much money thrown around with the leveraged buyouts and hostile takeovers. We made huge fees and lots of interest income. Nice bonuses too. Whatever happened to all of that?"

"You know, a few people got a little too greedy. Drexel, Burnham went out of business, and the government basically shut everything down. Of course, the investment bankers kept right on making huge amounts of money undoing what they had done."

"Andrew, do you think those days will ever come back? The hostile takeovers, the leveraged buyouts, and the huge amounts of money, I mean?"

"We'd need a change of administrations, I think. This President is clearly not going to allow all of that to come back. From what I understand, the Federal Reserve has a mandate to come down hard on any bank that tries to lend into one of these huge leveraged buyouts. And this guy Filipelli, chairman of the Fed, is a tough man. He regards Wall Street as a necessary evil. He's not going to allow the investment banks to use the commercial banks like that again, just to be able to line their own pockets with more cash at the risk of the national banking system."

"So the excitement is gone for good."

"At least for a long while."

Malley took a sip of coffee. He was beginning to sober up from lunch, and his focus returned to the interview. "Andrew, if you don't mind my saying so, one of the things I'd worry about if you were to come here is that the job wouldn't hold your interest. I mean, it wouldn't be exciting the way it was at Winthrop, Hawkins. Commercial banking without all of the leveraged buyouts can be, well, pretty boring sometimes. Oh, sure, we're trying to get into all that investment-banking stuff, underwriting stocks and bonds, advisory work and so on, but it will take years before we get anywhere. As you know, firms like Winthrop,

Hawkins have a lock on that business, and they aren't letting go of it easily." Malley gazed at Falcon intently, as if judging him. "I think this job is a quick fix for you. You need money because you lost what you had in that software company, so you'll accept our offer. But as soon as you have an opportunity to jump to one of the investment banks, you'll go. Please don't take offense to this, but I have to be honest. If it were up to me, I probably wouldn't offer you this job." Malley paused. "But it isn't up to me."

Falcon did not bother telling Malley that he had already visited almost every investment bank on Wall Street—even the very small firms—and no one wanted him. At first they would be excited about the prospect of recruiting such talent. But then, after the third or fourth round of interviews, just when they should have begun talking compensation, things would go cold, and the human-resource people would send him a thin envelope apologizing for the fact that he wasn't quite what they were looking for. It was difficult for him to understand. It was as if someone were following him, giving the firms information that caused them to back away from hiring him. But that was ridiculous. Just paranoia brought on by his dire financial situation.

Falcon looked Malley straight in the eye. "What do you mean it isn't up to you? You're the senior vice president in charge of all lending east of the Mississippi. You are the decision maker."

"Not this time, Andrew. You must have really impressed somebody upstairs, because I get the feeling that if you don't take this job, they're going to fire me. Who the hell did you talk to in the executive suite?"

Falcon shook his head. "No one."

"You haven't met Boreman or Barksdale yet?"

"You mean the chairman and vice chairman?"

Malley nodded.

"No. I met an SVP in human resources, but that was it."

"The merger was what, five years ago? Boreman wouldn't have

been at NASO at that point. But Barksdale was. Maybe he remembers you from the merger," Malley said.

"Maybe."

"How did you hear about this position, Falcon?"

There it was—the first time Malley had referred to him simply as Falcon, not Andrew. It was the classic evolution all business associates underwent, and it still bothered him after so many years. They called him Andrew for a short time, to be polite, and then instinctively began calling him Falcon. Friends called him Andrew. Business associates called him Falcon. But wasn't that what he wanted? A name people would remember. Wasn't that why he had given himself the new name after high school?

Falcon answered the question. "A headhunter called me out of the blue. Some guy I had never heard of before. He wouldn't tell me how he got my name, but that's typical for those guys."

"It's amazing how fast your headhunter became aware of this position. We fired the woman who headed the team we want you to take over only two weeks ago." Malley glanced at the open calendar on his desk. "Wednesday, the week of the twenty-first."

"Really? That guy did work pretty fast." Strange, Falcon thought. The headhunter had called him on Monday of that week, two days *before* NASO had actually fired the woman. And the headhunter had specifically mentioned the position the woman had held and that they had let her go, though of course he did not mention her by name.

"When did the headhunter call you?"

"That Friday. The twenty-fifth, I guess." For some reason Falcon did not want to be forthcoming.

"Uh-huh." Malley continued to stare at Falcon. "Well, the bottom line is that we want to hire you. We're willing to pay you a salary of one hundred twenty thousand a year and a bonus that could reach fifty percent of your annual salary."

One hundred eighty thousand dollars. That was it. The maximum he could expect to earn. It beat the crap out of food stamps, but it didn't come close to the $1.1 million he had earned at Winthrop, Hawkins. And it paled in comparison to what MD Link should have been worth by now.

"We want you to head up Team Two, which is responsible for marketing NASO's credit and noncredit products throughout Maryland, Delaware, Pennsylvania, and Ohio. Your title will be vice president, and you will have five professionals reporting to you, another four administrative assistants, and three secretaries—one of whom will be your personal secretary."

Just a vice president. There were probably two thousand VPs in the NASO organization. "I would report to you?"

"Yes."

Well, there was an opportunity. Not to wish any harm to him, but he'd probably be dead of that heart attack in a year. Maybe the bank would move him into Malley's position. "I'd like to be able to hire my own secretary." Falcon thought of Jenny. She still hadn't found a job yet either.

"I don't think there would be a problem with that. Can I take that to mean you're going to accept the offer?"

"It means I would like to take a couple of days to think about it."

Malley nodded uneasily.

The woman danced effortlessly to the heavy beat of the bass booming from huge speakers positioned throughout the trendy Upper East Side nightclub. Several men danced around her, though none had been invited to do so. They moved wildly, attempting to catch her attention, but she remained impassive to their gyrations. She was lost in the music.

Falcon watched her move behind and between the arms and legs of her uninvited suitors. She was gorgeous, absolutely gorgeous, and he was impressed. She was tall, perhaps five-eight, and the bun atop her head, formed by her long, silky, ebony hair, made her appear even taller. Her beautiful face was accented by huge, dark eyes, high cheekbones, and full, red lips. Her long black dress plunged deeply between small but well-formed breasts. Her skin was dark, but it was difficult to determine in the low light of the club just how dark she was. Greek? Perhaps even Spanish. He didn't care.

Out of all the beautiful women at the club, this was the one the men watched most carefully. They watched her every move. The insecure men pointed and poked each other, fantasizing because they knew they stood no chance with her. The confident men hung back by themselves, calculating. And the stupid ones tried to dance with her.

It was not simply her physical beauty that attracted Falcon and the rest of the men to her. It was the way this creature carried herself. She danced beautifully, never too quickly, never too slowly, always in time with the music. As though she were making love to it. She completely ignored the men about her even as new suitors approached with each song, and the ones who had tried to gain her attention for a few minutes faded into the mass of dancing flesh in search of easier prey. Her head and arms swayed rhythmically. Falcon gazed, mesmerized.

He had positioned himself against a column, close to where she moved. He found that he could not take his eyes from her. It was as if a lightning bolt had struck him, and he was too intoxicated to worry about his pride at this point. Every few moments he swore that she glanced at him through innocent eyes. But he knew it was simply the alcohol and his imagination.

Suddenly a large, dark man moved through the crowd with greater purpose than any of the other suitors. He did not dance or circle around her until finally coming close, as the other men did. He walked directly to her, cutting through the gyrating male bodies, who were at first irritated at the new competitor but quickly melted away as they became aware of his huge size.

Falcon's pulse quickened as the man took the woman by the wrist and began to pull her toward a door at the back of the club.

He watched them go, standing straighter as they moved away. She did not complain, but neither did she readily accept her fate, tugging slightly against the man. As they reached the door, the woman turned to take one more glance at the dance floor. And then she was gone, pulled into a private room by the dark man. Falcon watched the door close.

For several minutes he stood staring at the door. When it became obvious the woman was not coming back, he turned again toward the dance floor. There was nothing else to compare to the dark-haired vision. Was that all it had been? A vision?

Falcon politely declined a buxom blond woman who asked him to dance. She was pretty, but his mind remained full of the beautiful girl with the dark eyes. He watched the blonde return to the dance floor as he brought the scotch to his lips. It was his sixth drink in the last three hours.

A hundred and twenty thousand dollars in salary. A fifty percent bonus. A hundred and eighty thousand dollars a year in total compensation. Most would be ecstatic. Not Falcon. It had been the wrong decision to leave Winthrop, Hawkins. There could be no denying that any longer. He had attempted to contact Granville twice after their confrontation at the Harvard Club, hoping that the older man would soften on his promise to never again allow Falcon to work at Winthrop, Hawkins. But Falcon's calls were not returned. He had tried one last time after leaving NASO this afternoon. But nothing. By now he would have been earning several million dollars a year instead of the paltry compensation NASO was offering. He had thumbed his nose at Granville, and now Granville was thumbing his right back.

The music seemed to grow louder. Falcon glanced at his watch. Two forty-five in the morning. Whenever he awoke later today in the one-bedroom Queens hovel he had rented to facilitate his job search, he would call Malley and accept the offer at NASO. What choice did he have? He was eating hot dogs for breakfast, lunch, and dinner. In another month he wouldn't be able to afford rent.

The day after tomorrow, when the terrible hangover had subsided, he would take the ten-thousand-dollar signing bonus NASO was offering and rent himself a real apartment in Manhattan.

Falcon turned to go, to find a taxi that would take him all the way back to Queens. But as he turned, she was there, blocking his path. To his surprise, he found himself staring into the same dark eyes that had fascinated him so from the dance floor. She was even more beautiful than he had first thought.

Falcon was vaguely aware of the circle of suitors—her constant entourage—but they were irrelevant now, and the dark man was nowhere to be seen. Falcon was the focus of her attention. She smiled slightly, tilted her head back and to the side, and took his hand. And suddenly Winthrop, Hawkins, NASO, the bankrupt MD Link, and his financial problems evaporated.

Phoenix Grey lifted the soft drink to his mouth as he stood in a dark corner of the club. He had been watching Falcon for two weeks and felt as if he knew the man intimately. Suddenly he sensed the change in Falcon's demeanor. The girl, with one look, had lifted him out of his depression. She could become a problem. He would have to report this development to Rutherford.

6

The chairman of the Federal Reserve System of the United States of America. His power was absolute and irrevocable. Once appointed by the President and confirmed by the Senate, he was beholden to no one, just as Supreme Court justices, once confirmed, were insulated from the electorate. His term lasted only four years, and he could be replaced at the end of it by another Presidential appointee, but that didn't happen often. Any President who dared consider the idea of replacing a sitting Fed chairman against his will risked the wrath of the "I" bankers, who would crater the stock and bond markets. The Street placed grave importance on an independent Fed chairman, and every President was painfully aware of this.

Carter Filipelli sat alone at the head of the huge mahogany table in the middle of the Federal Reserve's formal boardroom. He was awaiting the arrival of the other nineteen people who would sit at this meeting of the Federal Open Market Committee, or, as the Street called it, simply the FOMC. They should have been a powerful group, but Filipelli did not allow them to exert their authority to any great degree.

The boardroom was cold and imposing, hardly conducive to back-and-forth exchanges between the participants, and Filipelli used this sterility of setting to his advantage. Frowning brass eagles, polished so that they shone even in the dim light of the large room, perched on the upper edge of the chandelier that dominated the space above the long table. The walls were covered by maps of the twelve Federal Reserve districts that sliced the country into strange and asymmetric shapes. Behind Filipelli was a huge fireplace in which lay several large logs that had been on the hearth for at least a decade. Over the fireplace was another brass eagle, this bird much larger than those on the chandelier. One talon clutched arrows, the other an olive branch. The air in the great room smelled like that of an ancient library, musty and bookish.

Filipelli laughed aloud, and the sound echoed in the huge room. He was the Fed chairman, arguably one of the most powerful people in the world. With only sporadic resistance from one or two of the other members of the FOMC, he set monetary policy for the United States by controlling interest rates and bringing to bear the Fed's vast cash reverses. He could raise rates to head off inflation, thereby inducing a recession, causing pain and suffering; or he could lower rates, spurring economic growth and putting billions into the collective pockets of the country.

Many Americans did not understand the absolute power of the Fed chairman: his ability to act independently and without constraint, his ability to single-handedly create prosperity or poverty. It flew in the face of every tenet of democracy. And this blatant disregard for the American system of government was not advertised by either political party or by Wall Street. It was perhaps the only thing in the world these three constituencies could unanimously agree upon. And with good reason. If the general populace came to understand the Fed's unchecked structure, they might demand change, which would spell disaster for the country. No Fed chairman could be shackled by a democratic process and be expected to react to the split-second machinations of modern financial markets.

Because of his tremendous clout, financial analysts and investors worldwide attempted to interpret Filipelli's every move. An utterance, an offhand remark, a *sneeze*, for Christ's sake, could set off panic buying or selling in markets around the globe. He laughed again. It was an incredible country where a poor Italian family, only two generations removed from the heart of Brooklyn, now hailing from a backwoods Alabama town, could produce a son able to rise to such a position of influence without the use of military force. Perhaps it really did matter who you went to kindergarten with.

Typically, the chairman of the Federal Reserve and the President worked at arm's length. But President Buford J. Warren, former Democratic Senator from Alabama and a self-proclaimed Washington outsider, had proven to be an atypical President, a man unwilling to abide by tradition simply for tradition's sake. He had deemed that the country, mired in an economic malaise brought on by the huge federal budget deficit, needed action when he took over the executive branch.

So when the existing Fed chairman's term expired three months after Warren's election, he bucked the system and kicked the man out, calling on his old friend, Carter Filipelli, who, at the time, was chief executive of Alabama's largest savings and loan, Great Southeastern Savings, to run the Federal Reserve. The President needed Filipelli to take firm control of the country's central bank and assist him in implementing his domestic and foreign policies. Now, after three years at the helm, after all the financial pundits had initially predicted doom for the country as a result of the President selecting such an inexperienced man for such a terribly important job, and after Wall Street had initially crushed the New York Stock Exchange and the government bond market upon the announcement of Filipelli as chairman, he was one of the most respected men in Washington. Not liked, but respected. And he had the President to thank. Filipelli would be loyal to the man until the day he died.

In twos and threes the other members of the FOMC began to trickle into the boardroom, their conversations ending immediately at the large oak door. They moved silently toward their assigned seats. The room was intimidating even to these people of importance, so they did not converse once they entered it. Finally, all but one representative had taken his or her seat in the stiff, straight-backed chairs.

The FOMC met eight times a year on a regularly scheduled basis in the Washington boardroom, and on an ad hoc basis if market conditions warranted. The primary job of the committee members was to decide what action, if any, was needed to stimulate or retard the growth of the United States economy. They were also responsible for the health of the member banks of the national banking system and for calming jittery financial markets in times of turmoil. The committee was composed of Filipelli and the six Federal Reserve governors, the twelve bank presidents of the United States Federal Reserve districts, and the assistant secretary to the board. Only eight of the members—Filipelli, the six governors, and the New York Fed president, Wendell Smith—had permanent votes on the committee. And only twelve members voted at any meeting—the other four votes were filled on a rotating basis by the eleven non–New York bank presidents.

Filipelli looked around the room, making eye contact with each person individually, and the man or woman formally nodded back at the chairman before he would relieve them of his fierce glare. Each member's vote theoretically carried the same weight, but Filipelli so dominated the proceedings that any vote had become little more than a formality. Filipelli ruled the twenty-member committee with an iron fist, leaving little room for negotiation. His manner was gruff, and he wasn't afraid of ruffling a few feathers. Though not overtly advertised, Filipelli had a promise from the President to undermine the authority of any FOMC member who was not loyal to the chairman, and each member knew it.

When an FOMC member made a statement he did not care for, Filipelli's reaction was immediate and forceful. He would bang the table with his huge black gavel and then sneer or simply interrupt the speaker and inform him that his time had elapsed. Filipelli did not care if he was perceived as a rube. He was in Washington to do a job, and so far it was going pretty damn well.

The large grandfather clock next to the door chimed nine times. As the ninth chime faded, Filipelli rose quickly, removed his plain suit coat, hung it over the back of his chair, and rolled up the sleeves of his blue dress shirt as he sat down again. The other members watched carefully. No one else would even consider removing his suit coat, much less rolling up his sleeves.

Filipelli would not have been a physically imposing man—he was just five feet nine inches tall and of medium build—except that his features were sharp and well defined. This definition intimidated people. The raven-colored hair lay perfectly flat on the top of his head, slicked straight backward with styling gel to reveal a wide and sloping forehead. But in the back it stuck out, like porcupine quills. Brown eyes darted beneath thin, razor-straight eyebrows. His nose was long and pointed, and his mouth was set in a permanent scowl matching that of the huge eagle over the fireplace behind where he now sat. He rarely smiled in this room.

The black gavel, trimmed with gold paint, smashed onto the table. "The meeting will come to order." Despite his southern upbringing, Filipelli's nasal accent still reflected his Brooklyn roots.

The eighteen other members in attendance straightened in their chairs and attempted to match Filipelli's scowl. None was able to do so.

"It is nine o'clock and the meeting will begin as scheduled." Filipelli spoke with purpose. "President Smith of the New York Federal Reserve district has chosen not to join us today." Filipelli pointed at the empty chair at the end of one side of the table. "He did not bother to inform me of his absence. However, we will continue with our agenda anyway. I thank the rest of you for being punctual. President Obrecht of the Minneapolis

"I'm here, Chairman Filipelli." Wendell Smith sarcastically emphasized the word "Chairman." He moved smoothly into the room, smiling suavely at the other FOMC members. He stopped to shake hands with Obrecht, whispering an apology to the man, who was obviously relieved at Smith's last-minute appearance. Finally, he sauntered to his seat.

The other committee members glanced at one another and leaned back in their chairs. Obrecht was not the only one who was relieved. Smith was the second most powerful member of the FOMC, and without his attendance, Filipelli would have run through the meeting like a freight train.

Filipelli watched Smith open his leather attaché case and arrange several papers before him on the grandiose table. He despised Smith. He was part of the Yankee Establishment and flaunted it. A distant relative of John D. Rockefeller, Smith lived in a gorgeous Darien, Connecticut, mansion with his wife, Traci. Smith was worth at least forty million dollars—more than the rest of the committee combined—and he wasn't bashful about informing others of his wealth. More than once Filipelli had overheard Smith at an official Fed function telling someone about his chalet in Switzerland, the yacht in West Palm, or the Rolls. He was blond, blue-eyed, six feet two inches tall, permanently tanned, and without any outstanding physical features. His clothing was expensive but conservative, except for his neckties and suspenders, which were loud and provocative. His suits were cuffed and never double-breasted. He wore no jewelry save for a plain watch and a plainer, thick gold wedding band. Wendell Smith was a walking WASP billboard.

Filipelli tapped his fingernails on the waxed tabletop as Smith eased back in his seat near the chairman. "Are you ready to begin?" Filipelli asked insincerely.

Smith nodded politely, revealing no emotion whatsoever. His dislike for Filipelli matched Filipelli's dislike for him. But Smith didn't overtly express his hatred the way Filipelli did. That would have been undignified.

Smith's lips curled slightly as he stared at the little Italian. To him, Filipelli was nothing more than a hood. He wore cheap suits, hair gel, cologne, a bracelet, and even a goddamn pinky ring. Smith grimaced. And he was chairman of the Federal Reserve. America had gone too far. Much too far.

"Thank you so much for your cooperation, President Smith." Filipelli rolled his eyes. "The first order of business this morning will be Transtar Savings Bank in Boston. As you all know, Transtar has taken a bath on New England real estate. For all intents and purposes it is insolvent. We need to take control of it before the situation gets worse. Do you agree with this assessment, President Flynn?" Filipelli glared at Mary Flynn, president of the Boston Federal Reserve district. Clearly he wanted no discussion on this point.

Flynn cleared her throat. "I don't disagree. It will be a small bailout. Three or four hundred million at most."

"Is it wise to go in so quickly?" Smith interposed, unwilling to concede quite so fast. "My sources tell me that Transtar may, in fact, be able to raise some fresh outside capital. Maybe we could save the taxpayers the three or four hundred million by waiting a couple of extra weeks." He spoke in a tight-jawed, aristocratic voice.

The rest of the committee gazed at Smith. As president of the New York Federal Reserve, he was much closer to the investment bankers and the markets than any other member of the FOMC—including Filipelli. And because of his wealth, the other members assumed he knew a good investment when he saw one.

Filipelli strummed the table again. He wanted this to go no further. "And I suppose you will be one of these new investors in Transtar."

Harold Butler, president of the Atlanta Fed, snickered. He was the only obvious Filipelli supporter on the FOMC, and the others had nicknamed him the "Lieutenant." Filipelli and Butler were longtime friends.

Smith inhaled slowly and pursed his lips. It was a Filipelli tactic to hurl insinuating missiles. None of the members was allowed to invest for his or her own account because of the possibility of a conflict of interest, and Filipelli knew this. He was simply trying to break the Smith calm. He tried to do so at every meeting. "I resent that, Chairman Filipelli."

Filipelli laughed. "Well, you resent everything about me anyway, so this doesn't surprise me."

"You're right. I do," Smith said. He didn't mind playing the game with this little rube. He didn't mind telling him the truth either.

The other committee members glanced down. Never had a meeting become so personal so quickly. It was well known among the members that Filipelli and Smith did not like each other, but usually they were able to keep their emotions in check.

"Do we have to have further discussion on the matter?" Filipelli pounded the table. He was impatient to move on.

"I don't think so," Butler said. "Open-and-shut case as far as I'm concerned."

"I'll withdraw my objection," said Smith. There was no reason for him to burn powder on this issue. He glanced at Butler, who was smiling at him. What a jackass.

"Good. All in favor of taking over Transtar Bank. All opposed." Filipelli did not even bother to look up from his notebook as he took the vote. "Mr. Secretary, please let the record reflect an eleven-to-one vote in the affirmative on the issue. Next issue." Filipelli glanced up. "Interest rates. Let's get some discussion going."

No one spoke immediately. Smith glanced around, hoping he would not have to lead off. It would be better to be reactive today rather than proactive. He would have a better chance at garnering votes that way.

Finally, Flynn began. She had already been in the fray once and felt slightly more comfortable than the others about jumping in again. "Mr. Chairman, at your strong direction we have followed a rather restrictive course of action over the past three years in order to fight the high inflation that was roiling the markets when you were appointed. But given the inflation data of the past six months—it has been almost nonexistent—perhaps we should inject some reserves into the system to allow for growth. It would certainly benefit my area of the country." Flynn looked around for support.

Smith brought a hand to his face to hide a smile. Flynn's comments would be music to Granville's ears. If the Fed would only open up the money tap, the investment bankers could get busy and make some real money again. Smith rubbed a finger over his lips. Of course, even if they could override Filipelli on interest rates, the leveraged buyout issue remained. Filipelli wasn't about to allow that little game to come back. He and the President of the United States had made that quite clear.

Filipelli shot a glance at Smith, then refocused on Flynn. He sensed the same thing Smith had sensed, that the others might relent and vote for faster growth. "Should I take this to mean, President Flynn, that you are going to quit the Federal Reserve and enroll in an investment banker training course?"

"That isn't fair, Chairman," Smith interjected before Flynn could respond. He could hold back no longer. "Every time we're here, you put down the investment bankers. But they perform a very necessary function in our economy," Smith said calmly.

"They're money hungry. They don't care what they do to the economy as long as they pack their pockets with cash," Filipelli retorted quickly.

Smith disregarded Filipelli's criticism. "Let's open up the spigot and allow this country to grow again, Carter."

The others glanced up at Smith. First names were rarely used in this room. In a strange way it had become a more formal way to address another member of the committee than using his or her title. It meant the speaker was extremely serious about his point.

Filipelli leaned across the gleaming table and pointed a finger at Smith. "The reason this country's economy is in the position it's in, one of strength and stability, is because of me. Maybe GDP isn't growing meteorically, but inflation has gone down to two percent from eight percent since President Warren took office. And do you know why? Because I was willing to take the heat from the press when I kept interest rates high and drove inflation out of the system. When you all were hiding behind me." He thrust a finger into his chest emphatically. "Now the economy has stabilized, inflation is almost nonexistent, and I'm not letting it come back! I worked too hard to drive it out!" Filipelli straightened in his chair. He could feel himself losing control of his temper, and that would be embarrassing for President Warren. "I'm not going to let you ruin the economy for the common people just so your New York investment-banking buddies can make more money." He said the words matter-of-factly, then folded his hands on the table.

Smith hated Filipelli with every fiber of his being, but he wasn't going to allow the man to get the better of him. Not inside of this room. He began again in a measured tone. "Mr. Chairman, let's try to put our personal differences aside and do what's best for the country. Let's try to work for the good of the—"

But Filipelli did not allow Smith to finish. "Don't give me that holier-than-thou crap!" He could control himself no longer. Smith had won the war of nerves. "You're interested in one thing, Wendell. One thing. And that's Wendell Smith. You make me sick, you son of a bitch!" The last words echoed in the great room. Immediately Filipelli regretted the outburst. A mistake. He never should have said the words.

Slowly, Wendell Smith rose from his seat. He nodded politely at everyone but Filipelli, then without a word headed toward the door, his footsteps on the wooden floor following Filipelli's insult into the recesses of the room.

The chairman watched Smith leave, then turned back to face the rest of the committee. They were appalled. He could see it in the way they were looking at him now. It would be on the Bloomberg screens in a matter of minutes, and then there would be hell to pay. This time he had gone too far.

7

Falcon rose from the seat as the stiff-looking maître d' led Jenny through Chez Martin, a trendy new French restaurant on Manhattan's Upper East Side. He watched her carefully as she approached. She looked as pretty as ever in an off-the-shoulder, knee-length dress that revealed her delicate upper frame and only a slight hint of the cleavage below. Falcon breathed deeply. He needed to maintain control. He wanted her to be his secretary, not his lover.

"Hi." She kissed him gently on the cheek as she reached the table.

He returned the kiss, noticing a subtle trace of tasteful perfume. "Hi, yourself. You look ravishing. Is that a new dress?" He guided her into the booth. She seemed nervous, unsure of herself in these surroundings.

"What?" Jenny looked around quickly, taking in the sights and sounds of the restaurant.

Falcon laughed. "I asked if that was a new dress."

"What, this old thing?" Jenny touched the material lightly, then gazed directly into his eyes. "Of course it's a new dress, Andrew. I spent my entire life savings on tonight. It's not as if I'm asked out to a five-star restaurant by a handsome young investment banker every night." She paused, then smiled. "I didn't really spend my life savings." She touched his hand lightly. "Don't look so concerned."

"I'm not concerned." He realized that he had been staring at her. She looked more beautiful this evening than he could remember—she had turned several heads as the maître d' had led her through Chez Martin. He liked the way her mouth curled when she smiled. And he liked that she was impressed by the restaurant. He took a sip of the Scotch and glanced around. He shouldn't drink too much this evening. Not if he wanted the situation to stay simple.

"Do you like my dress?" she asked.

Falcon looked back at her but didn't answer right away. He was lost in thought.

"Andrew!" Jenny touched the back of his hand again.

"Yes. Yes, I like it."

"Good. I know you don't really like my wardrobe very much. I bought this one with you in mind."

"Madam, would you care for a cocktail?" the maître d' interrupted Jenny rudely. He wanted to return to the front of the restaurant.

Jenny glanced at Falcon. "What do I want?"

She wanted him to order for her. Somehow he found that appealing. "Want a drink? We'll have that nice bottle of Bordeaux you pointed out to me earlier, René."

The man nodded and glided away quickly.

As Falcon took a long drink from his water glass, Jenny leaned toward him. "Thanks for sending the limousine to New Brunswick. My father was very impressed, as was the rest of the neighborhood."

"Oh, sure, sure. I thought it would be fun. I didn't have time to come down and get you, what with the new job, and we couldn't have you coming up on a New Jersey Transit train, now could we?"

"I would have come any way I had to."

"And did the driver bring the champagne as I asked?" He ignored her admission.

Jenny nodded. "Please don't ask how much I had. I'm embarrassed."

Falcon grinned. So she was already tipsy. She had seemed a little unsteady coming through the restaurant, but he had thought it just his imagination.

"Don't smile at me like that," she said as she moved closer to him. "You look like the cat who ate the canary. That smile makes me nervous."

He glanced at her perfectly manicured fingernails. She was so different from the other women. Her attention was focused on him alone. She wasn't trying to see who else in the place she had impressed. She was there to impress him, and only him. And she was so vulnerable, which somehow made her more alluring. "Don't be nervous." He smelled her perfume drifting through the air again. The scent was much stronger now. He had to be careful. He cared about her as a friend and that was all. A relationship with Jenny would take him in a direction he did not want to go.

"Your wine, sir?"

Falcon turned quickly. "Yes! Ah, yes. The wine." He glanced at the label. "Lafite-Rothschild. Very nice."

Jenny moved slightly away from Falcon and smiled at the couple at the next table.

After the steward had finished pouring the wine, Falcon returned his attention to Jenny. "You're enjoying the evening, aren't you?"

"Very much. I hope you are too." She raised one eyebrow seductively and lifted her wineglass. "Here's to your new job." Her voice became serious. "I'll miss you very much. I already do."

Falcon broke the short silence. "Here's to you, Jenny." He lifted his wineglass to hers. "You were a wonderful executive assistant at MD Link. I'm just very sorry that you had to go through that awful scene with Reid. That the job ended that way."

Jenny waved her hand as she took another long sip of wine. "Don't worry. I'm a big girl. I'm just sad about Reid." She paused. "But I can take care of myself. I'll find another job."

"Which is one of the reasons I asked you here tonight."

She looked at him curiously.

"I want you to be my executive assistant at the bank I'm joining. The National Southern Bank. I've already cleared it with my senior people. I can offer you forty-five thousand dollars a year plus a commuting allowance."

Jenny stared at Falcon incredulously. "Are you serious?"

"Yes."

Her eyes lit up. "Well, my answer is yes. I don't even have to think about it. My God, you're a wonderful man." She leaned over and kissed him gently on the cheek. "Forty-five thousand. I can't imagine what it's like to earn that kind of money. That's more than what my father makes, I think. Forty-five thousand dollars? Really?"

Falcon smiled. "Really." He stared into her eyes. She was so outgoing and full of life. So beautiful. Stay in control, Andrew, he told himself over and over. Stay in control.

8

Buford J. Warren, President of the United States of America, stared at Carter Filipelli sternly from behind the great desk of the Oval Office. For several moments he said nothing, and then he began to laugh. "Jesus, Carter. I knew you were a little hot-blooded, but for God's sake, did you have to call him a son of a bitch in front of the entire FOMC? Couldn't you have taken him in your office and delivered the tongue-lashing?"

"I'm very sorry. There isn't anything I can say. I completely lost my temper. Nothing like that has ever happened to me before. The guy is just so damn worried about himself and his Yankee buddies he gets to me. He really gets to me. I mean he's worth millions, and all he cares about in the world is turning that into millions more. The greed factor is written all over him. And he doesn't care about anyone who isn't like him. Catholic, Jews, Italians, Blacks. He hates them all. If you're not in the social register, he doesn't want to talk to you. He's a self-serving Establishment bigot! The kind of person you and I came to Washington to destroy."

"Why don't you tell me how you really feel about him? Don't sugarcoat it, Carter, just in case the Republicans are listening in." The President winked.

Filipelli's eyes flashed around the room. "I know I've put you in a bad position. I'll give you my resignation, if that's what you called me in for." Filipelli spoke in bursts, like a machine gun.

"Nonsense. I need you to stay right where you are. I worked too hard to have you confirmed. I do understand your anger and frustration at a man like Wendell Smith. I did come to Washington to fight the power and influence of men such as him because you're right, he is a self-serving Establishment bigot and this country can't move forward until his kind have been pushed out of the way. *Pushed* is the word. *Destroyed* might be too harsh." The President stared at the ceiling for a few moments. "Maybe *destroyed* is the right word. Anyway, I don't want you to resign. But I do want you to apologize to him."

Filipelli glanced out the window at the White House Rose Garden. The bushes were in full bloom. It was an impressive spring display, but he could not appreciate it. His mind was on a million different things.

"I know it will be difficult for you, Carter, but you've got to do it. I need you in your position, and I need you to be influential in your position. Do you understand?"

"Yes, Mr. President." There was no room for argument.

"Unless you take immediate corrective action, Wendell will have a huge opportunity the next time he enters that boardroom. All of those FOMC members will be looking to give him the sympathy vote, and he may be able to influence them as he was not able to do before because of it. Don't get me wrong, they'll still be afraid of you. But he'll have that opportunity unless you go all out to head him off."

Filipelli sighed. "Okay, I'll publicly apologize to him."

The President pointed a long finger at Filipelli. "You won't just apologize. You'll take him to lunch for the assembled press corps. You'll compliment him on everything from his cuff links to his nose hairs. You'll never directly agree with any of his financial policy views, but you'll laud his insights."

Filipelli smiled slightly.

"See, Carter. Smiling isn't so difficult." The President beamed. The wayward son had come to the mountain and seen the light. "Come on, a little wider. Christ, I smile a thousand times a day if I smile once. I hate it, but I do it because people like to be around people who smile."

"You can't trust financial people who smile a lot."

The President disregarded Filipelli's comment. "Make nice, Carter. It's time for your metamorphosis from a pit bull into a diplomat. There could be other jobs for you in my administration, but you've got to tone down your act. I don't need an enforcer anymore—I need a politician. Do you understand?"

Filipelli cringed at the thought of becoming a politician. "Yes, sir."

"And by the way, in the next six weeks you will be taking each and every other member of that committee to a special luncheon or dinner in his and her honor too. Individually."

Filipelli began to object, but the President held up his hand. There would be no further objections.

"Is that all, Mr. President?" Filipelli rose.

"No. I want your opinion on something."

Filipelli sank back into the captain's chair in front of the great desk. "What?"

"I'd like to think I'm a fairly modest man." Both men grinned at the thought of the President having any measure of modesty. "As egomaniacs go." They chuckled. "Pragmatically, I'd say I'm a pretty good bet to win another term this fall."

"With the kind of approval rating you've got, I'd say you're a lock."

"Right. So, why in the hell are the Republicans serving up one of their rising young stars for me to slaughter in November? This guy Bob Whitman is the best thing to happen to the Republican party in quite some time. He was governor of Connecticut at thirty-four and has served one term in the House and one in the Senate. He served in the military. He comes from a self-made family. He has a truly magnetic personality. He is wise beyond his years, and he's squeaky clean. There's nothing in his closet. No women, no drugs, no payoffs, nothing. My people have been all over him for months. They can't find a thing. I've met him a couple of times. Try as I might, I couldn't dislike him. He's going to win the GOP nomination in a cakewalk. Hands down." The President paused. "But he doesn't have a chance against me. Why would the Republicans allow him to run and be defeated? They're not stupid over there."

"They want him to gain experience." Filipelli lamely attempted to solve the riddle.

"That's why you aren't my campaign manager, Carter." The President laughed quickly at his own joke and then continued. "If I'm a Republican guru, I keep Whitman in the Senate for another few years. I keep him in Triple-A ball, where he's striking out everybody he faces, building confidence, and making a bigger and bigger name for himself each day. I don't bring him in to face Babe Ruth in the ninth with the team already way behind and Babe swinging for the fences just to pad his statistics for next spring's contract negotiations. I don't let him run in 1996. I wait to see what's happening in 2000. Whitman certainly isn't going to have a problem winning another Senate term in 1998. The long and short of it is that running against me this year is political suicide. He doesn't have a chance. The only thing people will remember about him, if they remember anything at all, is that he's a loser."

Filipelli shrugged. "All I know is that we've stuck it to the Establishment where it hurts them the most—in the brokerage account. And we're going to do it again when we win in November. I can't wait to see Wendell's face the day after the election. I've already scheduled a meeting for that morning."

The President beamed. "We have pissed them off, haven't we?"

"Yes, Mr. President, and I love it. I grew up poor, and I don't mind admitting that I enjoy seeing how worried Wendell and his cronies are about their money. He sees that we're going to win again, and he knows we're going to take a serious amount of his net worth away from him when he dies."

A silence hung over the room.

Finally the President spoke. "So, Carter, you are going on vacation next week."

"Yes. I'm going fishing. Fly-fishing in Montana."

"How did a guy like you learn to fly-fish?"

"I'm a well-rounded sophisticate, Mr. President." Filipelli smiled again.

The President chuckled. "That's a good one. You've got more rough edges than a sheet of sandpaper. Of course that's why I need you." He bit his lip. "Well, leave a number. And make certain you take Wendell to lunch before you go."

9

As was his custom, Falcon arrived promptly at 7:15. It was ridiculous to come to his office at NASO this early because there wasn't even enough work to keep him busy from nine to five. Corporate banking was even easier than he had imagined. But he couldn't sleep past six o'clock in the morning. He never had been able to do that.

As he draped his suit coat over the back of one of the visitors' chairs in front of his desk, Falcon glanced out the window of his fortieth-floor office. Humidity hung over the buildings of midtown Manhattan like a circus tent. It was going to be a long, hot summer in New York City. The subways were already stifling. And it was only May.

Jenny moved into the office carrying several papers. She too arrived early, not to impress Andrew Falcon anymore, but other people at the bank. The fling with Andrew was over, she kept telling herself. She shook her head. She should have been smarter, because she wasn't the type of girl who had flings. She should have known the tryst at the Four Seasons after dinner that evening would mean nothing to him. She should have been more suspicious of why they hadn't gone to his apartment.

Falcon glanced at the copy of the résumé he had been putting together and covered it quickly with a folder as Jenny walked into the office. He did not want her to see that he was still trying to get back into investment banking and out of this boring corporate banking career. And at this point she would probably be only too happy to mention it to the human-resources department.

"Hello, Miss Cagle!" His voice boomed through the office unnaturally as he tried to be overtly friendly. "How are you this morning?"

"Fine, Andrew." She put the papers down onto his desk. "I need your signature on these." Her voice was flat and indifferent.

"Hey, let's go to lunch today. Just you and me. I think we need to do that."

"Can't, busy." She flashed a quick, cool smile.

"Tomorrow then."

"Busy tomorrow too."

"Jenny . . ."

"Could you just sign the papers please?"

"We need to talk."

"No, we don't!" Her voice rose sharply.

Falcon stared at her for a few moments. He wanted to tell her how bad he felt about taking her to the hotel after dinner. How he wished it hadn't happened, because now, just as he had anticipated, their relationship was strained. He wanted to tell her that he truly cared about her. That he found her terribly attractive. And that in another situation perhaps they could have had a meaningful relationship. But he didn't tell her. It wasn't his nature to be so direct in personal relationships. In business, yes. But not with friends or lovers. Perhaps it was a good thing she had declined the lunch invitation.

He removed the Cross pen from his shirt pocket and signed the papers. She scooped them up from the desk and stalked out. He watched her go until, without asking him, she closed the office door behind her. Jenny would have been able to see him from her workstation, and she didn't want that.

Falcon gazed at the closed door for a few minutes. They had been so good together at dinner—and in the hotel bed.

He breathed deeply, then reached across his desk to switch on the Bloomberg terminal. Immediately the screen flickered to life, and as it did, he smiled. It was an amazing machine. It relayed every tidbit of information available to humankind in milliseconds—at least to an experienced user. It gave up-to-the-minute stock, bond, and currency quotes from exchanges around the world. It gave brokerage reports, general corporate information, airline schedules—hell, it could tell you the latest exhibit at the Louvre if you asked it nicely. It was his most reliable asset in the office. NASO personnel, at least the ones he had come into contact with so far, were morons compared to this machine.

Falcon eased into the comfortable leather chair he had brought with him from MD Link and spread out a copy of the *Financial Chronicle* on top of his desk. The *Chronicle* focused primarily on business news, as did the *Wall Street Journal.* However, it differed from the *Journal* in two important ways. First, the *Chronicle* also included an expanded sports section. This meant that businessmen did not have to purchase two papers from which to obtain their most critical news. Second, the newsstand price of the *Chronicle* was only two-thirds that of the *Journal.* These differences had enabled the *Chronicle* to grab a healthy portion of the *Journal*'s daily circulation in just two years of publication.

Falcon knew a bit about publishing after working with several media companies at Winthrop, Hawkins, and he did not understand how the *Chronicle* could operate profitably at its current newsstand price, but somehow it had become tremendously successful. It didn't make sense, but then you couldn't analyze everything in life because if you did, you would end up in the mental ward at Bellevue. He had learned that early in his career.

The phone buzzed, and he punched the speaker button.

"Andrew Falcon."

"Mr. Falcon, this is Eddie Martinez in the Funds Transfer Group." Eddie's Brooklyn accent was thick so that every "er" sounded like an "uh."

"Hi, Eddie." Funds Transfer was a back-office area of the bank, responsible for making certain that the billions of dollars a day that flowed through the institution ended up in the proper accounts. The back office was staffed by lower-middle-class stiffs from Brooklyn and Queens. The positions didn't pay much, and there was little hope for significant advancement within the organization. Falcon felt somewhat sorry for Martinez, but there wasn't much he could do. "Please don't call me Mr. Falcon. Just Andrew."

"Oh, okay. Hey, I'm just calling to thank you for the case of beer."

Last week Falcon had delivered a case of beer to Martinez for being particularly helpful with a wire transfer of one of Falcon's accounts. The wire had become lost in the system, and Martinez had quickly located it. The transfer amount was large, and the client's chief financial officer had gone ballistic at the news that the money was unaccounted for. "My pleasure. You came through." It was important to let people know they had done well.

"Anytime you need help, let me know."

"I will, Eddie."

Falcon ended the call by pressing the speaker button again. Almost immediately the line buzzed a second time. "Andrew Falcon."

"It's me."

"Alexis?"

"Yes." Her gentle laugh flowed pleasantly to his ears. "You are too stiff sometimes, Falcon. You need to relax."

"I'll try to do better."

"Please do."

Falcon smiled. He could not get enough of that distinctive Italian accent.

Alexis had overwhelmed him as no other woman ever had. They had danced until five in the morning that night at the club. He had been too embarrassed to take her back to his studio apartment in Queens and had rented a room at the Waldorf instead. A room he could not then afford. From that point on, they had become almost inseparable.

His mind drifted back to last evening. Like every other night since he had met Alexis, it had been filled with lovemaking. It wasn't the best he had ever had—she wasn't passionate like Jenny. But so what? She was exciting, played very well with the people he needed to impress, and seemed totally devoted to him. Plus, she was awfully nice to be seen with. Besides, sex wasn't everything, he told himself.

Alexis had helped him find the new apartment on the Upper West Side, helped him decorate it, and then announced that she too would be living at the same address. Falcon had no objections. She loved to dance and drink. And she was more than willing to help defray the costs of a Manhattan lifestyle with earnings from her modeling jobs. It was, in a word, bliss.

And she was the perfect business partner. At NASO social functions she moved easily among the corporate executives he was trying to woo, impressing them with her beauty, charm, and intelligence. In only a few weeks he had picked up several important deals because of her, though he would never admit it to her.

"What are you doing?" Falcon asked.

"I'm lying naked in your bed, and I'm bored. Why didn't you wake me before you left?"

Falcon picked up the receiver quickly. There was no telling what Alexis might say through the speaker. She was gentle and ladylike. But she was also direct. European, she would say. "I thought you would be tired. You put in a long night last night."

Alexis stretched and Falcon could hear her moan. He pressed the receiver tightly against his ear.

"I'm just your little toy, aren't I? You don't really care about me, do you, Falcon?"

"Not at all."

"Come back home to me now," she said insistently.

"Alexis, I . . ."

"Come home, Andrew. I need your body next to mine. Come home."

"Don't you have a shoot in Central Park?"

"It's not until two this afternoon."

Falcon hesitated. Her offer was tempting, and these days he could be tempted. He had no client appointments today, no meetings at all until after lunch, and he had missed their normal prework interlude this morning.

"Maybe."

"Do I have to beg? You like it when I beg, don't you? I'll let you do anything you want to me if you come home right now."

"Anything?"

"Anything."

Falcon glanced at his watch: 7:35. If he left now, he could be back to NASO by eleven. Jenny would cover for him. Or maybe she wouldn't. But no one would miss him anyway. That was the worst thing about this job. No one ever missed him. Malley rarely called because he was too intimidated, and the very senior people never came down from the ivory tower in a huge commercial bank. "I'll be there in a few minutes."

Falcon put down the phone, stood, pulled his wallet from the inside of his suit coat but left the coat hanging over the back of the chair, and headed toward the closed office door. As he opened it, he nearly ran into Jenny.

"What the . . . ?"

"I have one more thing for you to sign." Her voice was stone cold.

He wondered if she had been listening to the conversation on her extension. "I'll sign it when I get back. Listen, I forgot something back at the apartment. It may take a while to find it when I get there." He stared at her. "Be a sport and cover for me."

And he was gone, trotting down the corridor toward the elevator bank.

Jenny watched him leave. She knew exactly why Falcon was going home. And she hated him for it. She should quit, she told herself. There was no reason to put herself through this every day. She sighed. But where in the world was she going to find another job that paid the kind of money she was earning now? Nowhere else. It was that simple.

The ceiling fan rotated slowly above the brass bed. Falcon watched it spin for a few moments, then glanced at his watch. Ten forty-five. Time to go.

"Don't you ever take that watch off, Falcon?" Alexis stood at the bathroom door, naked.

Falcon moved both hands behind his head and stared at her dark nipples, partly covered by the straight hair cascading down from her shoulders. "Only for sex."

Alexis looked at him strangely. "Isn't that what we just had?"

"Oh, that's what you call that." He said the words as if he had just made a great discovery.

She rolled her eyes. "Falcon, give me a break. I'm sorry if I'm not as good as some of your past conquests. Maybe someday I'll measure up."

"Just kidding." But he wasn't.

Alexis moved seductively from the doorway to the bed. When she reached it, she pulled back the sheets, knelt down on the mattress, and kissed him just above the dark line of his pubic hair. She moved up his body and slid her tongue into his navel, then lay down, rested her head on his lower chest, and looked up at him. She smiled, defining her exquisite cheekbones. "I'm trying to be sexy."

Falcon stared into her eyes. They were soft and feminine like

Jenny's, but there was something steely to them too. Jenny's eyes betrayed her vulnerability even when she was at her coldest. There was no vulnerability to betray in Alexis's eyes. "I see that." He wanted to know more about her, but as yet she had been unwilling to open up except for some hazy comments about an unhappy childhood in Milan. And of course if he did push, she would expect him to be more forthcoming about his own background, which he did not want to be.

"Do you like it?" Alexis asked.

"Yes. How about another round?" Perhaps he did not need to go back to the office quite so soon.

Alexis shook her head and rolled away. "I've got to get ready for that shoot in Central Park."

"Come on. We could experiment."

She rose from the bed and moved to the window overlooking 82nd Street. "No." Her voice was firm.

That was the problem, he thought. She didn't like to experiment. She simply wanted him to move on top of her and have it over with. During foreplay she could be sensual and somewhat imaginative, though she was not particularly knowledgeable as to the trigger points of the male body. But once intercourse began, she became indifferent, almost frigid. It was strange.

"What time do you have to be at the shoot?"

"One o'clock. It starts at two, but I have to be there early." She ran her fingers through her hair and leaned back. The black tresses fell almost to the small of her back. "Falcon, why don't you get rid of that secretary of yours? I don't like her attitude when I call your office."

Falcon sat up in the bed immediately. "What do you mean?" She turned from the window and stalked to the bathroom, slamming the door behind her.

He gazed openmouthed at the door. Where the hell had that come from?

* * *

"How is Falcon?"

"Not challenged."

"Is he still sending out résumés?"

"Of course, but no one will hire him."

"Obviously. Granville has seen to that. Falcon must suspect something."

"I don't think so. We would be aware of it."

"Is he working diligently or simply putting in his time?"

"Working hard. In fact, he's actually generated some attractive business for NASO. He's using contacts from his days at Winthrop, Hawkins. I believe he was able to win the agency role away from Chemical Bank on a new syndicated revolver for the Black and Decker Corporation. But overall, he hates what he's doing. He doesn't like the slow pace or the lack of compensation."

"So he's ready for this project, Bill?"

"More than ready, Turner. He'll drop everything else immediately, with NASO's blessing, of course. And he's so starved for something he considers mentally stimulating that he won't question NASO's seeming overindulgence in the transaction. More important, we will make it worth his while not to question NASO's huge commitment."

"I still don't like this. I think it is a big risk to have Falcon involved just because Granville holds a grudge. And I think we should have anticipated the fact that the other young man, um, what was his name?"

"Bernstein."

"Yes, Bernstein. We should have anticipated that Bernstein would commit suicide after our people tampered with the software. It was everything to him."

"There was no way to anticipate that. It was simply an unfortunate side effect."

"Side effect? Jesus Christ, Rutherford! Do you think his family considered it simply an unfortunate side effect? First West, then

Jeremy Case, now Bernstein. It's not what we're supposed to be about. Where does it stop? This is getting out of hand, don't you think?"

"Not at all. Sometimes things have to be done that may seem distasteful. Sometimes people have to be sacrificed. It's part of the deal. Everything is under control."

"And what if Bernstein had killed Falcon during his little tirade?"

"Then we would have simply used someone else. According to Boreman, there are others out there who could legitimize our project."

"We should have used someone else other than Falcon from the beginning. In the end we may pay for Granville's indulgence. One should never allow feelings to influence business. I'm getting nervous. There's a lot on the line here. And a lot of ways this thing could go wrong."

"Everything will be fine."

"What about this woman Falcon has taken up with, Bill? Could she be a problem?"

"No. She's simply a diversion. Believe me, he's very ready for this project."

"I understand Carter Filipelli reacted strongly to Wendell's criticism."

"He did. So strongly that he tried to influence the markets on his own, without the agreement of the rest of the FOMC."

"That's insane. He isn't supposed to do that. Filipelli is out of control."

"Yes, he is, along with the President and the Treasury Secretary."

"I suppose Filipelli would not appreciate what we are about to do."

"I think that's a safe bet."

"How did you find out that Filipelli was acting on his own?"

"Didn't you know?"

"Know what?"

"Chambers' son works for Filipelli."

"We have eyes everywhere, don't we, Bill?"

"Yes, we do, Turner."

10

"Falcon?"

"Yes."

"This is Phil Barksdale, vice chairman of NASO."

"Yes."

"I'd like you to come up and see me as soon as possible."

"May I ask what this is about?"

"I'll tell you when you get here. If you didn't already know, I'm on the twenty-seventh floor. Oh, and by the way, I'd rather you not tell anyone that you are coming up to my office. Including your secretary."

Falcon hung up the office phone. "If you didn't already know." What an asshole. And what the hell was this all about anyway? Did they know he was shooting résumés all over the country? Had Barksdale called because the bank was pissed off about it? But why would Barksdale call? In his first few weeks at the bank, Falcon hadn't even met Barksdale or Wallace Boreman, the chairman. So why would Barksdale call? It should have been some moron from personnel, or "employee representation," as those people liked to be called now. Suddenly Falcon was interested. He hurried to the elevator.

Barksdale met Falcon at the doorway of his huge office. He was tall, over six-four, balding on top of his head, with patches of gray hair above the large ears and dark, bushy eyebrows over his sad hazel eyes.

"Hello, Falcon." His voice was deep and melodious. It reminded Falcon of a disc jockey he had listened to growing up in Philadelphia. The voice was friendly, but the face was not. Barksdale did not smile as they shook hands.

"Good morning." Falcon's hands were not small, but they were enveloped by Barksdale's grip.

Barksdale leaned into the outer office. "Grace, no calls." He closed the door quickly, not awaiting a response from the older woman positioned outside his office like a sentinel. "Let's go over here, Falcon." He motioned toward several comfortable chairs arranged around a mahogany coffee table in one corner of the office.

Falcon glanced about the room. He had seen a thousand offices exactly like this one in his career. Pictures everywhere. Barksdale's family, his friends, the sailboat, the dog, a couple of politicians. On the credenza behind his desk were hundreds of transaction mementos—Lucite tombstones identifying the deals—half of which Barksdale probably hadn't even worked on. Falcon glanced around. Thirty feet by thirty feet at least, he guessed. What a waste of space.

They sat in chairs on opposite sides of the table. "Coffee, Falcon?" Barksdale pointed at a tray on the table.

"No, thank you."

"Well, I'm having some."

Andrew quickly reviewed his mental notes on Barksdale as he watched the older man pour a steaming cup of coffee. Barksdale had been with the Trust Company of Alabama prior to its merger with First Atlanta. He had been headed for the chairmanship of the combined entity until the bank ran into severe problems in Brazil three years ago. Barksdale had taken the fall for those problems, because at that time he had been responsible for the International Division of NASO. So the board had shoved him aside by making him vice chairman and then turned to an outsider, Wallace Boreman, to head the bank. Boreman was regarded on Wall Street as a savvy manager willing to take reasonable risks in the name of sizeable profits. Boreman had been credited with solving the Brazilian situation quickly and with transforming the stodgy, conservative southern institution into a solid commercial bank, on the way to bigger and better things. He could have fired Barksdale because of Brazil. The board would have looked the other way. But he hadn't. Barksdale owed Boreman his career.

Barksdale had been left behind in the process, but it wasn't all that bad a life, Falcon thought: in at 9:30 in the morning and out no later than 5:30 in the afternoon; two or three rounds of golf a week in the summer; Manhattan's finest restaurants three or four nights a week; and over half a million dollars a year of annual compensation in the process, according to the proxy. It was not a gigantic income by New York City standards, but certainly one that enabled the man to live comfortably.

Barksdale took a sip from the cup and replaced it on the china saucer. "So how's the job?"

"Fine. Just what I expected." Falcon was not particularly enthusiastic, but he was past the point in life where he had to be insincerely excited about everything.

"Bored, aren't you?"

Falcon took a breath. He didn't like the sound of that. It sounded like something a superior might say if he weren't happy with a particular employee's performance. Being out of a job again did not interest Falcon, especially since no one was paying attention to the résumés he was sending out. "Not bored. No, I wouldn't say that."

"You're lying." Despite the melodious voice, Barksdale was gruff in his manner.

"I'm not lying." Was Barksdale about to fire him? Falcon felt a sudden wave of discomfort.

"Forget it. I'd be bored too if I were you." Barksdale waved a hand as if in disgust. "Look, I need your help. NASO has the opportunity to become involved in a very nice transaction. One in which we can make a lot of money. You have experience in the area of the transaction. Not many of us around here do. Hell, I'll be honest. No one around here has the experience you do in this particular field."

Falcon moved back in the large chair. He was relieved. "What kind of transaction is it?"

"A leveraged buyout."

Falcon's pulse quickened. A leveraged buyout? That could actually be interesting. "You say NASO has the opportunity to become involved in this transaction. In what capacity?"

"As financial adviser, arranger, lender, underwriter. Whatever capacity we want. I think it's an opportunity for us to really put NASO on the map in terms of competing against the investment banks. And if this thing works, if we are successful, Boreman wants to set up a mergers and acquisitions advisory group here at NASO. Boreman would want you to head it up. It's quite an opportunity."

The words were music to Falcon's ears: mergers and acquisitions advisory. "Tell me more about the transaction."

"You must keep all of this strictly confidential—"

"Phil, I mean no disrespect by cutting you off. You obviously know my background, the fact that I was a partner at Winthrop, Hawkins in that firm's M&A group. Is that right?"

Barksdale nodded. "I'm even aware that you were involved when NASO acquired the Bank of Manhattan."

"Right. I've been through this drill before. I know about keeping things confidential."

"Of course, of course. I just felt I had to say it." He paused. "We—by 'we' I mean Boreman. It's really his relationship. Boreman has a very strong relationship with an investment group out of Germany."

"Which one?" Falcon would know the group. He could feel

adrenaline suddenly pumping through his body. It would probably be a small deal, but so what? It was a chance to get back in the game. God, it had been so long. If this was a real opportunity, he would make certain the transaction closed. He would make certain that Boreman allowed him to set up an M&A group at NASO afterward. And he would make certain that Granville rued the day he had not returned his calls.

"You will meet them. Soon. But for now I would like to keep their name out of this. Boreman's orders. You must understand that."

Falcon was not pleased. "Okay." His voice betrayed his irritation.

"Look, I can't violate a direct order from Boreman."

"Fine. So this group wants to acquire someone here in the United States. Probably a basic manufacturer. Auto parts, specialty steel, chemicals. Something like that."

Barksdale hesitated. "That's right. How did you know?"

"The deutsche mark has strengthened considerably against the U.S. dollar lately, which makes a U.S. acquisition by a German company relatively inexpensive in mark terms. As far as the industries I referred to, those are industries the Germans traditionally like. Basic manufacturing. So, what company is the target?"

"Penn-Mar Chemicals."

Falcon stared at Barksdale. "What!"

"Yes." Barksdale took a sip of his coffee.

"Penn-Mar Chemicals? The Penn-Mar Chemicals headquartered in Toledo, Ohio?"

"Yes."

"Penn-Mar is the second largest chemical company in the United States, Phil. It's a behemoth." Falcon rose from the chair and moved to the Bloomberg terminal he had spotted on a table beside Barksdale's desk. He typed Penn-Mar's stock symbol on the keyboard and waited. Almost immediately the information he sought flashed onto the screen. "My God, Penn-Mar has over four hundred million shares outstanding, and the share price is thirty and a half. That makes its market equity value over twelve billion dollars." He looked at Barksdale uncertainly. "And to acquire a company, any public company, you don't just go out and pick up the shares at the current trading price. To gain control, we'd have to pay an acquisition premium. It would cost these people sixty to seventy-five dollars a share to successfully close a public acquisition." Like so many times before, he was calculating as he spoke. "That's a total of twenty-five to thirty billion dollars to buy Penn-Mar's equity. And that assumes Penn-Mar's management is amenable to the takeover, which I doubt they would be. An unwilling management team would translate into an even higher acquisition price."

"I certainly hope the Germans don't have to pay thirty billion. Jesus Christ!" The older man almost spilled his coffee.

"They will. Count on it. I hope they have a lot of money to put into this thing." Andrew returned to the chair.

"A billion. They will put a billion into the acquisition of Penn-Mar."

Falcon gazed down at the carpet and shook his head. "I don't want to make it rain on my own parade, believe me, Phil, but that isn't nearly enough to seed the acquisition. The Germans, assuming they are real and they do have money to put into this transaction, could borrow *some* of the purchase price, but I doubt we would be able to raise twenty to thirty billion dollars of debt on top of only one billion in equity. Banks are skittish. They were burned in the eighties in highly leveraged deals, and, in case you haven't heard, the chairman of the Federal Reserve, Carter Filipelli, is not keen on the idea of banks lending into highly leveraged, risky transactions. And 'not keen' is putting it mildly. He's made speech after speech about how he won't allow banks to dive into the LBO business again. About how he and the President aren't about to let a go-go eighties mentality return to the market."

"You mean he wouldn't be terribly happy about NASO funding a Penn-Mar LBO."

"Of course that's what I mean." Falcon shook his head. "It doesn't matter anyway. We haven't got the firepower if all the Germans have is a billion."

"NASO will strongly support the transaction in whatever way it has to so that the transaction is completed." Barksdale said the words quietly, almost inaudibly.

Falcon glanced up at Barksdale. "What did you say?"

Barksdale stared steadily back at Falcon. "I said that NASO is willing to commit a significant amount of capital to this transaction."

"How much are we talking? What is a 'significant amount'?"

"Whatever it takes."

Falcon allowed the words to hang in the air between them for a few moments. "You realize, of course, that there are legal lending limits involved in banking."

"Thanks so much for that sound bite. To think, after forty years in this business I'm finally learning about legal lending limits."

Falcon ignored Barksdale's sarcasm. "Seriously, NASO can only lend a maximum of fifteen percent of capital into one transaction. How much capital does the bank have at this point?"

"About fifteen billion dollars."

"So NASO could commit a little over two billion. That doesn't come close to what we need."

"I told you, we are willing to do whatever it takes. First of all, we have a securities subsidiary that can underwrite junk bonds. I figure we can do five or six billion in the securities subsidiary alone. I've already spoken to Hennings, who heads up the Section Twenty Group. He thinks they can do that amount." Barksdale could see that Falcon was doubtful. "Second, we manage several equity funds thanks to recent deregulation. I think we could pull another three billion from those entities. And finally, there is no love lost between Wallace Boreman and Carter Filipelli. If we went a bit over our legal lending limit, I doubt Boreman would be too troubled. Besides, there is little the Fed could do to us. We're too big."

"They could fire your asses."

"Only if they find out." Barksdale sipped on the coffee. "So, let's add up those figures. For fun, let's say we committed four billion in bank debt, six billion in long-term junk bonds, and three billion in equity. That's thirteen billion dollars. With the Germans' equity of one billion, we'd have a total of fourteen billion to pay for the acquisition. We'll need more, but remember, now the acquisition vehicle has four billion in equity and six billion in subordinated debt. We ought to be able to raise a helluva lot of bank debt on top of ten billion of deep capital."

"You're serious?" Falcon looked at Barksdale in disbelief. Even Winthrop, Hawkins would not have been able to commit that kind of money to a deal. "Has Boreman presented this to NASO's board of directors? I would think this kind of commitment would require board approval."

"Sure. Certainly he has."

"You were at the meeting?" Falcon was unconvinced.

"Of course I was."

Barksdale was lying, and Falcon knew it. "You realize that if for some reason Penn-Mar went bankrupt with NASO holding a thirteen-billion-dollar investment, the bank would be out of business in a minute. There would be people lined up for miles outside the doors to this place trying to get their money out. And the bank wouldn't be able to give it to them. And NASO's crash would send the financial markets into chaos. The stock market, the bond market, the currency markets. They'd all crater."

The older man put down his coffee cup and said smoothly, "The Federal Reserve would step in. They would put in whatever money was necessary to keep the bank solvent. Hell, the savings and loan crisis cost the United States government three hundred billion dollars. Thirteen billion pales in comparison."

"But the S&L crisis involved thousands of different savings banks, which didn't all fail simultaneously," Falcon argued. "And those institutions weren't big players in the currency or derivative markets, the way NASO is. NASO has literally thousands of contracts with other financial institutions around the world to deliver currencies at specified dates. Thousands of situations where the bank is the other side of options contracts and interest rate swaps. If there were a run on NASO because the word got out that we couldn't meet our deposit obligations, the Fed would have to react in seconds, literally. If there was any delay, any at all, the system could disintegrate. The entire banking system. Other financial institutions would encounter liquidity problems immediately because we couldn't meet our obligations with them. Investors would pull their huge deposits, and banks would start failing all over the place. It wouldn't be just a thirteen-billion-dollar problem. It would be catastrophic."

"You are exaggerating."

"Bullshit! This country has never had a large bank go down. Sure, Continental Bank in Chicago had some problems in the early eighties, but the Fed had plenty of advance warning. It was a situation that developed over a prolonged period. The Fed had time to step in. And things weren't so incestuous at that point either. Institutions weren't so interdependent. The system is like a house of cards now. Every institution depends on the others. Literally, the chain is only as strong as the weakest link. Phil, if we invest thirteen billion dollars in Penn-Mar and for some reason Penn-Mar goes bust, we could cause havoc in the U.S. financial markets. A bank just isn't supposed to invest all of its capital in one deal. For very good reasons."

"Look, Falcon, I'm not proposing that NASO hold all thirteen billion. We would make the initial investment and then sell most of the securities to other institutions, thereby spreading the risk through the system and making us a nice profit at the same time."

"So we would presell the deal?"

"What do you mean, 'presell'?" asked Barksdale.

"I mean that we would send the money out to pay for the shares, but then the other institutions would send money to us immediately. In other words, we would take this to hundreds of other banks and insurance firms and make certain of their commitment before we sent the money out to pay for the shares. So that we knew we wouldn't really be on the hook for thirteen billion."

"No! We can't do that. We will talk to a few firms, but only to obtain the balance of the money we can't come up with ourselves. The Germans and Boreman have been very specific about that. They don't want anyone knowing about the deal before we announce our offer to purchase, other than people who absolutely have to know. They are paranoid that if word gets out about this deal, someone else like DuPont or Hoechst will preempt them. The Germans want a fully financed offer in place before we announce the takeover. After the takeover is complete, we can sell the paper to other institutions."

"So then we will be taking a risk. A huge risk. It will take us at least thirty days to sell the paper. Probably sixty. And that's extremely optimistic. What if during that period something happens? What if we can't resell the paper after we send the money out the door because Penn-Mar suddenly develops a bad case of pneumonia?"

"That's why you are involved, Falcon. To make sure Penn-Mar is clean. To make certain that we and the Germans don't overpay for it. And to make very certain that within no more than sixty days after the close of the transaction, NASO holds less than two billion of the paper. You can sell the bank debt, the junk bonds, and the equity. Once we've won the bid, you can call any contacts you have. Hennings will do the same. Work together. Work separately. Pull in our people in the bank's syndication group. I don't care. But sell the stuff. We have to be able to get rid of it fast!"

"It would be a huge effort."

"Are you saying you don't think you can do it? Are you trying to tell me, now that you have something real to work on, you're backing off on all of that talk about how good you are?"

"You aren't going to intimidate me, Phil. It won't work."

"Push things as close to the edge as possible. Wasn't that what you told Malley you did at Winthrop, Hawkins in your interview with him?" Barksdale wasn't going to let up. "Let me see you work that edge now, Mr. Falcon."

"I'll need a top lawyer. I have a good friend at Davis, Polk who would be perfect—"

"No. We'll use Dunlop & Latham." He finished the coffee and pulled out a pack of Salems. "Smoke?" Barksdale thrust the pack at Falcon.

Falcon ignored the offer of cigarettes. "Dunlop & Latham? You must be joking. I mean, Phil, they are an excellent labor relations firm, but those guys wouldn't know the difference between takeover documentation and a dime-store novel." Falcon maintained his calm exterior, but inside he was beginning to boil. He couldn't hope to complete a transaction of this magnitude without experienced legal help.

Barksdale pulled a cigarette from the package, lit it, and threw the pack toward the desk. It fell short. Several cigarettes bounced out of the pack and onto the carpet as it hit the floor. "I'm not joking. It's already decided. And we don't want them brought in until the last minute either. Until just prior to when you need to file the offer to purchase. Until just before we launch the tender. Next question."

"We'll have to file Hart-Scott-Rodino antitrust papers."

"Dunlop & Latham can handle that too."

"I'm telling you, they don't know that stuff." Falcon was becoming exasperated. "Let me ask you a question. Do you actually want to win this thing? Do you want the Germans, whoever the hell they are, to get control of Penn-Mar? Because if you do, you've got a funny way of going about this thing. This is the big game. I'm a first-string quarterback. But you are giving me the second team with which to win the game."

"Next point." Barksdale exhaled and smoke began to envelop the room.

"I can't stand smoke."

"It's my office. Next point."

"I'll need analytical help. An associate to crunch the numbers and do the research."

"Out of the question. As I told you, we want as few people knowing about this as possible. In fact, after today I want you to work at home. I will set you up with everything you need there. By tomorrow afternoon you will have in your apartment a personal computer complete with a laserjet printer, and you will have a Bloomberg terminal. If you need Securities and Exchange documents, call Disclosure and have them deliver the papers directly to your address. Do not have them delivered to NASO."

Falcon hadn't expected this. "Where am I supposed to be?"

"At a seminar."

"You can't really expect me to do this without working closely with the people in the securities subsidiary before we make the offer. You were talking about six billion dollars in junk bonds."

"Anything you need to say to Hennings goes through me. Don't take it personally, Falcon, but Boreman and I want to keep this thing confidential until the minute we go public. We want all of the information to flow through us so that if there is a leak, we'll know exactly where it came from. You haven't been at NASO that long. We don't know you that well yet." Barksdale blew more smoke into the office. "Win this one for us, and we'll know you very well. It's worth five million dollars to you, Falcon. You personally, that is. It's worth five million, your managing director title, and the chance to head up an M&A group. And wouldn't that be a nice thing to wave under Granville Winthrop's nose?" Barksdale paused, knowing the arrow had hit its mark. "The computer equipment will be at your apartment by noon tomorrow. I believe you live at 232 West 82nd, Apartment 1004. Is that correct?"

Falcon did not acknowledge Barksdale's question except to lift one eyebrow. These people had checked him out very thoroughly. Very thoroughly. They knew which buttons to push and when to push them. He had underestimated them, and that irritated him. But five million didn't. Nor did the chance to get back in the game.

NASO's executive washroom was magnificent, replete with showers, sauna, inlaid tile, and an elderly gentleman who did nothing all day but distribute towels and collect dollar bills. Falcon washed his hands in the warm water. He took his time. He did not want to go back into Barksdale's smoke-filled office. But they had a great deal more work to do.

In the mirror Falcon spotted one of the stall's marble doors opening. The man who emerged was dark-haired and tall. His face was deeply tanned so that it emitted a healthy glow in the mirror. He wore a white-collared, blue pin-striped shirt and a sharp tie. Wallace Boreman. Falcon recognized the man's picture from the inside cover of NASO's annual report.

Boreman nodded at Falcon in the mirror, almost imperceptibly, but said nothing. His face remained impassive as he moved to the sink next to the one in which Falcon was washing his hands. Boreman rolled his shirtsleeves above his elbows, then moved his hands beneath the running water.

Falcon glanced casually in the mirror at Boreman's left hand to see if he wore a wedding band. He knew Boreman was married, but you could tell a great deal about a man by his wedding band, and a great deal more if he didn't wear it. But before Falcon's gaze reached Boreman's hand, he noticed something peculiar on

Boreman's inner right forearms. It appeared to be a small mole at first. Andrew looked more closely. It wasn't a mole. Too well defined and not raised off the skin. Something else. A brand? Suddenly Falcon noticed that Boreman was staring at him in the mirror. Falcon's gaze dropped quickly to the bottom of the sink. And somewhere deep in the recesses of his brain a small, faraway voice began to murmur as yet unintelligible words.

11

Sharon Cruz sat quietly at one end of the long conference-room table. Very soon she would become the center of attention. It was a distinction she did not relish. This was strange for a litigator, because trial attorneys were by definition perpetually the center of attention. It was strange that she could so easily stand before an unknown judge, a hostile jury, the press, and a partisan audience and tenaciously argue the innocence of her client or the guilt of her opponent's client without a hint of self-consciousness; yet a presentation to her partners caused her such anxiety that she could barely speak by the time she was called on.

Her stress came because she cared about the partners' opinion so much. She wanted acceptance. If a jury found her client guilty, so be it. She had tried her best and that was all there was to it. But if the partners were not immediately enthused, she was crushed.

From her seat, Sharon could see the waters of Baltimore's harbor glistening in the afternoon sunlight. The harbor was thirty-one stories below this conference room of the renowned law firm of Cleveland, Miller & Prescott. She wished she were down there enjoying the afternoon sun. She wished she did not have to speak to them today.

Even after nine years at the firm, she was still uncertain about their true feelings toward her. She was Hispanic, and they, except for Grover Tipton, were white. Suddenly, Sharon longed for New York City, where people were more readily accepted. But the money, as a third-year partner, had become addictive. Two or three more years, and she would have the financial wherewithal to begin her own practice. She promised herself she would spend at least fifty percent of her time representing minorities who didn't have the means to obtain a decent lawyer themselves.

Sharon's gaze fell back on the blue-green waters far below. Who was she kidding? The only way she wouldn't be staring out the same window two or three years from now would be if Cleveland, Miller & Prescott had relocated its offices in the interim.

"Ms. Cruz?" Turner Prescott's controlled tone knifed through the room from the other end of the table.

"Yes, sir." The image of the blue-green waters evaporated. Prescott stared at her sternly over wire-frame glasses balanced precariously on the end of his nose. "Yes, sir." Sharon said the words again more slowly, making certain that she enunciated each syllable. In her first few years, the partners had complained that she spoke so rapidly they weren't able to understand her. She had actually visited a speech therapist to address the problem, and it had been corrected—for the most part. But from time to time, when she wasn't concentrating, the speed with which her native Spanish was spoken returned.

"Please update us on the Bradlee matter." Each Friday the twenty-two partners reviewed every case for which the firm had been retained. It was a benefit of a smaller firm, she felt, that they could all meet together in the same conference room. One of the other partners had been speaking for the last five minutes. Now it was her turn.

Sharon stared at Prescott for a moment. He was sixty-four but seemed much younger, and he was quite dapper in the matching bow tie and suspenders. As the senior and managing partner of the firm, he was responsible for strategic planning and administration. Despite Prescott's extra duties, he still managed to originate more business than any other attorney at Cleveland, Miller and logged more than his share of courtroom time. Brilliant, tireless, and quietly commanding, Prescott had guided the firm to national prominence as litigation specialists over the past twenty years. He liked her, but more important, he accepted her, and he continually placed significant responsibility in her hands.

Sharon felt the eyes of the partnership upon her.

"Wait a minute."

Sharon glanced up from her notes. The speaker was Lyle Frames, an overweight, balding man who appeared older than his forty-four years. He whined when he spoke and was not generally liked by the other partners. But he was a stickler for details and was always one of the top earners at the firm.

"What is it, Lyle?" Prescott cut in.

"Turner, I don't remember a discussion at any of the new business meetings with respect to Bradlee."

"There was no discussion, Lyle. I made the decision unilaterally. It is a terribly important case, and it was absolutely essential that confidentiality remain strict until this time. Anyone have a problem with that?" Prescott scanned the room.

But Frames would not let it go. "I think there should have been at least some back-and-forth about who worked on the case if it is so important."

"Are you questioning my judgment with respect to using Ms. Cruz?" There was an edge to Prescott's normally smooth voice.

Frames heard the edge, and though he was a stickler for procedure, he was not stupid enough to push Prescott. Cleveland, Miller was a partnership in name only. In reality it was a dictatorship—for the most part benevolent. Frames shook his head.

"Please continue, Ms. Cruz." The edge disappeared. Prescott smiled politely at her.

She smiled back and then began. "Cleveland, Miller & Prescott has been retained by the Bradlee Company to represent it in litigation with regard to a dispute involving environmental problems." Gradually the perspiration covering her palms began to dry.

She glanced up from the papers. The partners were staring at her, as she knew they would be. Ogling was a better word. She was attractive. Short and slim with dark hair and a nice figure, she made a pleasant fantasy. She knew that. Half of them probably weren't listening to her at all, just gazing at her body. Men were so predictable.

Sharon returned to the papers before her. "Bradlee is located on the Eastern Shore of Maryland. Until a year ago, it was a dairy farm operated by a husband and wife—a small outfit, only five hundred head of cattle."

"I remember reading about that." Ann Peifer, the other female partner at Cleveland, Miller, interrupted. "The entire herd was poisoned. No one could figure out what happened. That farm is located near Centreville, twenty miles south of Chestertown. Isn't that right?"

Sharon smiled at the other woman. They were close friends, out of necessity. "That's right."

"Please continue," Prescott said impatiently.

"As Ann mentioned, the entire herd died within a few days. With the help of local authorities, the Bradlees were able to trace the catastrophe to a poison in the cattle's water supply. Fortunately, the barns' wells were supplied by a different underground stream than was the Bradlee home. Anyway, the authorities found that the underground stream from which the well drew its water was poisoned. However, they were unable to locate the source of the contamination.

"The Bradlees were ruined. They had business-interruption insurance, but the insurance company had gone bankrupt, and as it turned out, the insurance broker had been simply pocketing their checks. He never told them that the insurance company had gone down.

"The insurance broker is now in jail, but the Bradlees were unable to collect anything from him. They were forced to declare bankruptcy themselves. They were completely wiped out as a result of this." Sharon paused and looked up.

The partnership was breathless. They trusted Prescott. They knew there was more to this than just the death of a dairy farm. They sensed a deep pocket from which the Bradlees could extract a huge sum of money and, more important, from which Cleveland, Miller could extract its pound of flesh.

Sharon continued. "Several months after the cattle died, Roger Bradlee received an anonymous telephone call. It came at night, and it lasted only about thirty seconds. The caller simply told him that they ought to dig in a certain place on the farm next to theirs. That if they did, it might be the answer to their prayers."

The room was as quiet as a tomb.

"Bradlee and his two sons went out immediately with a front-end loader to the spot. Apparently the caller was very specific with respect to the location. They didn't bother calling the Parker family, the owners of the property, because they were afraid that if they notified the Parkers, whatever the anonymous caller had told them about might somehow disappear. As it turned out, they didn't have to worry. It only took the Bradlees about fifteen minutes to find what they were looking for." Sharon looked up again.

The partners were on the edge of their seats.

"Fifty-five-gallon drums filled with toxic waste."

There was a collective murmur from the partnership.

Sharon continued. "As soon as they hit the first few drums, Roger Bradlee had the good sense to stop digging. He sent one of his sons into Centreville for the authorities. He sent the other one home for shotguns and rifles. Somehow he knew that he had uncovered something very big and very bad. Something for which a number of parties were probably responsible and probably would do anything to cover up. He also realized that this might be his family's salvation, and he did not want it to slip away. The site was on a fairly remote part of the Parker property, so no one saw them working.

"The local sheriff was at the site in a half hour. He determined that there was indeed cause to investigate further and obtained a search warrant from the local judge at three in the morning, enabling him to proceed. He then called members of the Environmental Protection Agency and the Maryland Environmental Safety Board at home. Woke them up out of a sound sleep. At five in the morning, the EPA arrived, and by four that afternoon they had discovered over five hundred fifty-five-gallon drums filled with some of the nastiest stuff known to mankind."

Grover Tipton intervened. "So the Parkers were using at least part of their property as a hazardous-waste dumping site."

"Well, someone was using the property that way. The practice has become widespread on the Eastern Shore. It's still pretty desolate out there. Mostly dairy cattle, chicken farms, and crops. The locals have figured out that they can bury a couple of loads of hazardous waste on their property and make more from that in a night than they can farming all year. And with a lot less effort."

Lyle Frames broke in. "So then the Parkers allowed someone to dump toxic waste on their property for a fee?"

"The Parkers have owned the land for years. They claimed to know nothing about the site. They own about four thousand acres outside of Centreville, and they said that someone must have directed trunks to that location and buried the waste without their knowledge. It seems far-fetched that they wouldn't know, because it would take lots of truckloads to transport five hundred drums. But to give them the benefit of the doubt, it *is* a very remote location. I visited the farm. Of course, the EPA doesn't believe they didn't know. The EPA has searched the entire property with metal detectors, but they haven't found anything else yet. The EPA has also searched another two thousand acres the Parkers own farther down the Eastern Shore, near Cambridge. But they've found nothing there either. The IRS is performing an audit to review the Parkers' cash receipts over the past few years. They are looking for unusually large deposits."

"The poison in the Bradlees' water supply. Did it come from those drums?" Frames asked.

"Tests carried out by the EPA show conclusively that the waste in the cattle's drinking water was the same as was contained in the drums on the Parker land. And it gets better. The EPA tracked the underground stream that supplied the Bradlees' cattle herd. It went directly beneath the illegal dump site, at a depth of less than a hundred feet."

"Were the drums leaking?"

"Yes."

"Who dumped the waste on the Parker farm?" It was Tipton who asked the vital question. Cleveland, Miller wasn't going to earn a huge fee from a judgment against the Parkers—even if they could prove that the Parkers knowingly buried the waste. It sounded as if they were land rich, with six thousand acres on the Eastern Shore, but that could be meaningless. Farmland outside of Centreville and Cambridge might not be particularly valuable, and there might be a hefty mortgage attached to the property that would have to be repaid before the Parkers could use the net proceeds of a land sale to make restitution to the Bradlees. What the Bradlees, and therefore Cleveland, Miller & Prescott, needed was a deep corporate pocket: a multimillion-dollar industrial corporation, preferably headquartered outside the state of Maryland, unquestionably guilty of sending the drums to the Parker land and, by logical extension, guilty of poisoning the Bradlees' cattle herd. Even if the large corporation produced legions of attorneys to proclaim their client's innocence, in the end the local jury would find the corporate defendant guilty and award the Bradlees a large judgment. The corporation would appeal the judgment, and Cleveland, Miller would recommend that the Bradlees settle for a lesser amount. It always happened that way. Depending on the size of the corporation and its financial wherewithal, Cleveland,

Miller might be able to settle at ten to twenty million dollars for the Bradlees. And Cleveland, Miller & Prescott would receive a third of that amount. That was standard. Three to seven million out of one case. Maybe much more if the corporation responsible for the waste was large. The partnership licked its chops. But everything was contingent upon being able to identify that corporation.

"Have you been able to determine who sent the waste to the Parker farm?" Tipton asked the question again.

"We have. But before I continue, let me say this. There is a restraining order on all of the parties with respect to publicly discussing the case. That is why none of you has heard anything about it in the press. That order will be in effect until the trial begins, but since you are all partners, Turner feels you should know what is going on, especially in light of the fact that we are going to trial next week."

She paused for effect and then addressed Tipton's question again. "Of the five hundred or so drums, only two had any identification. Names on the rest of the drums had been filed or sanded off. However, two drums bore the name Penn-Mar Chemical Corporation."

"For those who may not be familiar with Penn-Mar Chemical Corporation," Prescott interjected, "why don't you give them a little background, Sharon?" He wanted to make certain that the partnership was duly impressed.

"Penn-Mar is a multinational chemical corporation with properties all over the world. For the fiscal year ended December thirty-first, 1995, Penn-Mar reported worldwide revenue of over forty billion dollars and net income after taxes of over a billion. Ranked by revenues, it is the second largest chemical company in America."

Another audible murmur raced around the conference room. The partners leaned toward one another and nodded. A settlement far in excess of ten to twenty million dollars might be possible.

"But before we all start thinking about new beach houses in the Virgin Islands and so forth, I think you should know that there are a few problems with the case." Sharon spoke loudly to restore order. "We have been able to specifically link only the two drums with Penn-Mar's name on them to the company. The contents of the other drums were exactly the same as the contents of the drums bearing Penn-Mar's name; however, the waste at the site in Centreville is common to many commodity chemicals produced by a wide variety of U.S. chemical companies and U.S. subsidiaries of foreign chemical companies. In addition, neither of the marked drums was leaking. Only about half of the drums at the site had leaked, and the two traceable to Penn-Mar were not among them."

The partnership began to settle back in its seats. Suddenly the ten- to twenty-million-dollar settlement was looking very iffy.

"All is not lost, though." Sharon was taking the partnership on a roller-coaster ride, and she was enjoying it. "Penn-Mar has a large facility located on the outskirts of Wilmington, Delaware—a facility which, in the manufacturing process of its chemicals, produces the exact same waste found at the Centreville site. We believe that the toxic waste found in Centreville came from this facility. Penn-Mar's next closest facility is in Pittsburgh, and we're pretty sure it didn't come from there. Anyway, we have found a truck driver who will testify that he made at least three trips from the Penn-Mar facility at Wilmington to the Parker property in Centreville. That's at least a hundred drums. He has received immunity from prosecution. That's why he's willing to testify."

"He'd better be under twenty-four-hour police protection too," Tipton said emphatically.

"As a matter of fact, we have hired several bodyguards for him. Not that we really think Penn-Mar would try to interfere with his testimony. All in all we believe we have a pretty good case. Penn-Mar has offered the Bradlees a settlement amount."

"How much?" Frames asked.

"A million," answered Sharon. "Frankly, we had no problem recommending to the Bradlees that they not accept the offer. That kind of money would just barely pay off the debts they have incurred over the past year and leave them with nothing else."

"Where is Penn-Mar headquartered?" Frames wanted to know.

"Toledo, Ohio."

"Have you been able to determine whether or not the corporate officers knew about this toxic dump site?"

"At this point we have not been able to establish a link between senior management and the illegal dumping. If we could establish that conspiracy, and if we could establish that all of the drums at that site were Penn-Mar drums from the Wilmington facility, we'd probably be able to win a huge settlement. Right now it appears that we'll be able to prove only that there were several very irresponsible employees at the Wilmington facility who sent two containers to the Parker land."

"Has anyone been able to figure out who the anonymous source was? Who made the telephone call that led the Bradlees to uncover the toxic waste that night?"

Sharon shook her head. "We don't know."

The manila folder lay on Prescott's desk. It was the key to the Pleiade Project. The key to everything. Without it, they could not bring down the President. With it, they would throw the financial markets into chaos, and destroy this heinous administration.

Prescott shook his head. He was worth perhaps fifty million dollars including the partnership interest. It wasn't anywhere near what Granville stood to lose, but it was enough. With the tax overhaul the President had announced as the major initiative for his second term, that fifty-million-dollar net worth, what he had labored a lifetime to build, would all but evaporate at his death, appropriated by the Internal Revenue Service. They were going to close all the loopholes and raise the inheritance tax rate to ninety percent on all wealth over three hundred thousand dollars. And any money flowing from personal and trust accounts to offshore accounts would be subject to withholding tax rates equal to or higher than the inheritance tax rates. He had already checked that possibility. It was insanity. But the President would get that new tax bill through Congress. Most of America didn't come close to a net worth of three hundred thousand dollars when they died. For them, it would be a painless way to significantly reduce the deficit. For Prescott, it would be catastrophic.

The file before him would change all of that. It would save Prescott's perception of the American Way. He didn't put much stock in truth and justice. His years in the judicial system had taken care of that. But a man ought to be able to pass on the wealth he had built over his lifetime to his designated heirs.

The file contained tremendously valuable documentation that they had obtained from Jeremy Case. The information proved conclusively that senior management of Penn-Mar was well aware that toxic waste from the Wilmington plant was being sent to the site on the Parker farm in Centreville, Maryland. In fact, seventeen Penn-Mar plants across the United States and Europe were systematically sending drums of toxic waste to unauthorized sites, saving tens of millions of dollars a year in the process. Legal storage of toxic waste involved construction and the ongoing monitoring of sites set up to handle the waste. That would have totaled hundreds of millions in capital expenditures—which they were saving.

The evidence was truly damning. Jeremy Case had given them memorandums listing the illegal sites, listing the individuals at the Penn-Mar facilities responsible for arranging the illegal disposal, and describing just how much money they were saving each year. There was even a memo from the chief operating officer to the chief executive officer outlining the COO's concerns about continued illegal disposal. It was beautiful. Prescott couldn't ask for a stronger case.

The information contained in the file—the file that had been inside the package Phoenix Grey had retrieved from the strip-mall pavement in Temperance, Michigan, after killing Anwar Ali—would destroy Penn-Mar and, thereby, an administration. It was too bad that they had to kill Jeremy Case after he had provided them so much information, but it was absolutely necessary. Just as Rutherford said, sometimes people had to be sacrificed to complete the mission. There could be no clues leading back to them.

Who had been that anonymous caller to the Bradlees that night? Prescott laughed. He had driven all the way from Baltimore to Wilmington to place that call from a phone booth outside the Penn-Mar plant. That way, when officials checked the Bradlees' telephone records, they would see the call coming from Wilmington. He would present that bit of evidence in court. It would be thrown out as circumstantial, but it would have its effect on the jury anyway.

He had made the call, but only after Rutherford had assured him that the two drums with Penn-Mar's name clearly painted on the side had been buried on top of the unmarked drums already in the ground there. The people at the Wilmington plant would never know.

Prescott laughed loudly. Rutherford was incredible. How the man accomplished some of these things, he would never know. He probably didn't want to know. Granville had been correct to recruit Rutherford. Prescott had objected to Rutherford at first. They all had. But Granville was right. They needed him.

Prescott had been cynical as well when Winthrop had proposed the plan to the other six of them two years ago. "The Pleiade Project" Winthrop called it—the term *Pléiade* originally referred to a group of seven French poets of the sixteenth century who favored the use of classical forms. But now the term referred to any group of seven brilliant persons. Granville liked that word—*brilliant.*

They had all been cynical at first. Now they were all believers. They were farther than they had ever dreamed they would be. Now it was up to Boreman to bag the elephant.

"Turner?"

Prescott looked up quickly. "Sharon, what in the world are you still doing here? It's after nine-thirty." She had caught him off-guard. The Case file lay open on the desk, and he did not want her to see it.

"I just wanted to make certain I was as prepared as possible for Monday. I hoped I might find you still here too."

"Beautiful night, isn't it?" Prescott nodded toward the office window overlooking Baltimore's now illuminated Inner Harbor.

"Beautiful." Sharon followed his gesture, as he knew she would.

Quickly Prescott closed the file and allowed it to drop silently to the carpet behind his desk. "Sharon, why don't we have ourselves a nice dinner? To celebrate the long-anticipated beginning of the trial. I think we can safely say that there is no way the other side can postpone it again at this late hour."

"Dinner would be very nice, Turner. But I don't want to keep you from your wife."

Prescott smiled. "She's at our summer home on Martha's Vineyard. I'm not going this weekend because of the trial."

"Oh." Sharon felt her knees go weak. "Fine." Suddenly she was nervous. They had spent a great deal of time together over the past few months preparing for the trial, but never once had they dined together alone.

"Good. Let me finish up a few things, and I'll be around in a minute. We'll go to the Brass Elephant. How is that?"

"Great." She hesitated momentarily. She wondered what was in the manila folder Prescott had subtly closed and pushed to the floor.

12

Falcon sat in the desk chair of his apartment and stared at the equipment. Barksdale had been true to his word. The men had installed everything in the apartment. Fax machine, personal computer, a Bloomberg terminal, a modem so that he could interface with the bank's mainframe, giving him access to brokerage reports, LEXIS/NEXIS, and Lotus One Source. The bank had even arranged for a separate telephone line so that Alexis would not miss calls related to her modeling jobs. Barksdale must have a very senior level connection at New York Telephone because, as a rule, it took at least two weeks to have a line installed in the city.

Falcon rubbed his eyes and yawned. He had worked straight through the weekend. Finally, late yesterday, Alexis had prevailed upon him to interrupt work and enjoy Sunday evening out. They had eaten at Henry's End, an exotic out-of-the-way place in Brooklyn Heights, then walked to the Promenade to view the lights of downtown Manhattan across the East River. He barely enjoyed dinner and did not enjoy the Promenade at all. He was preoccupied. There was too much to do.

Alexis wanted to go out afterward to a club, but Falcon nixed the idea initially. He needed to get back to work. He had lost valuable time already just by going to dinner. The first meeting with the German investment group was scheduled for the end of the week, and he was far behind. She had cried in the taxi on the way back to the Upper West Side, saying that she could not cope with his lack of attention. Now Falcon realized why he had never had a serious relationship in New York. But he also realized that he didn't want to lose Alexis.

So they went out despite his reluctance. And she had kept him away from the apartment until four o'clock in the morning at a hot new Argentine club, flirting and dancing with several men—the first time she had ever flirted with anyone in his presence. Finally, he had dragged her, literally kicking and screaming, from the dance floor. They had ridden home in the taxi in silence and had not spoken a word to each other since arriving at the apartment. Alexis had gone straight to the bedroom and locked the door, and he had sprawled on the leather couch in the living room.

His shirt, slacks, socks, and shoes lay in a crumpled mass on the floor next to the sofa. All he wore now was a pair of blue boxers. He was tired, hungover, and irritated. He rubbed his eyes again. What a great way to start the most important week of his life, a week that could ultimately be worth five million dollars.

Suddenly, Alexis burst from the bedroom. "I'm leaving!" she announced.

Falcon brought his hands to his face. Her voice knifed through his head like a high-powered laser. "Fine." He was in no mood for this.

"What do you mean, 'Fine'?" She stopped at the door of the room, hands on hips, staring at him.

He allowed his hands to drop from his face. She looked stunning in her tight top and short skirt. "I mean, go ahead," Falcon said calmly. "I've got lots of work to do and just four days to do it. Feel free to stay out all day and most of the night too." He gestured grandly toward the door, as if bowing before her as she entered a huge ballroom.

"I hate that superior attitude of yours sometimes. That Falcon control."

He leaned back in the chair, crossed his arms, slowly raised his left eyebrow, and broke into a sarcastic grin.

Immediately Alexis turned, picked up her pocketbook from the spindly wooden chair near the door, and hurled it at him. Falcon ducked to avoid the missile, then bolted from the chair and caught her as she attempted to rush from the apartment.

"Get off of me!" Alexis struggled to free herself from Falcon's grasp, but she could not. He was much too strong.

In one motion Falcon scooped her up like a baby and threw her onto the couch. Immediately he was on top of her, holding her hands down above her head. She continued to struggle for a few moments, then stopped as it became obvious that her effort was useless.

Their faces were inches apart. "Don't ever flirt with another man in front of me again. Do you understand?" Falcon hissed.

Alexis stared at him. She had never seen the fire burn this way before. "Let my hands go," she whispered. He did and she brought them to the back of his neck. "All right. I just did it so you'd pay some attention to me and not that damn computer." Falcon smiled, then pulled her lips to his.

Fifteen minutes later she had gone off happily on a shopping spree, and Falcon was back at his desk. He stared at the computer. There was so much left to complete: projections, discounted cash-flow analysis, debt-capacity analysis, comparable-transaction analysis, comparable-company analysis, review of Delaware and Ohio takeover statutes, review of all relevant newspaper articles relating to the company, and a review of Penn-Mar by division to determine what, if anything, could be sold to reduce the debt on the off chance that they were successful in acquiring the company. "Damn it." Falcon leaned against the back of the chair. He needed something for this headache.

The cordless phone on the desk whistled obnoxiously. "Shut up," he said, then picked up the phone and pressed the answer button. "Yeah."

"Andrew?"

"Yes."

"It's me, Jenny."

"Hi." Falcon's expression brightened immediately. He stood and moved to the kitchen to fix another glass of Alka-Seltzer. "It's good to hear your voice."

"Thanks." Her tone betrayed no emotion.

Falcon let out a long breath. She was still acting "professional," as she called it. "Lighten up, Jen. Come on. I miss the old Jenny Cagle. This one's too formal."

"Sorry. It's the only one there is. How do you want me to act?"

"Like yourself." Falcon dropped the tablets into cold water.

"I thought I was."

It was useless, he could see that. Well, the hell with her. The hell with everybody this morning. "What do you want?" He became curt, something he had never before been with her. Perhaps that would elicit a reaction.

"I have a couple of messages for you." The edge in her voice became more noticeable.

Falcon drank the entire glass of fizzing liquid in one gulp. So she could be stubborn. That made two of them. "Who called?"

"Gill Raines from Goodyear and Helen Dragas from H. J. Heinz. Do you need their numbers?"

"No. Look, Jenny . . ."

"Good-bye, Falcon. I'll let you know if anything important comes up."

"Jenny!" The line clicked in Falcon's ear. "Jesus Christ, that's all I need now." He replaced the phone slowly, fighting the urge to slam it down. Suddenly he realized that it was the first time Jenny had ever called him Falcon. So she didn't consider him a friend anymore. Well, good for her. Alexis was mad at him and so was Jenny. They'd both get over it in time.

The telephone whistled again almost immediately.

"Yes, Jenny," he said in a patronizing tone.

"Falcon?"

"Yes?"

"It's Barksdale."

"Oh. Sorry."

Barksdale ignored the apology. "I hope all that expensive computer equipment is hard at work. What do you have for me? How much can we pay for Penn-Mar?"

Falcon breathed deeply. "The thing is worth sixty dollars a share . . . sixty-five tops."

"We won't win with a bid that low. DuPont or Hoechst will come into the bidding process at those prices. We have to pay more."

Oh, so now he was an M&A expert, Falcon thought. "It isn't worth any more than that. At least not according to what I can tell from all of the public information I've gathered. Look, why don't we try to contact senior management at Penn-Mar? Maybe there is more value than sixty dollars a share. Maybe they've got a new product or a new process that will significantly boost revenues. Or maybe they've got some land on the balance sheet well below market value. A conversation with senior management might get me to a higher offer price."

"They won't meet with us." There was impatience in Barksdale's voice.

"You don't know that. They might be very happy to meet with us if you really think DuPont or Hoechst is going to jump into the fray. Penn-Mar's senior management shouldn't want to see either of those two companies win a bidding war. Those companies already know the chemicals business. The first thing they will do is kick out Penn-Mar's senior people to save a good bit of money. We, on the other hand, need them. We don't know anything about chemicals."

"In fact, we do know a good bit about the chemical industry. By that I mean the Germans and their representatives do. Besides, Penn-Mar probably has all kinds of golden parachutes and rabbi trusts in place to protect those guys in case of a hostile takeover. They'd be only too happy to see the price go higher to make their stock options worth more." Barksdale was throwing out a couple of terms he'd heard at a cocktail party, as if he really knew a thing about M&A.

"Penn-Mar doesn't have anything like that in place. A shareholder rights group got them to rescind all of that last year," Falcon said, slamming Barksdale's little foray into the game.

"I don't care." Now Barksdale was on the defensive and he became authoritative. He was vice chairman and Falcon was just a vice president. "We're not going to contact them before we announce our offer to purchase. It would give them time to find another bidder. Maybe another buyout group that would give them all kinds of incentives and options we're not willing to give. I don't want to give them any more time than I have to."

"Phil, if we pay more than sixty dollars a share, the equity people in the buyout couldn't expect to receive more than a twenty to twenty-five percent annual return, and that's optimistic. Equity players usually need forty to fifty percent a year. It would hurt our credibility in the—"

"Falcon, we're going to pay seventy-five dollars a share."

"What?"

"Seventy-five a share. You said it yourself last week when we first discussed this thing. We can't win unless we pay seventy-five a share."

"That was before I knew what a dog this thing is. I can't in good faith recommend seventy-five a—"

"That's what we're paying, damn it."

"Why not start out at sixty? It's a respectable premium over the current price. Don't give away the farm on the opening salvo."

"I want to bear-hug them. I want no chance that this company slips away from us."

Falcon could hear the stress in Barksdale's voice, and he tried another tack. "Is Boreman driving you to this? Is he telling you the price has to be seventy-five a share? He's the one who is friends with the Germans, right?"

"What else have you found, Falcon?" Barksdale asked, ignoring him.

There was going to be no further discussion on price. Falcon could either be a part of the team at seventy-five or not. It was his choice. And he wasn't going to miss this party. No way in hell. It was his chance to get back to the big time, his chance to start an M&A group at NASO, and there was the five million they were going to pay him if the deal went through. He wanted that five million. Plus there was the added incentive of rubbing the biggest takeover in history right in Granville's face—right under his nose. So what if Boreman and Barksdale wanted to play Russian roulette with the Federal Reserve? That was their business, as long as he got his five million and had time to put it into J. P. Morgan or one of the Swiss banks. And what the hell? What was he worried so much about seventy-five dollars a share for anyway? Maybe the Germans knew more about Penn-Mar than he did. Maybe they had inside information. It wouldn't surprise him at all.

"What else have I found? Let's see. Penn-Mar is headquartered in Ohio, but it's incorporated in Delaware, as many of the Fortune 500 are. If Penn-Mar's board does not embrace our offer, if the offer is hostile in other words, we'll have to get at least eighty-five percent of the stock in the initial tender or the Germans won't be able to touch Penn-Mar for three years."

"What do you mean they won't be able to touch it?"

"Hands off. No meddling. Management gets to keep operating Penn-Mar the way they want to even though the Germans own it. It's called the Delaware Statute in M&A parlance."

"So what does that mean for us?"

"It means that we'll have to make this an all-cash offer. No security-for-security deal. Those deals have much less chance of getting more than eighty-five percent in the initial tender because shareholders are leery of what you're trying to pawn off on them.

Everybody knows what cash is worth. Especially the arbitrageurs. And they'll be the only ones left at the end. You'll need them."

"So it's an all-cash deal. Good, I like that. I assumed it would be all cash anyway. What else?"

"I checked their SEC documents for poison pills, staggered terms for the directors, and lockup provisions, the normal shark repellents. They don't have any. That's good. I also looked at what we might be able to sell after the transaction to reduce the debt. They've got a couple of noncore divisions. I love these big companies. When you start digging, you find they're into everything. Anyway, I think we could probably raise about three or four billion dollars from the sale of divisions which have nothing to do with chemicals. And we could do it quickly, within four to six months. I know people who would buy those divisions."

"Falcon, you've been busy. I'm impressed." Barksdale relaxed. Falcon had come to terms with the price. There would be no further trouble. "I knew there was a reason I wanted you involved with this thing. Anything else?"

"Not right now."

"All right. I'm going to let you get back to work. You will be ready for Friday?"

"I'll be ready, Phil. But before you go, I've got a couple of questions."

"Yes?"

"Well, we need to line up the financing internally and externally."

"I'm taking care of that. The equity is ready to go. The Germans have already deposited their billion at NASO, and Boreman has made arrangements for our three billion from the funds we manage. Hennings thinks he can do at least six billion in junk bonds. And I'm talking to the head of the credit department, Ron Jones, with respect to the senior debt NASO will commit."

"Four billion?"

"What's that?"

"Four billion. That's what you said NASO would commit in senior debt when we talked about it last week. Four billion."

"Right, four billion."

"And Ron Jones is going to approve four billion dollars on top of six billion in junk bonds even though four billion is way over our legal lending limit?"

"Let Boreman and me worry about that."

"Okay. But that's still only thirteen to fourteen billion dollars of financing in place. If we're really going to pay seventy-five dollars a share for Penn-Mar, we're going to need a lot more. Like another eighteen billion."

"We are talking to ten other banks. Several here in the United States, a couple in Europe, and a few in Tokyo. We are talking to these institutions only at the very top levels. We're looking for three billion dollars from each. They are all interested. Very interested. But they need your leveraged buyout analysis and you to talk them through it. I need you to finish that analysis as quickly as possible."

"Then let me get back to work."

"My thoughts exactly, Falcon."

"One more thing, Phil."

"What's that?" Barksdale said, starting to become exasperated.

"What are we going to assume for fees in this deal?"

"You tell me, Falcon. You're the investment banker."

"The commercial banks will need at least two percent up front. I'm sure Hennings will charge three to four percent up front on the junk bonds. That leaves just the advisory fee. My fee for the bank."

"What's typical?"

"One percent."

"One percent of what?"

"One percent of the deal amount, including any existing debt that is refinanced."

"That would be one percent of thirty-two billion dollars. Is that what you're telling me your fee is?"

"Yes. That's the standard fee."

"That would be three hundred twenty million dollars. That's outrageous. Besides, I told you. You will get five million personally if this thing goes through. Not a penny more."

Falcon was relieved. They were still planning on paying him the five million. That was why he had raised the fee discussion in the first place. "I know. The rest would go to NASO."

"I think Boreman would have a hard time convincing the Germans that the advice of you or NASO was worth three hundred twenty million. How about fifty million?"

"You're the boss."

"Anything else, Falcon?"

"No."

"Good. If you need me, don't hesitate to call. I'll be here until around four-thirty. I've got a dinner at Remi."

"You lead a tough life, Phil."

"Someone has to do the dirty work. Bye, Falcon."

"Bye."

Falcon clicked off the phone. As he gazed out the window down at 82nd Street, the little voice that had murmured to him that day he had come face to face with Boreman in the executive washroom whispered to him again. Except it was more insistent now. Something didn't smell right.

Falcon removed the internal NASO telephone book from the top left-hand drawer of the desk. He found the number he was looking for and began to press the sequence onto the pad. Abruptly he stopped. This was stupid. Barksdale had been emphatic about not talking to Hennings, or anyone else from NASO, except Jenny. As Barksdale had said, they didn't know him very well yet—which meant they didn't trust him. The line could easily be tapped, or there could be a bug in the equipment they had delivered.

Five minutes later, Falcon was standing at a pay phone in the lobby of the Portland Hotel, across the street from his apartment building.

"National Southern Bank. Funds Transfer Group."

"Eddie Martinez, please."

"Just a minute."

As Falcon glanced casually around the lobby, he caught a man staring at him. Or perhaps their gazes had simply crossed for a second? Falcon watched as the man turned to speak to a Barbie doll look-alike behind the front desk. There seemed to be nothing unusual in his actions.

"Eddie Martinez."

"Eddie, this is Andrew Falcon." He spoke in a subdued voice, not quite certain why.

"Mr. Falcon. How are ya?"

"Eddie, call me Andrew."

"Sure."

"Eddie, I need a favor."

"Anything for you, Mr. Falcon."

Falcon did not bother correcting Martinez again. "I hate to make this so secretive, but you've got to keep this very confidential. Just between the two of us. Can you do that?"

"Of course."

Falcon listened carefully to Eddie's voice for any sign of discomfort about the confidentiality issue. But there was nothing. "I'm very serious about that."

"Not a problem," Martinez said quickly.

"Okay. Look, I need you to find a wire that would have come into the bank in the last month or so. The total amount is a billion dollars. It wouldn't surprise me if the money came in as several different wires, maybe lots of them. So as not to attract attention."

"Wouldn't surprise me either, Mr. Falcon. A billion-dollar wire.

Hell, yeah. Somebody would've said something. Where was this money coming from?"

"Supposedly from Germany. But again, it wouldn't surprise me if it came from several different places. Look, I know I'm not giving you much to go on, but I need your help on this one." Falcon checked the front desk again, but the man was gone.

"S'okay. I'll do what I can. I got some ideas. What exactly do you want to know about the money if I find it?"

"One very simple thing. The wire's source. Who sent the money. I don't care if you talk to people at other institutions, but don't talk to anyone else at NASO. Okay?"

"Yeah, sure. I gotcha. I'll call you when I find something."

"No. I'm not going to be in the bank for a couple of weeks. I'm at a, uh, seminar. Don't call me, I'll call you. All right?"

"Uh-huh."

Falcon could hear the slightest apprehension creep into Eddie's voice. Eddie wanted to ask questions, but didn't. "Thanks, Eddie. I'll be in touch."

Falcon hung up the phone. He checked the NASO phone list he had brought with him from the apartment. He wanted to call Hennings and Jones to see if Barksdale and Boreman were really working with them. But that was too risky. If in fact they were working with Barksdale, they would call him immediately to let him know that Falcon had breached confidentiality. He glanced one more time about the lobby and headed for the door.

Jenny hurried down Seventh Avenue toward Penn Station. She glanced at her watch as she waited on the corner of 39th Street for the light to change: 5:32. Eight minutes to make the New Jersey Transit train back to New Brunswick.

She had missed Falcon at the office lately. As difficult as it was to admit, the place seemed empty without his crackling energy. Most of the people in the building walked around like zombies. For the hundredth time she wondered why he was suddenly working out of his apartment. It seemed so strange. After all, he hadn't been working at NASO all that long.

The light changed, and she darted across the street. The sidewalk was thick with office workers scurrying toward trains, buses, and cabs. Making progress in the melee was difficult.

Suddenly a man bumped into her, sending her large black handbag spinning to the pavement. The contents of the bag spilled across the sidewalk.

"Damn!" It had not been a good day. As she knelt to retrieve her belongings, she turned to curse the man, but then realized that he had stopped to help her.

He knelt beside her. "I'm very sorry," he said in a gravelly voice.

Jenny stared at the man. He was nondescript: average height, average build, average everything. "It's okay."

In seconds they had reloaded the articles into Jenny's bag. She turned to go, but the man caught her by the arm. "We want to know about Falcon. Everything he does. Everywhere he goes. Your phone is tapped at the office and at your home. But if Falcon tries to reach you some other way, we want to know about it. Immediately. Don't try to find the wires, and don't tell anyone about this conversation either. That is, if you value your life. Here is a number." The man pressed a small piece of paper into Jenny's palm, then closed her fingers around it. "Call this number if there is anything you think we would be even remotely interested in. Don't tell Falcon about this conversation. And don't try to resign from NASO. I'll kill you if you do." She gasped in shock, and Phoenix Grey smiled harshly. "By the way, this could turn out to be very profitable for you if you cooperate. You hate Falcon anyway. At least you ought to. He used you very badly."

Jenny stared at the man as he melted into the crowd. She gazed down at the piece of paper the man had pressed into her hand. She noticed the familiar pattern, the familiar color. It was a dollar bill. No, not a one-dollar bill. She unfolded it fully. A thousand-dollar bill. Jenny searched the crowd. But he was gone.

"I'll kill you if you do." He had said it that casually. Like "Have a nice day." She began shaking. What was Falcon involved in? She stared down at the thousand-dollar bill. What was *she* involved in?

"Falcon left his apartment to make a call this morning. He went to the hotel across the street."

"What?"

"Yes."

"Why in the hell would he do that? Could he have found the bug? He must have. That's the only explanation."

"He couldn't have found the bug. That would be impossible. It's inside the computer. He knows nothing about electronics."

"Then why did he leave the apartment?"

"I don't know."

"What did he say on the phone?"

"I'm not certain. I couldn't get close enough to hear. I don't know who he called either. But I put a wire into that phone after he left."

"Good. Let me know if anything else comes up."

"Right."

Rutherford scowled as he replaced the receiver. Perhaps Turner Prescott was right. Perhaps he should have resisted Granville's decision to take Falcon down as part of this. He stared out at the sunset over Boston's South End. Time could not move fast enough now.

13

"Do you honestly believe Penn-Mar is an attractive stock?" Victor Farinholt stared out the window past Peter Lane, toward the Capitol's huge dome rising above Washington.

"I do." Lane was insistent. He was pressing too hard. Farinholt would hear that in his voice. "I really do," he said more soothingly. It had to be a softer sell. Otherwise, Farinholt might become suspicious.

"And you think Penn-Mar should be part of the President's portfolio?"

"I think it should be part of his and several of the Senators' portfolios as well. Look, you know we are extremely restricted in terms of what we can put any of these elected officials into. No foreign stocks, no defense stocks, no this, no that. The list is endless. But Penn-Mar isn't restricted. It's just a basic manufacturing company, a chemical company located right here in the good old U.S. of A. Sure, the company has some foreign operations, but almost eighty percent of revenues are generated in this country. It's headquartered in Toledo, Ohio, for Christ's sake. How much more American can you get?"

"Fine, but is it a good investment?"

"I think it is. In the last couple of months the share price has run up a bit, but there's still a great deal of upside left in the stock."

"What do you mean, 'it has run up a bit'?"

"At the beginning of the year, the stock was around twenty-four dollars a share. It closed yesterday at thirty-one."

"Peter, that's a twenty-percent increase in six months. That's a lot. And we're not talking about a high-technology stock here. Penn-Mar isn't going to have the kind of dramatic earnings growth that a computer company might have. It might be out of gas by now."

"I understand your reaction. But Penn-Mar's management has cut production costs and increased efficiency dramatically. They could increase the top line another fifteen percent and not hire another factory worker or buy another piece of capital equipment. It's amazing and it hasn't been widely publicized. Yet. But I think the word is starting to get out. And with the economy beginning to come around, Penn-Mar will see significant increases in revenues because chemical companies traditionally lead the economy."

"I know . . . I know." Farinholt had heard the same arguments hundreds of times before. He had been in the money-management business for thirty years, since graduating from Yale in 1966. Farinholt peered down at the charts Lane had prepared. "Let's see, since January one the Dow Jones average is up eight percent and the S&P 500 Index is up nine percent. Christ, you're right. Penn-Mar is up over twenty. I don't know, Peter . . ."

"But look at DuPont and Dow. Both of those stocks are up over fifteen percent. And compare the price-earnings ratios of DuPont and Dow versus that of Penn-Mar. Penn-Mar is a strong opportunity, Victor."

Farinholt relaxed into the chair and considered the argument. He had founded Lodestar Investment Management twenty years ago, after ten laborious years at a large Boston money-management firm. For most of those twenty years Lodestar had languished as a small-time financial advisory firm, barely generating enough fee income to stay in business. But three years ago the President had called Farinholt and asked him to manage his money. By law, elected officials were not allowed to invest themselves, because of the possibility of conflicts of interest, so they entrusted the money to third parties. Blind trusts, they were called. The President and Farinholt had attended prep school together in the early sixties and had maintained a professional friendship ever since. But it was still a shock to Farinholt when the newly elected President, the toast of Washington, called for his help.

Word spread that Lodestar was managing the President's money, and suddenly the whole world wanted Farinholt to manage its money too. Farinholt moved the office from Atlanta to Washington two years ago to accommodate the growth in business. Now, besides the President, Lodestar counted as its clients seven Senators, thirty-two Representatives, a Supreme Court justice, and hundreds of institutions. And Farinholt was worth millions. He rather liked this sudden success, and he was not about to foolishly endanger his gravy train.

"Any scabs on this thing, Peter?" Farinholt tapped the table. He had hired Lane away from Merrill Lynch a year ago. He was a helluva securities analyst. But you had to be careful with Peter. Sometimes he told half-truths. Of course, that was the trouble with the securities industry as a whole. Everyone told half-truths—and thought nothing of it.

"Not of any substance. They've got a lot of environmental litigation pending against them. In fact, there was some news about a suit against them in Baltimore this morning. That little tidbit came across the wire just before I came in here. But shit, Penn-Mar's a fucking chemical company. They're bound to have environmental problems."

Farinholt winced. Lane had a terrible mouth. That was another thing he didn't like about people in the securities business. "What are the particulars of the suit you mentioned?" Farinholt didn't really care about the specifics of the action. Who knew how legal action that had just begun was going to turn out? But he did want to see how well Lane had researched Penn-Mar.

Lane was agitated. His leg bounced up and down beneath the table. "Something about some people on the Eastern Shore of Maryland who had their dairy herd killed by polluted water. They claim that Penn-Mar illegally dumped toxic chemicals on this farm, the drums leaked, and the shit got into the cows' water supply. So they clean up the site, pay the people some compensation for the loss of Elsie and the rest of the herd, which probably ended up as dog chow, and everybody gets on with their lives. The thing will get settled before it ever gets to the jury. Every one of these things gets settled. Penn-Mar pays a couple a million bucks, and it's over. It isn't going to affect the stock price one way or the other. Penn-Mar is too big. Besides, I'm not recommending a long-term strategy. I'd keep it in the President's portfolio for six months. The juice will be out of it by then."

Farinholt drew in a long breath, then exhaled loudly. He did not like to tinker with the composition of the President's portfolio. It was full of blue-chip companies because the last thing he wanted was a real problem with one of the President's stocks. Just keep up with the Dow. That was all he wanted to do with that portfolio. But the truth was the President's portfolio had not kept pace with the Dow. It had increased just four percent since the beginning of the year, half the Dow's performance. He needed a winner. "All right. Buy twenty thousand dollars' worth. And some call options. That will be ten percent of the President's portfolio, enough to make a difference if you're right. Yet it won't hurt us too badly if you're wrong. And you'd better not be wrong, Lane. Sell IBM to get the money. Use Alex Brown. You got that?"

"Sure, sure." Lane rose to go.

"What's the upside on this thing, Peter? Short term."

"It will be at forty-five dollars a share by Christmas. I guarantee it."

* * *

"Twenty thousand dollars at thirty-one is done!" the Alex Brown broker screamed the words into Lane's ear. "That's six hundred forty-five shares. I'll send you a confirmation later."

"And I need one other thing too."

"What?"

"Call options. What's the strike on the Septembers?"

"Uh, hold on." People screamed in the background. "Yeah, thirty-five."

"Price?"

"Three and a quarter."

"Still a hundred options to a contract?"

"Yep!"

"Buy me fifty contracts. For the same account."

"Done. I'll send you the confirm on that transaction too."

"Take your time."

"Good-bye."

"Yeah. You have a nice day too," Lane said sarcastically. He hung up the phone. A wave of relief coursed through him. For a moment he had been worried that Farinholt was not going to give the approval to purchase the Penn-Mar shares. Then he might not have received the five hundred thousand dollars. If these people wanted Penn-Mar in the President's portfolio, so be it. He didn't care. He had no particular political affinity, except that he was beginning to approach the level of income where he would run into this President's new tax rates.

Even if Farinholt had turned down the recommendations, he could have simply lied and told the woman that they had put the President into Penn-Mar. But something about the woman's eyes told him that might not be a good idea. "We'll be listening" was what she had said. Lane didn't know exactly what that meant, but he had an idea. Bugging devices were common in Washington.

Five hundred thousand dollars. In cash. No taxes. He would quit and go lie on a beach somewhere. Lane wiped a bead of perspiration from his forehead. Farinholt had bought the crap about cost-reduction programs at Penn-Mar so easily. God, people were gullible.

Money moves over the wire effortlessly, nothing more than electric pulses travelling between huge computers installed in the back offices of financial institutions around the world. As long as the notification is properly encoded, no questions are asked, and the money flows directly to its destination. Sometimes it moves through several institutions before it reaches its ultimate destination, depending on who has a correspondent relationship with whom. But it always arrives.

The amount was not large, thirty thousand dollars. A minuscule amount compared to the billions that come and go each day. Not enough to create the slightest suspicion. That was the way they wanted it.

The wire transfer found its way into NASO as a snake would enter the basement of a home. Silently. Smoothly. Through the darkest passageways. Searching for prey. But the wire, the thirty thousand dollars, did not remain at NASO for long, as the snake, locating no prey in the basement of the first home, would exit through another darkened passage, searching for another basement in which to hunt.

The wire remained at NASO just long enough to nestle into an account that had been set up for Falcon only the day before. An account of which he was completely unaware. The wire moved into the account and then moved almost immediately back out again into the system, into the numbered Citibank squirrel account, which even the bankruptcy judge had been unable to find upon the demise of MD Link. It was an account Falcon should have closed many months before but hadn't. They appreciated his uncharacteristic lack of attention to detail. The money did not remain in the unclosed squirrel account for long either. Just long enough for Citibank to record its presence.

Then it moved on again, this time to a Chase Manhattan general clearing account. The Chase account was maintained by Winthrop, Hawkins and used as a depository for clients' funds. The funds were used by large institutions and wealthy individuals to purchase stocks and bonds through Winthrop, Hawkins security brokers.

Winthrop, Hawkins bought and sold securities only for large institutions and very high net-worth individuals. Normally, Falcon would not have met the minimum net-worth requirements for using Winthrop, Hawkins brokers. But today he was being offered a special opportunity, an opportunity of which, again, he was not aware. He would have given anything to know what was happening and who was behind the movement of money and the "gift" that found its way into the special brokerage account at Winthrop, Hawkins. Because if he had known, he might have been able to avert the disaster.

Thirty-two dollars a share. Nine hundred and thirty-seven shares. A gift to Falcon from an anonymous donor. A gift that could potentially provide him a forty- to fifty-thousand-dollar gain—as well as a five- to seven-year prison sentence. A sentence he could not survive.

The camera bulbs popped and flashed at Carter Filipelli and Wendell Smith as the two men stood on the steps of the Federal Building, across Wall Street from the Stock Exchange. It was from the Federal Building that George Washington had addressed a nation after being elected its first President. As a sign of respect, and at President Warren's direction, Filipelli had made a special trip to New York, to Smith's territory, to host a conciliatory luncheon at Tavern on the Green—Smith's favorite restaurant. In attendance were other senior members of the New York Fed, local politicians, and top investment bankers.

After dessert, Filipelli gave a short speech, praising Smith's service to the Federal Reserve, his knowledge of how markets interacted, and his economic insights. Then they had travelled to

Wall Street together, by limousine, for the photo session with the press. The two men stood close together, hands clasped in what had become a five-minute handshake.

"Lots of people here!" Smith yelled the words above the din of the screaming reporters' questions. He nodded approvingly as camera bulbs flashed all around them.

"Yeah, they'll be calling this Fed Bowl in the morning," Filipelli yelled back.

"You know, you're not such a bad guy!" Smith screamed at Filipelli.

Filipelli smiled broadly for the cameras and leaned toward Smith's ear. "Yeah, but you're still a son of a bitch!"

14

The square-shaped boardroom on the top floor of the NASO Headquarters building, forty-seven stories above Park Avenue, was easily large enough to accommodate NASO's sixteen directors and invited guests during the bank's quarterly board meetings. The ceiling, at least twenty feet high, was covered with exotic Philippine seashells. The insides of the shells reflected all colors of the spectrum as spotlights, hidden behind the cornice molding, slowly rotated.

Like the room, the table, covered entirely by beige felt cloth, was square. The shape made the middle of the table completely useless, Falcon thought as he stared at the beautiful centerpiece of fresh roses. It was the wrong room for this meeting. There would be just four people in attendance today. This room would overpower the presentation, and Falcon was keenly aware of how vital aesthetics were to a successful presentation. But Barksdale wanted the meeting here, so here it would be. He had selected this venue primarily because there was an elevator that ran directly from the basement to the forty-seventh floor, making no stops in between. Today's attendees, including Falcon, would be able to come and go anonymously.

Falcon moved to the huge window on the south side of the room. Despite the thick midday humidity, he could see all the way downtown, his view only slightly obstructed by the Chrysler

Building, and behind it, the Empire State Building. The World Trade Center's towers soared skyward in the distance to the right, seemingly not so much taller than the NASO building at this great distance. To the left, in the center of the downtown area, rose the spires of the AIG headquarters and the uncharacteristically modern J. P. Morgan building at 60 Wall Street.

New York. It was an incredible city. A city in which one was tremendously happy or tremendously unhappy. Exuberant today and despondent tomorrow. There was no middle ground here. And Falcon had revelled in that volatility when he was younger because the short down periods made the highs even more intense. It had made him proud to survive in New York. Now it just made him tired.

During the last few days, huddled over the computer, one question kept reverberating through his mind, over and over. If he had money, five million dollars, for instance, would he stay in this godforsaken city? A city he derisively nicknamed the Bad Apple? The answer kept coming up no. The answer was to escape as quickly as possible. He would take the money, two million after taxes, sink half a million into a comfortable but conservative farm in the outer reaches of Vermont, and live out his existence on the remainder of the money and whatever else he could earn out there.

Alexis probably wouldn't agree to that life. She would be horrified at the thought of being more than a few miles from a major metropolitan center, horrified at the thought of being more than a few minutes from Fifth Avenue. But so what? Maybe he didn't want her to go. He flexed his left hand. Maybe Jenny really ought to be the one. In Vermont, her background wouldn't matter.

Falcon gazed out over the concrete wasteland and suddenly began to laugh. It was a dream, a goddamn pipe dream, to think he would go to Vermont. He'd be living in New York chasing the almighty dollar until the day he died. Not because he necessarily required what those dollars could buy, but because money was the yardstick of success or failure in this society. It was the constant against which every individual could be measured objectively. And he would be damned if he wasn't on top when the measuring was done. He was too driven. It would be his undoing someday. Granville's words kept coming back. He hadn't known until now what the older man meant.

"Falcon." Barksdale's melodious voice filled the boardroom.

Falcon turned. He had not heard the elevator door open. Following Barksdale toward him were two other men, who looked neither to the left nor the right, but maintained their gaze steadily upon Falcon. They came to where he stood, and he was strangely irritated that they would invade the space in which he had been fantasizing about the idyllic Vermont farm.

"Falcon, this is Devon Chambers and Werner Prausch. Werner is a partner in the German-based investment firm Westphalia Nord. Devon represents Westphalia's U.S. affiliate, Veens & Company. Veens will be the entity making the acquisition."

"Good afternoon." Falcon shook the German's hand first. The man was blond, blue-eyed, and of average height. Falcon judged him to be around forty. "I've not heard of Westphalia Nord or Veens & Company," he said.

Chambers stepped in front of the German without offering his hand to Falcon. "It was formed two years ago. It specializes in chemical-company acquisitions both in Europe and in the United States. It is very private and very publicity averse. We have completed several small purchases since our inception. Our money comes primarily from institutions within Germany with which our chairman has strong connections." Chambers spoke in a low whisper, through labored breaths. "You will receive more detailed information later for your perusal."

Falcon tried to summon the trademark crooked smile as he stared down at Devon Chambers, but somehow he could not. Chambers was small and frail, and the charcoal-gray suit appeared to be pinned to his body in certain places. The dress shirt fit loosely around his neck, as if it had been purchased at a time when Chambers' neck was healthier. The man's skin was pallid, almost devoid of pigment, and the dark hair contrasted sharply with the pale skin. He looked like a walking corpse.

Finally, Chambers took Falcon's outstretched hand. Chambers' hand was actually cold to the touch, and Falcon had to make a conscious effort not to recoil.

"Good afternoon, Devon." It seemed unnatural to address this man by his first name, but Falcon forced himself to do so. It was a quick way to put those much older on equal ground in a business setting. He had learned that long ago. But it had to be done authoritatively.

"Hello." The same low whisper. Chambers' lips, thin and dry, barely moved. He exhibited no friendliness at all.

Chambers' eyes did not leave Falcon's and did not blink. It unnerved Falcon, and he felt the small hairs on his neck rising. But he betrayed no emotion.

"Why don't we all sit down?" Barksdale was acting too friendly. He was visibly agitated, Falcon noticed. Chambers intimidated him. "Let's have some coffee." Barksdale guided the two clients to one corner of the huge boardroom table.

Falcon followed them to the table and sat around the corner so that he faced them.

"Falcon, as you know, Wallace will be unable to join us today." Barksdale turned to the other men. "Wallace is in Tokyo speaking to the chairman of the Long Term Credit Bank about the transaction."

The other two men nodded solemnly.

"Why don't we get right to it?" Chambers said bluntly.

"An excellent idea." Falcon slipped into his presentation mode. "But if I could first be so bold as to ask about your background, Devon."

"Falcon, you'll get all of that—"

"It's all right." Chambers cut off Barksdale. His gaze was

overtly unfriendly for the first time. "I was chairman of DuPont until six years ago, when I retired. I played golf and travelled for a while after that, but it wasn't enough." Chambers paused to breathe. "I was fortunate enough to make the acquaintance of Werner and his partners. It has given me an opportunity to get back in the game."

Falcon stared at the man. "Of course. You spoke at Harvard Business School. You spoke to my second-year business policy class."

Chambers nodded. "I did that every year. We at DuPont tried to remain very active at Harvard. DuPont recruits heavily from both the undergraduate and business schools."

"Did you graduate from HBS?"

Chambers nodded. "Harvard undergraduate as well. Now, can we discuss Penn-Mar, please?"

Falcon glanced at Werner. He wanted to ask about Prausch's background but didn't. Chambers was clearly in charge, so Prausch's background probably didn't matter anyway.

Falcon passed each of the men a small bound booklet. "Devon, I would appreciate your comments at any point."

"I won't hesitate." As if saying this had caused him too much effort, the older man touched his chest.

Falcon took a deep breath, but before he could begin the presentation, Chambers began to cough—short, innocent coughs at first, as though he were simply clearing his throat. Chambers removed a handkerchief from his suit pocket, covered his mouth, and motioned for Falcon to begin the presentation. But the coughing deepened to an unpleasant hack which sounded as though it were tearing Chambers' lung tissue apart. The older man leaned onto the table, dropped the handkerchief, and grabbed the felt material tightly as he convulsed. His knuckles turned snow-white as what little blood circulated through his fingers drained away. "Katherine! Katherine, help me!"

Barksdale and Prausch stood quickly. They looked around frantically but were paralyzed by the attack.

"Katherine, the pills!"

Barksdale and Prausch looked at each other but did not understand.

Falcon moved quickly to Chambers' aide. He leaned down close to the old man's pallid cheek. "Where?" he asked urgently.

"Pocket." It was all Chambers could do to speak.

In the side pocket of Chambers' coat Falcon located a small vial. He pulled it out quickly, glanced at the prescription, and turned to Barksdale. "Water! Now!"

But Barksdale was still frozen. It was as if his shoes were bolted to the thick Persian rug. His mouth opened and closed but he made no sound.

Finally, Prausch responded. He sprinted to the far end of the room, where there was a dumbwaiter on which was a ewer of water. He grabbed the entire pitcher and a glass and ran back to Chambers. Falcon pulled Chambers to a sitting position, shoved two of the light-green tablets into his mouth, and forced water down his throat. When Chambers opened his mouth again to cough, Falcon saw that he had swallowed the pills.

"Call an ambulance!" Falcon yelled at Prausch.

"No!" Chambers coughed again. "No, I'll be all right." He steadied himself on the table.

Prausch hesitated.

"What are you waiting for? Go!" Again Falcon yelled at Prausch.

Chambers grabbed Falcon's hair tightly and brought his face directly in front of his own. "I told you not to send for an ambulance!"

Falcon stared into the yellow corneas. Death was very close to claiming this one. And though he had taken an immediate dislike to the man, he had to respect Chambers' tenacity to fight the inevitable. "All right. It's your life."

At Chambers' request, the three men helped him to his feet. For a few minutes he stood, leaning against the table as he sipped water and wiped his face. Then he sat, pronounced himself fit, and pointed at Falcon. "Get going."

Falcon hesitated.

"I said, get going, boy. What's the matter, haven't you ever seen someone with a little chest cold?"

Falcon stared at the man for a few moments, then sat down and began.

For the next forty minutes he explained the public-tender process, from the point Veens & Company would announce its offer to purchase—long, technical documents published in tiny print in the *New York Times* business section, the *Wall Street Journal*, and the *Financial Chronicle*—to the point at which Veens would take control of Penn-Mar. He explained that there were no significant concentrations in the stock—no individuals or related groups that owned more than five percent of Penn-Mar's shares. Which was good, because large holders could work together to drive the price even higher than what Veens wanted to pay. He explained the Williams Act—the body of laws regulating public-tender offers—the Hart-Scott-Rodino antitrust statutes, and the reams of Securities and Exchange Commission documents they would have to file. He explained the maximum per share value he attributed to the company and the process by which he had determined the valuation. He discussed potential competing bidders, the Delaware Statute, and the divisions he would recommend for sale immediately following the transaction, and who the most likely buyers for those divisions would be. He explained how Veens & Company would pay for the shares; what levels of debt and equity would be used; what interest rate and fees the banks and junk-bond investors would require for their money, which Veens & Company would use to pay for the shares; and what return Veens & Company could expect from its huge investment in Penn-Mar Chemical Corporation.

The three men did not interrupt him once. They sat and listened, as if mesmerized. Falcon's presentation was technical and concise, and when he had finished, he closed the booklet from which he had delivered his monologue and glanced about the huge room. "The acoustics are better in here than I thought they would be." His gaze finally came to rest on the three men. They were impressed, he could tell. He had seen the look on countless other faces before. "Questions?"

Finally Chambers spoke. He seemed to be completely recovered from the coughing attack. "Falcon, you stated that you believe the top value for the shares is seventy-five dollars."

"Yes. And that's generous." Falcon glanced at Barksdale, who was staring at his fingernails. It was more than generous. It was too much. But that was what Barksdale required.

"That is based on a discounted cash-flow analysis?"

"Yes. I projected the company's operations for the next ten years and discounted the resulting cash flows, assuming a terminal value for all of the cash flows after the tenth year."

"What discount rate did you use?"

"Ten percent."

"And what growth factor?"

"Four percent."

"That's your problem. That's why you are only coming up with seventy-five dollars a share as a value for Penn-Mar. The growth factor for the terminal value should be much higher than four percent. Penn-Mar has a new fertilizer product, which has been kept very secret. It will quickly add half a billion dollars in annual revenue to Penn-Mar's income statement. I also know that they are negotiating a long-term contract with the Russian government to provide certain industrial chemicals. It will involve the construction of four plants in Russia. That could double the size of the company in five years."

"Are you suggesting that we should pay more than seventy-five dollars a share for Penn-Mar?"

"I'm suggesting that we must be prepared to go higher," said Chambers. "I believe seventy-five is a fair bid and we should start at that price. But we shouldn't be surprised if our initial bid is topped. I don't think DuPont or Hoechst will allow Penn-Mar to slip away at that price without a fight. Both of those companies would enjoy tremendous synergies with the acquisition of Penn-Mar. They could fire thousands of middle managers and administrative people and add a great many new products without spending a dime on R&D." Chambers' voice was almost inaudible. He coughed again.

Immediately the other three men leaned forward, but there was no cause for alarm this time.

Falcon waited until he was certain that Chambers was not about to endure another coughing attack. "The Department of Justice would never let DuPont or Hoechst acquire Penn-Mar. Those companies would control one hundred percent of the market for certain chemicals if they acquired Penn-Mar. The antitrust people at the DOJ would have a field day."

"Mr. Falcon, you and I both know that the DOJ is almost as unpredictable as our President. We cannot count on them to protect us. Make no mistake. We need to acquire this firm. We must acquire it. Therefore we must be prepared to pay more than seventy-five dollars a share."

"I have to disagree—"

"Don't ever disagree with me, boy." Chambers pointed a bony finger at Falcon. "You're just the hired hand. You take orders from me."

Falcon leaned back in his chair. He didn't like the term *boy*. "You hired me to advise you."

"Falcon—" Barksdale began.

"Shut up, Barksdale!" Barksdale's head dropped immediately, and Chambers turned back to Falcon.

"To advise you," Falcon continued. "That's what I was hired to do. Although I didn't realize that the mandate included saving your life." Falcon's eyes narrowed.

For a split second Chambers smiled, and his face became instantly sinister. Then just as quickly, it reverted to its former shape. "When will we announce the takeover?"

"Boreman will be back from Tokyo tomorrow night." Barksdale spoke up, desperate to validate his presence at the meeting. "He tells me things are going quite well there. He stopped in Europe on his way to Japan, and he says that several of the French and Italian banks are very interested also. We did not bother going to the Germans. They are too damn conservative. No offense." Barksdale nodded at Prausch. "The banks will need a day or two to go through Mr. Falcon's numbers, but based upon his meetings so far, Boreman believes the banks will come through to fill out the twenty billion or so of additional bank debt we need. NASO is ready to commit thirteen billion through several areas of the bank and its securities subsidiary." Barksdale raised an eyebrow at Falcon. "I think we should be ready to go by Wednesday of next week."

"Fine." Chambers turned to Falcon. "I think it's time for you to begin working with the lawyers to draw up the papers."

Falcon nodded. It was premature, but he wasn't going to argue anymore. He wanted the five million and he didn't need any more of Chambers' condescension crap.

"Falcon, we'll need to send copies of your presentation to those banks in Europe and Japan that are interested in coming into the deal. I will give you a list after we are done here." Barksdale cleared his throat. "Then you'll have to be ready to talk to them. To take them through your analysis. It's going to be a busy few days for you." He tried to sound important, but Chambers was paying no attention.

"Not a problem. I look forward to it." Falcon glanced at Chambers. The man was staring at him as if he were trying to bore into his mind. He seemed somehow inhuman.

"I'll call Dunlop & Latham and tell them you will be in their offices first thing tomorrow morning to begin drafting the documents." Barksdale pounded the table. "I've had them on standby for two weeks."

"And you are certain they can maintain confidentiality?" Chambers seemed vaguely uncomfortable.

"Absolutely. We are close to them. They are trustworthy."

"Good."

"There's something else we need to discuss," Falcon said.

"What's that?" Chambers snapped.

"The Federal Reserve. Specifically, Carter Filipelli, the chairman."

"Why do we need to worry about Filipelli?" Chambers seemed annoyed.

"Once Filipelli gets wind of this thing, I think he's going to shut it down very quickly. And as chairman of the Fed he can do that. Besides hauling NASO into court for violation of legal lending statutes, Filipelli can make life for NASO very difficult in myriad other ways."

Chambers waved his hand at Falcon as if this point was irrelevant. "Is there anything else you can think of that is important for us to know about Penn-Mar?"

Falcon leaned back in his chair and smiled at Chambers. Fuck him. The Fed was going to come down on them. It wasn't a question of whether—it was a question of when. If he didn't want to listen, fine. "Well, Penn-Mar's not a very safe place to work if you are a senior executive. Especially if you are the senior vice president in charge of operations." Falcon laughed as he stretched.

"What is that supposed to mean?" Chambers moved forward in his chair.

Falcon thought he detected something odd, vaguely strained, in Chambers' voice. "I'm sure it's just coincidence, but the two people who have held that position in the last year have ended up dead. Both deaths involved strange circumstances."

"Go on." Chambers closed the booklet before him.

"About a year ago a man named Tom West was killed in a terrible automobile crash in Toledo, Ohio. West was SVP in charge of operations at Penn-Mar."

"An unfortunate occurrence, but I don't see what is so strange about that," Chambers hissed.

"The car was travelling at a great rate of speed down a hill in Toledo one night in June of last year. At the bottom of the hill, there was a fairly sharp turn, which West didn't make. The car flipped over on its top."

"Again, I don't—"

Falcon ignored him. "When the police arrived, old Tom was still strapped into the driver's seat by his safety belt. There was blood all over the place. Lots of it, in fact, on the back of the seat. Just one problem, though. The blood was dried, and it had flowed down the seat toward the floor of the car. But the car was flipped over on its roof. Evidently Mr. West was dead beforehand, and then someone put him into the car. The police never were able to pin it on anyone, though. They called it an accidental death, but it wasn't."

"How do you know all of this?" Barksdale asked.

"The story was on Bloomberg. The part about the blood I got from a very nice detective on the Toledo police force. I called them for fun. Doing all that work on the computer was sometimes boring, and I needed a break. I didn't really think I'd get anything out of them. But small-town cops can be pretty forthcoming if you know how to ask the questions."

"You mentioned that there were two people who had died," Chambers said pointedly.

"The second SVP was murdered recently in Temperance, Michigan, just across the state line from Toledo. His name was Jeremy Case. He was the person who took Tom West's position.

The circumstances surrounding Case's death were even more bizarre than those of West's. Case was a born-again Christian. When he wasn't at work he was at church with his wife and two all-American kids. Anyway, he turns up dead at a strip mall next to the body of an unidentified Iranian guy. There are all these pictures of some naked woman strewn around the bodies, not to mention two guns. It appeared that the two men killed each other, perhaps over the woman, but it didn't fit with Case's background. Here's this wonderful father, whom everybody in the community loves, killed at around one in the morning an hour away from his home at some remote strip mall. It made no sense. They never did identify the Iranian or the woman in the pictures. All of that was on Bloomberg too. Strange, huh?"

Chambers did not answer. He did not say a word. He simply stared at Falcon. But behind the stony exterior he cursed Granville Winthrop.

The late-afternoon sun shone down on 82nd Street, casting long shadows on the sidewalk. Falcon walked slowly, suit coat slung over his shoulder. Why was he so worried about the fact that these people were willing to overpay for Penn-Mar? They were every investment banker's dream. They didn't care if they overpaid. They just wanted Penn-Mar, at any cost. But why? Why was it that important?

There I go again, Falcon laughed. Take Chambers' advice. Shut up and be the hired hand. You'll earn five million dollars, and you'll make Granville green with envy. Once the deal is announced, it will be all over every business page in the country, along with my name as the lead investment banker. Granville will have one of his aides order the takeover documents filed at the SEC, and when he sees the fifty-million-dollar fee, he'll go ballistic. He'll think about that evening at the Harvard Club and wish he'd taken me up on my offer. He'll wish he'd returned my calls. Even if it will be just the money he'll regret missing out on.

And what a piece of shit Chambers was. Hadn't thanked him once for stuffing the pills in his mouth and averting a coronary.

Falcon looked up from the sidewalk. Jenny Cagle was leaning against the wall outside the entrance to his apartment building. She wore a light sundress that fell only to the middle of her thighs. She did not have the rail-thin body Alexis possessed, but suddenly he rather preferred Jenny's full figure. His mind drifted back to the night at the Four Seasons. She had been incredible.

As Jenny saw Falcon approaching, tie loosened, suit coat draped over one shoulder, and Wayfarer sunglasses protecting his eyes, she smiled and moved quickly to him. When she reached him, she touched his arm gently. "I'm sorry for the way I acted on the telephone. For the way I've been acting in general. I want you to accept my apology."

Falcon grabbed the olive branch immediately. "I'm the one who should apologize."

They stood facing each other, neither knowing what to say.

Jenny's eyes dropped to the pavement. "That's all. I guess I should get going. I don't want you to get in trouble with Alexis in case she shows up."

Falcon shook his head. "No, she's in Connecticut until late this evening. Very late." He knew he shouldn't have said it. He could have just as easily agreed and ducked inside the apartment building. The truce was made. They were friends again. He could have left it at that.

Jenny looked up from the sidewalk and smiled slyly. "Want to have a beer? Just one quick, cold beer at the end of a long, hot week to cement our understanding. Come on, it will taste really good."

"I've still got a great deal of work to do." But the truth was he didn't have any work to do. The packages would not reach the banks in Europe and Japan until late tomorrow, and their bankers wouldn't be ready to discuss the contents for a day after that, Sunday midday at the earliest. He didn't have to be in the offices of Dunlop & Latham until ten o'clock tomorrow morning, and there was nothing he could do to prepare for that marathon.

Jenny pouted. "Just one. I'm so thirsty."

So she couldn't stay mad at him. He removed the sunglasses and broke into a wide grin. "Okay."

"Great." She took his hand and began to pull him gently down 82nd Street. "I heard about this great Mexican place from a secretary at NASO. I think it's close."

Falcon stopped her. "I have a better idea."

Manny's Pool Hall was dark and mysterious. Jenny glanced toward the front of the place from her barstool. The lone window next to the door was covered with a thick curtain so that the bright sunshine of the afternoon could not invade this tiny corner of Trenton.

Jenny brushed her hair back with her fingers. It was a wreck, she was certain of that. But she was also certain that she wasn't going to use what was probably a cracked and dirty mirror in Manny's unsavory ladies' room to freshen up if she could help it. At least not without an armed guard standing outside the door.

Falcon had driven a million miles an hour down the New Jersey Turnpike, covering the fifty miles from Manhattan to Trenton in what seemed like just minutes, dodging the other cars as if they were playing a video game. He was trying to scare her, but it hadn't scared her at all. She loved going fast. And she sensed immediately that Falcon was in complete control of the vehicle by the way he handled the steering wheel and the way he used the gears more than the brakes to slow down the car. Jenny had also noticed how Falcon had driven straight to the pool hall, without directions from anyone. As if he had been coming here all his life.

"What'll ya have, little lady?" The bartender yelled the words condescendingly over the loud rock music blaring from the speakers positioned near the ceiling. The barrel-chested, hairy-armed man stared unapologetically at the exposed skin between her breasts. He smiled lewdly at her. This woman was out of her element. She was dressed much too nicely for Manny's. And he wasn't about to make her visit here any easier.

"How about a slow, comfortable screw?" Jenny ran the long nails of her fingers sexily across the wooden bar toward his chubby knuckles, but stopped just short of them.

The man straightened up and cleared his throat. So the woman wasn't going to be easily intimidated. Worse still, he didn't know how to fix that drink.

Jenny tapped her nails on the bar. She sensed the man's discomfort. "You don't even know what a slow, comfortable screw is, do you?" She checked the thin gold band of his ring finger and laughed to herself. His wife would probably vouch for that too.

"Beer and more beer. That's what people here want." The bartender wanted to get away from this woman quickly. He realized immediately that she was a great deal sharper than he, and probably making fun of him somehow.

"Okay then. How about a beer?"

"Oh, great choice," the man said sarcastically. "Wanna be a little more specific?"

"Heineken."

The man shook his head. "Budweiser or Miller. No foreign beer."

"Fine. Budweiser."

The bartender moved away, toward the cooler.

Jenny spun slowly on the vinyl-covered barstool. Andrew was immersed in a tricky shot on the pool table at the very back of the dank establishment. He brought the cue back smoothly and then forward just as easily. The white ball rolled the length of the table, kissed the eight ball, which dropped into a corner pocket, and came to rest in the middle of the green felt.

Falcon's opponent, a young man clad in a white T-shirt and dark jeans, shook his head dejectedly. The boy—Jenny judged him to be no more than sixteen—replaced his cue on the wall rack and reached for the pack of Marlboros tucked under a sleeve of the shirt. He removed a cigarette, lit it, replaced the pack under the sleeve of the T-shirt, then removed his wallet—attached to a belt loop of the jeans by a gaudy silver chain—threw several bills on the pool table, and stalked off. Falcon scooped up the money and began to count it, grinning as he did.

Falcon carefully inserted the money into his leather wallet, smiled at Jenny, and moved toward her.

"So how much did you take from that poor boy, Andrew?"

Falcon's face contorted into a look of disgust as he sat down on the barstool next to Jenny. "Poor boy? That's a good one. Kid's no boy. He's probably got a police record as long as your legs. But just for your information, I won eighty dollars."

"He thought you were an easy mark, didn't he?"

Falcon flashed the crooked smile. "Are you asking if I hustled him?"

"I'm not asking. I know you did."

Falcon shrugged. "You walk into a pool hall in this section of Trenton, you'd better be ready for whatever happens to you. Buyer beware and all that. He asked for the game."

"Yeah, after he watched you missing all those shots while you practiced."

"Good, wasn't it?" Falcon smiled widely. "But that wasn't what hooked him. We bet only twenty dollars on the first game. It was the way I just barely missed the shots to lose the first game. By that much." Andrew held up his thumb and forefinger, just slightly apart. "That's what got him to bet a hundred dollars on the second game."

"Well if you're so good, then you can teach a beginner like me how to play."

Falcon shook his head as he finished his beer. "I don't think so."

"Come on," Jenny said. She was feeling the alcohol and she

didn't want the afternoon to end yet. She sensed that he was ready to leave. "Please." She smiled sweetly and batted her eyes.

Falcon's face took on a pained look. He put down the glass. "All right, but we need to get back at some point."

They moved away from the barstools to the nearest table. Falcon racked the balls, then moved toward Jenny to show her how to hold the cue.

"It's okay. I can manage."

"Huh?" Falcon gazed at her.

"I know how to hold the cue. The question is, what's the wager?" She bent over the table and slid the stick back and forth through her fingers.

Falcon laughed. "You don't have to do this, Jenny. Really." He didn't like how smoothly the cue was moving in her hands.

"You think I can't shoot?"

Falcon shrugged. "You might be able to play a little, but you can't beat me. You'd be wasting your money."

"How about betting me that eighty dollars you won from the kid?"

"Jenny, don't do this."

"Is it a bet?"

"No."

"Are you afraid?" She knew that was the easiest way to get a man's attention, to question his virility. She had two older brothers—whom Andrew should have asked about by now—who had taught her how to play.

"Do you have any older brothers?" he asked.

"No."

Falcon stared at her, sensing that somehow he was making a mistake. He knew that a pool hall was no place to expect a straight answer from anyone, including Jenny Cagle. Sweet, adorable Jenny Cagle. He nodded at the table. "Okay. Eighty dollars. You break."

It was over quickly. In less than five minutes Jenny had pocketed all of the striped balls as well as the eight ball. She walked slowly to Falcon and took the four twenty-dollar bills he held up in his right hand. "You said something about walking into a pool hall in this section of Trenton. Be ready for whatever happens to you." She winked and sauntered toward the door.

Falcon watched her as she walked away. A pistol. No other word for her. What was it Granville Winthrop had said to him one night at the estate? "When you're done with all of the veneer, like the one sleeping upstairs, get yourself something real."

Falcon glanced at the bartender, who was leaning across the counter to catch the last glimpse of the fading sun coming through Jenny's dress as she walked out the door. "Hey, Freddie! Put your eyes back in their sockets."

Freddie raised his hands to show that he meant no harm.

"And tell your mother hello for me."

Freddie nodded.

They moved into the tiny room of the hotel, locked in a savage kiss. Jenny's tongue explored his mouth as her long fingernails ran through his hair. Falcon turned to close the door of the room, unclenching his lips from hers in the process. Her tongue and lips moved to his neck and he felt her fingers unbuttoning his white dress shirt. In seconds it was open. She pulled it apart and began to tantalize him with just the tips of her fingernails. Slowly she moved her fingers from his chest to his navel and then back. Falcon felt the pressure in his pants growing. He stood in the darkened room, head back, and allowed himself to enjoy her magic. Alexis would never do this for him. She wouldn't know how, and she didn't want to learn.

Jenny slid her hands along Falcon's shoulders and into the arms of the shirt. It and the suit coat fell to the floor as one. She bent over and began to bite his chest and stomach. Her tongue traced tiny circles on his tight skin.

"Jenny."

"Does it feel good?" she asked, her breath short.

"You know it does." Falcon's breathing was as fast as hers.

She sank to her knees before him. In seconds his pants were sliding down his legs. He could feel her lips on the inside of his thighs, and the coolness of the evaporating saliva aroused him wildly. She helped him off with the suit pants and boxers and then her mouth was on him.

Jenny's hands and mouth worked in unison and it would be only seconds before he would lose control. Falcon did not want that yet. He pulled Jenny to her feet and moved her back against the wall. He followed her, pushing his nakedness against her still clothed body.

"Mmm." She moaned as his mouth covered her soft neck. His hands moved up under the loose sundress and closed around her buttocks as he bit into the skin of her neck. "God, Andrew. You know . . . mmm . . . you remember I like it rough."

"Yes." He lifted the dress over her head and let it fall to the floor. He kissed her again on the lips hard, then turned her so that she faced the wall. He undid the bra, then with one quick pull, ripped the sheer G-string from her crotch and dropped it. "I'll buy you another one." He bit her ear gently as he whispered the words.

"I don't care. Just keep going. Don't stop." Her breathing was labored now. "Don't stop." She was reaching around her body for him, lifting herself onto her toes and pushing her buttocks high into the air. And then he was inside her.

It felt so incredibly wonderful. How could it be so different with her? It was flesh on flesh. That was all. Nothing else. Why was it so much better with Jenny than with Alexis?

"Harder, Andrew. Come on!"

Suddenly Falcon pulled her to the bed. He was down on her and within seconds she was writhing in a tremendous orgasm. Finally she screamed and rolled away from him. She could take no more. Falcon moved up her body and pressed himself inside her.

Her mouth caught his tongue and she did not let go. Moments later Falcon collapsed onto her body, exhausted.

Jenny lay quietly under the sheets with her head resting on his chest. She caressed his thigh lightly as he faded in and out of consciousness. They had been going at it now for two hours, and this was their first rest of more than five minutes. "Are you all right?"

He laughed. It echoed in his chest. "No. I feel like I might have a heart attack."

Jenny kissed his chest. "Good."

They were silent for a few moments.

"Andrew."

"Yes?"

"Does she make you feel this way?"

"No." His voice was almost inaudible. There it was again, the truth.

Jenny touched his face. "This is a pretty good deal for you, isn't it? Two women whenever you want them. It doesn't seem fair somehow."

"Jenny . . ."

She pressed a finger to his lips. "I wouldn't if I didn't want to. Are you enjoying it?"

"Yes, I am."

"Then I want to keep seeing you. And don't worry. When you come back to the office I will remain completely professional. No one will ever know. Promise. No more silly temper tantrums." She paused. "But there is a price." She feigned a serious expression.

"What do you mean?"

"I mean that I want to become at least a little bit more a part of your life than I am now."

That sounded strange. "How so?" Suddenly he wondered why she had become so understanding.

"I have a deal for you. You have me whenever you want, but we talk at least once a day. As long as you are out, you call me. When you get back, I get to come in your office once a day and just talk. For let's say ten minutes. Would that be so hard?"

Falcon shook his head and smiled. "No. I think I could do that."

"And one more thing. I get to learn more about you. If you aren't one of the most secretive people I've ever met, then I don't know who is. You've always been like that." She kissed his chest again.

"It's just the nature of my business, I guess. It makes me that way. The truth is, there isn't much to know. I'm pretty boring."

"You let me be the judge of that."

"Fine. If you think I'm so interesting, then ask me questions. Go ahead. Fire away."

Jenny put her head back down on his chest and slipped her hand between his legs. She felt his stomach muscles tighten involuntarily. "For starters, why don't you tell me about this project you are working on so diligently?"

15

The sun was rising quickly above the horizon and becoming hotter by the moment. Filipelli checked his watch. Just after 9:30. He removed the heavy wool sweater he had donned at the lodge early this morning to protect himself from the cool Montana morning. Even in July, Montana mornings could be chilly.

Filipelli scoured the sky. It was cloudless. "You think the weather will hold today, Bugsy?" Yesterday, Filipelli's first on the river, had started off clear and warm but by noon had turned cool and rainy. Now the weather was beautiful again.

"Don't know, Mr. Filipelli." Bugsy was busy rigging a nine-foot fly rod for nymph fishing and clearly did not wish to be disturbed. But here was a perfect opportunity to feed shit right down a city slicker's throat. It was too much to resist. "There's an old saying out here in Montana, Mr. Filipelli. If you don't like the weather, wait an hour. It'll change by then. Course, they say that over in Wyoming also. Idaho as well. I was out East one time many years ago. Maine, I think it was. They said it there too." Bugsy cackled for a moment, then refocused on the task of rigging the long fly rod.

Filipelli smiled. He rather enjoyed the fact that his crusty old fishing guide couldn't give a rat's ass that today's client was the chairman of the Federal Reserve. He could take a little ribbing from this crusty old salt. In fact, it was refreshing not to have people cowering before him. Hell, if he had asked the question back in Washington, people would have written reports or hooked up a live line to the National Weather Service. No, Bugsy couldn't care less about the Fed or the fact that Filipelli was a big swinging dick in world affairs. Bugsy lived in the real world. Montana. Where men were men and government officials were just lucky to be alive.

The air was crystal clear. Filipelli breathed in deeply. It was good to be out of Washington and the limelight for a few days. He had to go back Tuesday, but for the next two days he was going to forget about everything—Wendell Smith, the FOMC, even the President—and just enjoy himself.

Filipelli gazed out from the riverbank at the pristine waters of the Bighorn River rushing through the Yellowtail Dam a quarter of a mile upstream. The Bighorn spilled out of the mountain range of the same name rising up steeply on the southern horizon, then alternately tumbled and meandered to its meeting with the Yellowstone River a hundred miles to the north. On the long journey, these waters would converge with the Missouri and then the great Mississippi before ultimately flowing into the Gulf of Mexico south of New Orleans.

He watched the river drift by and wondered if General Custer had seen this same place on his way to the Little Bighorn. Even at this early stage the Bighorn was a large river, perhaps a hundred feet across, shallow enough to be waded in most spots, but very deep in some areas too. More important, the Bighorn was one of the most prolific trout rivers in all of the lower forty-eight states, filled with huge browns and rainbows.

Filipelli was an avid trout fisherman, when he had the opportunity, which unfortunately had not been often in the last several years because of his hectic schedule. Friends who also adored the sport had recommended this river to Filipelli on numerous occasions, but he had never had the chance to come. He had already fished many of Montana's other jewels: the Madison, the Gallitan, the Yellowstone, and even the spring creeks of Paradise Valley, but never the Bighorn. Now he was here and he was going to fully enjoy himself. His aides were under strict orders not to call unless something unprecedented occurred.

Filipelli was fishing out of Fort Smith, a town of no more than three hundred people located two hours southeast of Billings. When the West was being won, Fort Smith had been an outpost for government troops on the Bozeman Trail. Now it was little more than a trading post for the farmers and the Crow Indians of this desolate corner of the state. That and a base of operations for sportsmen such as Filipelli, who came in search of the huge rainbows inhabiting the Bighorn's depths.

Bugsy finished tying the knot attaching the clear monofilament leader to the thicker, bright-green fly line. He laid the graphite rod on one side of the fifteen-foot dory and glanced up at Filipelli. "Let's go. Time's wasting."

The two men pushed the heavily laden craft into the clear waters of the Bighorn. "Get in, Carter!" Bugsy screamed to be heard above the din of the water rushing through the dam just upriver.

Filipelli lifted himself awkwardly over the side of the boat. This movement was made more difficult by the aging rubber waders he wore to protect his body from the forty-seven-degree water. For a moment he balanced on the gunwale, almost capsizing the craft in the process, then tumbled clumsily onto the bottom of the boat. He pulled himself up quickly and sat in the bow facing back, toward the stern.

Bugsy gave the boat one more strong push, then pulled himself easily over the stern, climbed over the fishing gear littering the floor, and took his seat on the bench in the middle of the dory. He adjusted the oars, and began to row the boat toward the middle of the river. Filipelli marveled at the dexterity with which the older man had accomplished the entire maneuver. Bugsy was seventy if he was a day.

Bugsy smiled at Filipelli. "Little trouble getting in the boat there, Chiefy?" Bugsy rowed methodically as he flashed a nearly toothless grin.

"A little." Filipelli did not smile back. A little ribbing was fine, but it need not become routine. He was, after all, one of the most powerful men in the world. It was time to assert himself. And where had he come up with "Chiefy"?

The older man glanced over his shoulder at the other dory moving out into the river behind them. "Those guys gonna be with us all day?"

Filipelli nodded. "President's orders. I must have at last two Secret Service people with me at all times."

Bugsy grunted. "One of those bastards took the Colt Revolver I carry to shoot rattlesnakes. Told me I'd get it back when the day was over. I'd better get that gun back. It was my great-grandfather's."

"You'll get it back. Don't worry."

"So they thought I might try to shoot you, huh?" Bugsy began to laugh hysterically. It sounded as if he were having an asthma attack.

"You're a pretty rough-looking little character. Wouldn't surprise me if you had shot a few of your clients."

"Only the ones that don't catch the fish I find for 'em." Bugsy spat tobacco juice into the water. "Hope we don't run into any rattlers."

"Are there rattlesnakes around this river?" Filipelli scanned the banks nervously.

"Tons."

Filipelli could not tell if the little man was kidding or not. Bugsy bent down so the brim of the grimy Chevy Truck hat covered his face. Filipelli thought he noticed Bugsy's shoulders shaking as if he were laughing hard, but there was no way to tell. The heck with him. As long as they caught big fish, this little troll could enjoy himself.

The roar of the water rushing through the dam began to fade as the dory moved downriver, which in the case of the Bighorn was due north. Filipelli lay back against the raised bow, breathed deeply again, and took in the landscape. The prairie, covered by a carpet of light green grass, swept gently up and away from the riverbank. In the distance rose buttes and mesas, and beyond them the snow-covered peaks of the Bighorn Mountains touched the deep-blue sky. Big Sky Country. An apt nickname. You could see forever out here.

"Where was Custer massacred, Bugsy?"

"That battle was on the Little Bighorn, a tributary of this river. They meet about thirty miles north of here."

"Which Indians did he fight there?"

"The Sioux."

"But the Indians around here are Crow Indians, right?"

Bugsy nodded. "That's right. This section of the Bighorn flows directly through the center of the Crow reservation. Both sides of the river are owned and maintained by the tribe. Little advice for you, Chiefy. When you need to take a piss, don't go above the watermark on the bank."

"Why not?"

"Legally, the Crows is allowed to arrest you for trespassing if you do. We're allowed to walk on the riverbank to fish, but you can't go traipsing around them fields. By order of the federal government of the United States of America." Bugsy said the last sentence sarcastically. He knew more about Filipelli than he let on.

"Do they actually arrest people?"

"Sure. Wouldn't you? I mean, put yourself in their shoes. You see some joker walking around in your fields all decked out in fishing gear that probably costs more than you've been able to save in a lifetime. He pulls his pants down to piss all over your land, and all you can see is that lily-white ass sticking out at you. And that lily-white ass is probably related to one that came out here a hundred years ago to steal your land. So sure, they're gonna do whatever they can to harass you."

Filipelli laughed. "This land is so wide open, you'd see them coming for miles. I'd just go back to the boat."

"First of all, a little bit downriver the cover on the banks gets a lot heavier. Cottonwoods, bushes, tall grass, and the like. You wouldn't see them coming for the life of you down there. Second, an Indian could hide behind a blade of grass if he had to. Third, and most important, an Indian spends a good bit of his life carrying two things: a whiskey bottle and a gun. He often carries them together, which, let me tell you, ain't a great combination. He sees you pissing on his land, and he's likely to start taking potshots at us whether you're in the boat or not. I don't need that today. So just do me a favor. Stay on the riverbank and don't go no farther!"

"I'm a senior government official, and I go where I want to go. Besides, we have two highly trained Secret Service agents with us. We won't have any problems."

Bugsy glanced over his shoulder at the two agents struggling to keep pace. "Those guys would never see Indians coming either," he snorted. "They'd be dead before you could say Geronimo."

"Your tone leads me to believe that you are sympathetic to the way the Native Americans have been treated, Bugsy. That's good."

"Personally, I don't give two hoots about them, Mr. Filipelli. I've lived out here for fifty years and I ain't never seen one worth a lick. They're a goddamn pain in the ass is what they are. But I'm a pragmatic man. They're here and they ain't going anywhere, so I gotta live with 'em. And you know why they ain't worth a lick, Mr. Filipelli? Because you bleeding-heart liberals in Washington got this big guilt complex about what happened a hundred years ago, just like you got a big guilt thing over dropping the big one on Japan. So you feel like we gotta give everything to them. Land, cars, monthly stipends, and such. I'm not saying what we did to them people was right. No sane man could. Some of the stories I've heard about the butchering and the raping the soldiers did are incredible. Abominable is a better word. Anybody ever tries to tell me the white man represents the superior race, I laugh at 'em. But the problem is, when you give somebody everything he needs to survive, you take away his incentive. You take away his determination. These Indians take the money we give 'em and spend it on whiskey. They get all drunked up, and they end up beating their women and getting into car accidents. Ultimately they become alcoholics. You got to give a man something to strive for. Otherwise he's worthless. I don't care if he's Indian, white, Chinese, or black."

Filipelli wanted to respond. He was naturally drawn into arguments. But the boat suddenly began to pick up speed as it drifted around a bend in the river.

"Hold on, Chiefy." Bugsy pulled hard on the oars.

Filipelli turned in the bow. Before him was white water, boiling and churning over and through huge boulders. Skillfully, Bugsy guided the dory into the headwaters of the rapids. He stood in the boat, still holding the oars, mapping out his path through the rocks. Bugsy knew the slow water of the river intimately, but the fast water was constantly changing. As they reached the top of the rapids, he sat again and began to maneuver the craft through the frothy water.

The air became cooler over the fast-moving water. Filipelli grabbed the gunwales tightly and tried to anticipate the rocking and swaying of the boat against the rushing current. The rapids reached their peak, and then suddenly the dory slipped into smoother waters. Filipelli sank back into his position against the bow.

"That was great!" He was exhilarated, ready for anything, isolated in the wilderness and unavailable to the bureaucrats.

"That was nothing. This river doesn't have any real rapids. Least not this far south." Bugsy pulled a beer from the cooler behind his seat, cracked it open, and took a long swallow. He wiped his mouth with his sleeve when he was finished. "Want one?"

"No. Too early."

Bugsy grunted and shook his head. "Look over there, Chiefy."

Filipelli followed Bugsy's gnarled finger. At first he saw nothing. The glare of the bright sun off the water's surface was intense, even through the dark Polaroid lenses of his sunglasses. But after a few moments his eyes adjusted, and he could see why Bugsy was pointing. There were dorsal fins. Trout dorsal fins. Hundreds of them slicing across the top of the water as the fish fed on insects hatching at the surface. "Jesus Christ. There must be a hundred fish over there."

"Three hundred at least."

"That's incredible. And with the sun so high in the sky. I wouldn't think you would get a hatch like that until sunset."

"Oh, that's right, I forgot. You've never fished the Bighorn before. Well, get ready for a treat. They move like that all day long unless the weather is bad."

"What kind are they? Browns or rainbows?"

"Browns." Bugsy turned to look over his shoulder at the two Secret Service men, who were just now reaching the bottom of the rapids. He motioned for them to pull off the river. He did not want them disturbing the pod of feeding fish. They had nearly capsized three times coming through the boiling water and were only too glad to obey.

"All right, Chiefy, I'm going to pull us in here." Bugsy's voice had dropped to a whisper. It was his guiding voice. He scanned the water around the boat. "They're feeding on blue wing olives and midges. Small ones too. Size eighteen at most."

Bugsy was excited now. Filipelli could see it in his eyes and hear it in his voice. Almost as excited as Filipelli.

"Tie on an Adams pattern, Chiefy. Size sixteen parachute pattern. That way you'll be able to see your fly as it floats through the live bugs. That little extra bundle of wool, the parachute, will stick out like a sore thumb on top of the water. You'll be able to see when one of those big sons of bitches takes that pattern. Here." Bugsy handed Filipelli an Adams dry-fly pattern from a small fly box he had hidden in his tattered cloth fishing vest.

Filipelli reached and took the fly from Bugsy. Filipelli's hands were shaking and he took a deep breath. This was silly. These were just fish. But he was unable to steady his hands as he threaded the thin, clear monofilament line through the tiny eye of the pattern's hook.

Bugsy guided the dory quietly to the riverbank. The oars were silent as he propelled the boat through the water. Ten feet from shore, he slid over the gunwale of the dory into two feet of water and pulled it up the bank until it was half out of the water, securing the stern of the boat to the bank with a heavy metal anchor.

Filipelli glanced back upriver. The Secret Service men had pulled their dory out of the water seventy yards upriver, just below the bottom of the rapids. They were watching the chairman carefully.

Filipelli grabbed his fly rod and quickly started his casting routine. The tiny fly, a combination of feathers, animal hair, and thread, floated lazily along the surface. It was a dry fly, meaning simply that it was supposed to imitate an insect that had matured to its winged stage, a stage in which the insect would float on the surface before it took flight, as opposed to its nymph stage, when it resembled some prehistoric creature and would crawl or tumble along the riverbed in its insatiable quest for food.

Filipelli stared intently at the tiny pattern as if floated amid the trout boiling on the surface, waiting for the slashing strike from a hungry trout. The fly neared the end of the feeding area, but still there was no strike.

"Again." Bugsy whispered the words from his squatting position fifteen feet up the bank.

Filipelli lifted the long graphite fly rod, and the bright green, heavy fly line followed. It was this fly line that allowed the fisherman to cast the nearly weightless insect imitation great distances. The imitation fly was attached to a clear ten-foot leader, which was in turn attached to the fly line.

The fly jumped from the water. With a measured back-and-forth motion of the rod, Filipelli worked the fly line first back behind his body, then out over the water, simultaneously drying the fly and moving it into position to settle onto the surface of the water again. It was an elegant motion. It was an elegant sport. But not one for those lacking patience. The idea was to drop the fly onto the surface just upstream of where the fish were feeding and allow it to drift through the feeding area naturally, in the hope that it would attract a large fish along the way.

"Now." Bugsy grunted the order.

Filipelli gave the rod one more strong forward thrust, and the fly and line shot out over the Bighorn. The fly settled perfectly onto the water amid the live insects crisscrossing the surface. The imitation moved into the feeding channel smoothly.

"Looks good enough to eat." Bugsy followed the fly across the water.

"Let's hope." Filipelli's voice was hoarse.

Dorsal fins swirled around the pattern sucking down the live insects, but the huge fish paid no attention to Filipelli's Adams pattern. The pattern neared the end of the feeding channel again.

"Damn it." Filipelli began to raise the rod to begin another series of false casts. Just as he did a huge mouth closed around the Adams fly. Instantly the line became taut.

"Bang!" Bugsy stood and threw a clenched fist into the air. "You're hooked up."

Immediately, the trout realized something was amiss. With one flash of its tail the fish propelled itself from the water, shaking its head from side to side, attempting to free itself of the barb. But the hook remained embedded in the trout's jaw. The fish fell back into the water with a great splash. Again the fish leaped from the water, contorting its body, at the same time sending violent tremors through the line, the rod, and Filipelli's hands. Again it crashed back into the water.

"Christ, he must have gotten three feet clear of the surface on that second jump!" Bugsy was screaming, elated at the battle unfolding in the river before him. "That's a huge fish, Chiefy. Steady, man. Steady!"

Filipelli felt adrenaline surge through his body. It was just a damn fish. There was no reason to become excited. But he could not help himself. His breathing became short, and suddenly he found himself praying to whatever God there was that the line would not suddenly slacken, a certain indication that the great trout had torn the hook loose from its mouth or managed to break the thin leader at the very end of the line. He wanted to catch this fish badly.

"What kind is it, Bugsy?" Filipelli yelled at the older man without taking his eyes from the water.

"Rainbow! I can't believe it. I thought they were all browns in that pool. It's a beautiful fish. Must go eight to ten pounds. That's a big fish, even for this river, Chiefy."

Suddenly the line began to scream from the reel.

"He's goin' deep, Chiefy. Set the drag. Set the drag!"

Filipelli's hands shook wildly as he turned a screw on the reel to tighten the drag, making it more difficult for the fish to strip out line.

"Not too tight. Mother of pearl! That fish'll snap your leader in a heartbeat. That's only a seven-x leader on there."

The rainbow jumped from the water again, this time far out in the river. It had stripped out a huge amount of line.

"He's running downriver, Chiefy. Run with him. Run downstream with 'im or you'll lose 'im!"

Filipelli began to slog through the shallow water near the bank, holding the rod high to keep the line taut and maintain pressure on the fish's mouth. The waders made movement difficult, and he struggled to keep his balance, feeling for the rocks and sticks on the riverbed. Gradually Filipelli moved out into the river until the water reached his waist. It was easier to maneuver here. The riverbed was clearer of debris in the deeper, faster water.

Still the trout moved downriver, though it no longer stripped line from the reel. Filipelli glanced back upriver. In only a few moments he had moved downstream several hundred yards. He could barely see the Secret Service agents relaxing in their boat. Even Bugsy was fading against the background.

The rope wrapped quickly about Filipelli's ankles. At first he did not realize what was happening. Then suddenly he was pulled beneath the surface and completely submerged. For a moment he thought about holding on to the fishing rod, thinking that he must have tripped over some obstruction on the riverbed that he could not see through the murky water and that he would quickly regain his balance. But then he realized that he was being pulled toward the very deep water in the middle of the Bighorn, dragged by some unseen assailant.

Filipelli let go of the fly rod and began to claw for the surface. But already the attacker had pulled Filipelli into a pool ten feet deep, and Filipelli's fingers did not break through the surface of the water. He tried to kick the attacker, whom he could barely discern through the churning water, but the rope effectively inhibited this movement. Water poured into the waders, dragging him even deeper, and Filipelli panicked, realizing that he was going to drown unless he did something drastic.

Frantically he leaned forward for his ankles in an attempt to free himself from the rope. His lungs burned. His body craved fresh oxygen. He struggled for the rope, and suddenly one foot broke free. Filipelli kicked and struck something and then the other ankle was free. He pushed toward the light, clawing and screaming. The surface was close. Another second and he would be there.

Phoenix Grey's scuba mask was now around his neck, a result of Filipelli's wild kick to his face. But Grey did not bother to adjust it now. He reached for Filipelli and managed to grab one of his boots. He hung on. He had to. If Filipelli were to somehow reach the surface, it meant failure for the entire operation. And it meant his own death. Rutherford would see to that.

Filipelli kicked again. The surface was so close now. Inches away. Just inches. He felt as if his head must explode. Pounding. Pounding like hell. A pain he had never known. He screamed. He needed the air so badly. God, let me have one more breath. Why is this happening to me?

Filipelli's fingers broke through the surface. He felt the cool air on his hands. Surely the Secret Service agents would reach him in just a few more seconds. They must have noticed him disappear into the river.

Phoenix Grey mustered all his strength and smashed a large fist into Filipelli's solar plexus.

It was enough. Filipelli could no longer resist the natural urge to breathe even though he knew it meant death. The water poured into his lungs, and he began to choke. Grey pulled Filipelli back toward the depths.

Filipelli brought his hands to his neck. God, give me air. Please give me air. The pain is unbearable. I want to see my family again. One more time. There are so many things still to say. Please, God! He gulped another huge breath of water.

Gradually the light from the surface began to fade. And Carter Filipelli, chairman of the Federal Reserve, sank lifelessly to the bottom of the Bighorn River.

16

The Sevens of Harvard University trace their origins to the Civil War. In 1863, a number of undergraduate students formed a group that became known as the Federalists. Their solidifying philosophy was that the country had to come first, that it could not be torn apart and survive. It must remain united. So it was with unparalleled passion that they promoted support for the Union effort. And they were vocal in their condemnation of the Confederate insurgents.

The Federalists were fanatic as only young people can be. They nailed pro-Union propaganda to every tree on the grounds. They organized huge pro-Union rallies on the commons next to Winthrop Hall by inviting outspoken Federal proponents to speak, and they unmercifully harassed anyone on campus—student, faculty, or otherwise—who dared support the Rebel cause. They would issue threatening notes, throw rocks through windows, and offer other intimidations to those who held views contrary to their own.

The Civil War ended and the Federalists disbanded. But seven members of the society remained active. Secretly, because they believed they would be more effective acting anonymously, these seven men formed a new society. They had already learned a tremendous lesson: men acting in concert, with purpose and dedication and with a common goal, could influence the masses. This small group would carry on where the Federalists had left off and over the years would come to be known as the Sevens.

In 1893, Dr. Franklin Pearse died in Boston after a long battle against cancer. He died without heirs. His two children had died of scarlet fever in their teens, and his wife had succumbed to pneumonia the winter before his own death. During his life he had managed to save two hundred fifty thousand dollars, which at that time was a substantial amount of money. Having no heirs, Dr. Pearse donated his savings to his alma mater, Harvard University.

Along with the money was a note admitting that he was a Seven. The money, at that time the largest individual donation in the school's history, was dedicated to a scholarship fund for minorities, at Dr. Pearse's request.

On the night of Dr. Pearse's death, at exactly seven minutes before midnight, the bell in the tower of the university chapel tolled seven times. Harvard had recognized the Sevens.

The remaining six members of the society tapped a new member, a third-year student active in school politics. The older six members were rejuvenated by the newest Seven. The younger man immediately realized the opportunity he had before him.

The older men were all prominent individuals, several with significant Wall Street connections. The young student convinced the older men to use these connections to raise money secretly for the Sevens, realizing that Wall Street's Harvard alumni would revel in the opportunity to contribute to a secret society that could manipulate policy at their alma mater. And the youngest member increased the Sevens' visibility at the university simply by painting the numeral seven in white paint on the ivied brick buildings.

At the graduation ceremony of 1896, the Sevens made their first official donation to Harvard: one million dollars and seven cents, a huge amount of money at that time. The crowd was awestruck, and the newspapers covering the event barely mentioned that the keynote speaker was the United States secretary of state. Instead, the papers described in detail how an envelope had floated down from a fourth-story window of Grant Hall in the middle of the secretary's address, and how it was attached to a string in such a way that it dangled before the secretary as he spoke to the assembly of parents, students, and university officials from the porch of the building. The speech was interrupted while officials cut down the envelope, opened it, and announced to the crowd the contents. The crowd cheered for fifteen minutes, and the six older men and the graduating student watched with contained satisfaction.

After World War II, the Sevens became more politically active, allying themselves permanently with conservative ideology. They maintained the tradition of spectacular monetary gifts to the university, the amount always including a seven. But they focused their efforts primarily on influencing governors and Congressmen unfriendly to mainstream Republican political views.

A Seven was a Seven for life—there had been only forty-nine in the history of the society. At the initiation ceremony the man was branded on the inside of his upper forearm with the image of a tiny seven, truly legible only with the aid of a magnifying glass. Also at the ceremony a Seven took a blood oath of secrecy to which he committed himself for life and an oath to support all other Sevens in any way possible. Members were identified at death with a "7" at the end of their *New York Times* obituary and by the addition of their name to the others before them on a plain, unidentified plaque in the foyer of the Harvard Chapel, the importance of which anyone even remotely connected with Harvard knew.

The society never numbered more than seven members. When a member died, he was replaced within days by the top candidate from a long list of potential members who were constantly reviewed. New members of the Sevens were no longer tapped from the student body, as had been the tradition until 1945. The operations in which the Sevens had become engaged were too sensitive to be entrusted to a young person still unsure of his political persuasion. New members were individuals already in senior positions of large corporations, prominent law firms, government agencies, or Wall Street's most elite investment houses. They were worth huge amounts of money, were devoutly conservative in their political views, and were graduates of Harvard University. Those were the requirements.

Granville Winthrop scanned the room as he drew on the large cigar. Turner Prescott, managing partner of Cleveland, Miller & Prescott; Devon Chambers, former chairman of E. I. DuPont & de Nemours & Company; Wallace Boreman, chairman of the National Southern Bank; William Rutherford, former head of all European operations for the CIA; Wendell Smith, president of the Federal Reserve Bank of New York; and Bailey Henderson, president and CEO of the *Financial Chronicle*. Powerful men. All of them.

They were a homogeneous group. Caucasian, wealthy, and conservative, each had a wife and children. None was divorced, though several had mistresses. Each man belonged to an extensive list of civic groups and charities. And each hailed from a privileged background. Except for Rutherford.

Rutherford had attended Harvard on what amounted to a football scholarship (Ivy League schools supposedly did not give athletic scholarships but instead called this money financial aid to athletes) because he was not skilled enough to attend a football powerhouse such as Alabama or Notre Dame, and his family was not wealthy enough to afford Harvard. After a storied career as an all–Ivy League linebacker, Rutherford entered the army, where he rose quickly to the rank of lieutenant colonel. He was transferred to the CIA and four years later was promoted to head of all CIA operations for Europe. Rutherford spoke Spanish, Russian, French, and German fluently. He was skilled in the martial arts and versed in all intelligence-gathering technologies. He was steel tough, and the taking of another man's life did not bother him in the least.

In 1981 Richard Seale, acting administrator of the Sevens, had died in the Air Florida crash at the Fourteenth Street Bridge in Washington, D.C. The Sevens contacted Rutherford, who immediately accepted their generous request to join the society. His only job in life would be to run the Sevens' day-to-day activities, to assist Granville Winthrop, the number one. And he would earn more money in one year than he had in his entire army and CIA careers combined. Rutherford resigned from the CIA, effective at once, to join the Sevens and brought with him the services of Phoenix Grey, a man who knew more about killing than God or Satan.

The Sevens were meeting this evening at Prescott's twenty-five-acre estate in the Worthington Valley, a lush stretch of Thoroughbred horse country twenty miles north of Baltimore. They were meeting at Prescott's house, both because his wife remained in Martha's Vineyard so they could meet undisturbed and because Prescott had to be back in the courtroom at nine the next morning in downtown Baltimore.

"Gentlemen, let us bring the meeting to order." Winthrop's deep voice was naturally commanding. The room fell silent. "I thought it important that we meet one last time before the Pleiade Project enters the public arena." Winthrop paused. "I trust you have all heard of Chairman Filipelli's terrible accident Saturday in Montana."

The other six men nodded and snapped their fingers. Initially they had not all agreed that the assassination of Carter Filipelli was the correct course of action to follow. But as it became apparent that the President and Filipelli were serious about increasing the estate tax rate to 90 percent, the men agreed that the Pleiade Project must be successful, at any cost. If Filipelli had to die, so be it. He and the President were trying to steal what they and their families had worked for generations to build.

"Good. Devon, please give us an update on the takeover of Penn-Mar Chemicals."

Chambers drew in a long, labored breath. The malignant cancer in his lungs was growing progressively worse each day. Of the men in the room, only Winthrop and Rutherford knew how truly bad the cancer had become. Rutherford, at Winthrop's direction, had ordered Phoenix Grey to break into the office of Chambers' doctor to make copies of Chambers' file. Chambers would be dead by October. That was what the file said. Even Chambers did not know how little time he had. The doctor had been unwilling to tell him yet.

Chambers began. "We will announce our public offer to purchase on Wednesday. It will be in the *Wall Street Journal*, the business section of the *New York Times*, and, of course, the *Financial Chronicle.*" Chambers nodded at Bailey Henderson. "We will begin the tender offer at seventy-five dollars a share."

"Do you think DuPont or Hoechst will make a counteroffer once we announce our tender?" Prescott gazed over his half-lens glasses across the antique table. He looked crisp in the matching madras bow tie and suspenders.

Chambers turned stiffly toward Prescott. Even this slight movement was terribly painful. "I don't know, Turner. I've contacted my old friends at DuPont. Their strategic-planning people have looked at Penn-Mar several times over the past twenty years. It dovetails awfully well into their operations. They aren't currently looking at Penn-Mar. But if an offer was to surface, they could easily jump into the game." He paused to breathe. "They have three billion dollars of cash on the balance sheet and, with a double-A long-term debt rating, plenty of capacity to borrow on top of that. I'd say it's a pretty fair bet that they will look very hard at topping our offer at seventy-five. Of course, a combination of DuPont and Penn-Mar would raise serious antitrust objections from the Department of Justice. As far as Hoechst goes, they're a wild card. They may not have the ability to raise money as fast as DuPont. And once we start our offer, they would have only twenty days to react."

Winthrop began to speak.

"There's one more thing." Chambers interrupted him. "I wanted to bring this to everyone's attention. When I was at NASO at the meeting with Barksdale, Prausch, and Falcon, Falcon mentioned the fact that West and Case had died under suspicious circumstances."

The rest of the men glanced at Winthrop. They were all leery of Falcon's involvement, but they were more leery of Winthrop.

"So what?" Winthrop was defiant.

"I think he may try to find out more about these unfortunate accidents."

"Let him."

"But . . ."

Winthrop exhaled a large cloud of smoke at Chambers, who began to gasp for breath immediately. "You keep up your end of the bargain, little man. That's what I'm worried about."

Chambers nodded and reached for the green pills in his coat pocket. His face turned crimson as he held the cough in. He could not show weakness at this point.

"What about the financing, Wallace?" Winthrop pointed at Boreman, who was stuffing a ham sandwich into his mouth.

Boreman broke into a sheepish grin. "Excuse me. Today has been a long day. I got in this morning at five-thirty New York time from Japan. This is the first thing I've had to eat since a piece of crap omelet I forced down while on the plane." Boreman wiped his mouth with a cloth napkin. "The financing is basically in place. The equity and the junk bonds are ready to go. The bank debt too. There are just a few more details to work out with a couple of the Tokyo banks. Earlier this evening we received commitments from three American banks, three French banks, and two Japanese banks for three billion dollars apiece. That is another twenty-four billion dollars of senior bank debt along with four billion from NASO. As I said, there are just a few more things to iron out with the Japanese. Anyway, the transaction now has a total of thirty-eight billion dollars of financing. With that amount of money we could go up to almost ninety dollars a share if we had to. And we still haven't heard from two other banks, Credit Suisse and Credit Lyonnais." Boreman paused. "We had to give away some equity warrants to get the banks to commit so fast, but what the hell, after Turner is finished in the courtroom, Penn-Mar's equity isn't going to be worth a nickel anyway." Boreman waved what was left of the sandwich in Winthrop's direction. "I have to hand it to Granville on this one. Falcon did a tremendous job convincing these people that this was a strong transaction." Boreman did not want to make the same mistake Chambers just had.

Winthrop nodded approvingly as he exhaled cigar smoke at Chambers again. The others knew better than to complain about the thick smoke. Winthrop was not happy. He was unaccustomed to driving himself anywhere—his chauffeur usually took care of this detail but couldn't tonight because of the need for ultimate secrecy—and he had become lost in the rental car on the way from Baltimore's Amtrak station to Prescott's country home.

"Could we review once again what all this will do to NASO's financial position?" It was Bailey Henderson's turn to question Boreman.

"Certainly." Boreman took another bite from the sandwich. "Currently, NASO has approximately 15.2 billion dollars of equity and subordinated debt capital. NASO will commit thirteen billion to the Penn-Mar transaction, which, after Turner makes public the information about Penn-Mar's massive environmental problems, will become worthless overnight. Let me remind all of you that NASO also has another six billion of loans to real estate partnerships controlled by the Sevens. NASO will announce that they are worthless only hours after Turner lets loose his bombshell regarding Penn-Mar in Baltimore federal court. That's nineteen billion dollars of bad loans and lost investments announced in a few hours. The bank's capital will be erased in one day, and NASO will disintegrate. People all over the world will be screaming for their money, and the bank won't be able to give them a dime. We'll request emergency aid from the Federal Reserve, and it won't react immediately." Boreman nodded at Smith, who smiled broadly. "Wendell is now the de facto chairman, and he'll hesitate sending NASO any capital. That hesitation will send the markets from panic to meltdown. And of course Bailey over there will be reporting all of this—"

"And exaggerating the hell out of everything," Henderson cut in. "My reporter will make it clear that banks that are secured lenders to companies with environmental liabilities can be held liable for the environmental damage—and that Penn-Mar's environmental liabilities could run into the hundreds of billions. That ought to make NASO's depositors feel even better. Depositors at the other banks in the deal too."

Winthrop could barely suppress his excitement. They were drilled perfectly. They were a team. Each one knew his assignment. It was like clockwork, and repetition was the key. There was no substitute for repetition.

Henderson continued. "The next day, the day after we report NASO's destruction, the *Financial Chronicle* will report that the investment firm that manages the President's money, Lodestar Investment Management, entered into some questionable purchases of Penn-Mar stock just prior to the takeover by Veens & Company. Effectively trading on the inside. The story will be written so that the reader will infer that the President influenced Lodestar management into making the purchases because he had inside information. Has the memo been loaded onto the computer at Lodestar yet?"

Again Rutherford nodded.

"Bottom line—in the space of twenty-four hours, gentlemen," Winthrop said, "the President will be ruined. The financial markets will be in chaos and the economy will be in disarray. And the President will be fighting insider-trading charges. As a result, our candidate, Mr. Whitman, will win the Presidential election just a few weeks later, and then we'll all feel a lot better about the country's future and our own net worth." Winthrop snuffed out what was left of his cigar in a crystal ashtray on the table. "What about our friends here, Rutherford?" Winthrop pointed at Boreman and Chambers.

"It's all set up," Rutherford said. "The world will think Wallace Boreman couldn't handle the fact that NASO went belly-up, so he committed suicide by driving off a cliff. The car will explode when it hits the bottom of the ravine and the body will be burned beyond recognition, but the license tag will match Boreman's registration. It's the body that will be someone else's. With our three-billion-dollar cash hoard, we'll set him up for life. It'll be sort of like the witness protection program, only Wallace will be living like a king. The ranch in Wyoming has already been purchased."

Winthrop knew this, but he wanted the others to hear it.

"As for Devon," Rutherford continued, "I don't think he will have a problem. Turner is certain that no legal claims can be filed against him. There will probably be fraudulent conveyance claims filed by the existing creditors against Penn-Mar, but nothing personal against Devon. He may have to go to court to give testimony, and then again he may not." Rutherford stared at Chambers.

Chambers glanced at Rutherford. So Rutherford knew about the cancer. Bastard. But intelligence was his business. That was why they had brought him on board when Seale died in the airplane crash.

Winthrop lighted another cigar and turned toward Prescott.

"What about Veens & Company? Are you certain that trail is covered?"

"The day we win the takeover of Penn-Mar, Veens & Company will be merged into Penn-Mar, and Penn-Mar will be the surviving entity. All records of Veens will be erased."

"And Falcon?" Bailey Henderson leaned forward. "What exactly will happen to Falcon?"

Rutherford coughed. The smoke from Winthrop's cigar had enveloped the room. "We have arranged for Andrew Falcon to be found guilty of insider trading. Last Wednesday, Mr. Falcon purchased thirty thousand dollars worth of Penn-Mar shares, though of course he did not know about it. They'll send him to prison. A very tough prison. He'll be killed by another inmate."

"Why go through that trouble? Why not just kill him after the takeover has been effected? Why can't he just have a terrible accident the way Filipelli did? I'm sure Phoenix Grey can arrange that." Devon Chambers' breath was labored as he spoke.

"We don't want any questions. None. It has to look natural in this case. He must be discredited. And he must suffer. Physically and mentally." Winthrop rose to his feet and pounded the table. "I want that little bastard to suffer!"

The room became deathly still.

17

Rain, driven by violent gusts of wind, pounded the windows of Falcon's two-bedroom apartment. He opened the living room window as far as it would go, kneeled on the parquet floor, and pressed his nose against the damp screen. He surveyed 82nd Street from his perch ten stories above it. Far below, people scurried to their jobs. Hunched beneath umbrellas of all sizes and colors, they careened off one another in their mad rush to get to work.

As he peered down at them, Falcon was reminded of those childhood times when he had been condemned to the indoors by his father for a violation of some trivial household rule, forced to watch playmates outdoors from the window of his room. Charlie Richards. His father. Buddy, they called him down at the foundry. Buddy the bastard. Never smiled, never tried to make friends with anyone. Which was why so few people attended his wife's funeral. Nobody cared.

Falcon swallowed. His mother had been a sweet woman, her main concern the family—Buddy, Andrew, and the little girl, Sara. But Buddy was a tough man. And mean. He had abused her constantly. Perhaps it was better that she had run off the road that night coming back from a visit to her mother's home in Trenton. Falcon had always wondered whether it had really been an accident. There were no skid marks in front of the tree. But she would have known that she was killing Sara too—and she would never have done that.

Jenny's mother had died young also, one of the many things that had drawn Andrew to her. They had talked for hours about how it had affected Jenny growing up, making her stronger in some ways, weaker in others. About how she was convinced that someday they would be reunited in the afterlife. And in all that time Falcon had never told Jenny about his mother's terrible accident. Because he could never allow himself to become that close to anyone.

Falcon focused on one of the figures below him. He was different. He had no umbrella and was in no mad rush to get anywhere. In fact, he lay sprawled atop a blue sedan, arms raised to the heavens, laughing hysterically as the skies poured down on him. He recognized this man. It was West Side Willy, a huge, homeless man who regularly terrorized Upper West Side residents with his demands for cash and his filthy, intimidating appearance. Once a week the police would arrest West Side Willy for disturbing the peace or indecent exposure, but inevitably he'd be back on the street within twenty-four hours because he never committed a serious crime—which was nothing short of rape or murder in New York.

Suddenly, with no warning, the huge man leaped from the hood of the car and, screaming like a maniac, raced crazily at a group of people huddled together awaiting the crosstown bus. The human mass parted as he tore through them, then rehuddled immediately, slightly closer together now, for protection. West Side Willy stopped, turned to look back at the group, threw his hands into the air, and screamed more loudly than before. Then he ambled off, casually kicking cars as he walked away. Falcon shook his head and laughed. There was always one of a kind. Unfortunately, in New York City, it was usually more like a thousand.

Falcon rose from his kneeling position with a groan. He was

exhausted. He had been working around the clock to meet Chambers' Wednesday deadline. He and the attorneys had completed reams of paperwork; SEC documents, antitrust documents, bank credit agreements, the underwriting agreement for the junk bonds, and of course the offer to purchase—part of which would appear in all of the newspapers tomorrow morning, and the full copy of which would be mailed to every Penn-Mar shareholder of record as of the end of business today. He would have to review the offer to purchase one more time this morning before it could be sent to the *Financial Chronicle*, the *Wall Street Journal*, and the *New York Times* to be typeset.

Tomorrow morning the announcement would appear in those newspapers, telling the world of Veens & Company's intention to purchase any and all shares of Penn-Mar Chemicals. It would be the biggest leverage buyout of all time, eclipsing KKR's purchase of R. J. Reynolds in 1989. In fact, it would be the biggest acquisition of all time, period. Falcon laughed. They had put this thing together in less than three weeks. That was incredible. Even more incredible, he stood to make five million dollars. Please, God, just in case you're out there, let this one happen. It was funny how a man could so suddenly find religion.

Falcon moved into the apartment's small kitchen. Twenty-three hundred dollars a month and the refrigerator door only opened halfway. But that was New York. Love it or leave it because it wasn't going to give you any sympathy.

He pulled a half-full carton of milk from the refrigerator, lingering long enough at the door to take note of the disarray inside—thanks to Alexis—then shut the door and poured the milk over a bowl of Rice Krispies. As he listened to the cereal pop, a thrill surged through his body. Tomorrow he would announce the largest takeover in Wall Street history. Incredible.

It was zero stage. That was what he called it. The point at which the transaction took on a life of its own. You became reactive instead of proactive. The pace of the deal became supersonic, and you simply held on for the ride. So many things began to happen simultaneously that it became difficult to maintain control. But that was when a savvy investment banker earned his huge fee, maintaining absolute control over every aspect of what was going on. The investment banker became part psychiatrist, part army general, and part poker player. But above all, he maintained his calm. Traders could explode in volcanic eruptions, but not investment bankers. It was why Falcon had so easily gravitated toward this career. He maintained his calm naturally.

Zero stage. The Penn-Mar transaction had reached that point. Once the deal was announced to the Street tomorrow, everything would explode, and Falcon, Barksdale, Chambers, and everyone else even remotely involved would be swept up in the maelstrom. And what a maelstrom this was going to be.

He sensed Alexis's presence and looked up from the cereal. She stood before him stark naked. That was how she felt most comfortable in the apartment. She was unabashed by her exposure. It was a trait common to models, Falcon guessed, to be as comfortable fully dressed as naked. In any situation.

"Good morning, Falcon." Her voice was neither friendly nor unfriendly. She moved to him, gave him a quick peck on his unshaven cheek, and then squeezed past him to the refrigerator.

He watched her bend down to take out bacon and eggs. She had been helpful over the last several days, he had to admit. She had stayed out of his way and allowed him to work, realizing the importance of the endeavor. She had even cooked a dinner or two, and she hated to fix anything other than breakfast.

Alexis placed the food on the counter, then with much banging and crashing removed the pots and pans she would need to fix the meal. She glanced over at him. "Want some?"

Falcon shook his head and smiled.

She turned on a burner. "What's so funny?"

"You should start a cooking show on one of those five hundred new cable channels we pay so much for. You'd be a huge hit. Of course, we'd have to get you some kind of outfit. Maybe a see-through apron, with The Cook Looks Good Enough to Eat on it. That show would rake in the cash. I certainly wouldn't have to worry about being an investment banker anymore."

Alexis laughed. "What would you call it?" She dropped a huge piece of butter in the pan.

"How about the 'Godiva Gourmet'?"

"Ooooh, I like that. Would you be my agent?" She dropped the entire package of bacon into the pan without pulling it apart.

Falcon was always amazed at the fact that she could eat as much of anything as she wanted and never gain weight and never incur skin problems. Other models he had known developed deep psychological problems because they were so obsessed with their diets. Not Alexis. "If you pull the strips apart, they cook more uniformly."

"I don't care about uniforms, Mr. Neatnik." Her voice lost its playful tone. "Not all of us are anal retentive about neatness. I mean, my God, every suit in your closet has its own special hanger and its own special place. As do your shoes, shirts, socks, and ties."

He was easily her match. "Not all of us can function as complete slobs. I'd appreciate it if you'd straighten up the refrigerator after you've finished grazing. There's an avocado in there that's got more culture than the queen of England."

Alexis slammed the tongs she had been holding onto the counter, but did not look at him. Falcon backed out of the kitchen. He did not need an argument now. He had made his point and that was enough.

He moved to the desk with his bowl of cereal and surveyed it for a moment. Neat as a pin, he thought with pride, even in the midst of the biggest LBO in history. Organization. That was the key to success. That and about a million other things. Including a good deal of luck.

Falcon placed the bowl on the desk and scanned the front page of the morning's *New York Times.* He began to pull out the chair so he could sit down, but never did. His eyes were riveted on the headline: CHAIRMAN OF FEDERAL RESERVE DROWNED IN MONTANA.

Falcon blinked, and as he stared at the words, an eerie sensation crawled slowly up his spine. He shivered involuntarily as the sensation finally made its way to his neck and the base of his brain. Falcon had considered Filipelli the single biggest stumbling block to completing the Penn-Mar takeover. Filipelli could have intimidated the banks who had committed to fund the deal into backing out, and Veens and NASO would have been dead in the water, without enough money to pay for the shares. Filipelli was that powerful.

He had worried constantly about Filipelli and had voiced the concern to Chambers. Time and again Chambers would pass off Falcon's concern as trivial. Chambers was more worried about a competing bid from another large multinational chemical company. Falcon had wondered how Chambers could take such a cavalier attitude toward the threat of the Fed. Maybe he was staring at the answer.

Falcon stared at the page, and the words blurred before his eyes. Carter Filipelli was dead. This was crazy.

The green-and-white golf umbrella was obnoxious because it was so huge. But it kept Falcon dry under the onslaught of the pouring rain. Other pedestrians, less fortunate beneath their traditional-size shields, threw sarcastic remarks in his direction as they were forced to move aside before him.

Falcon moved past the Portland Hotel. He could have made the call from the lobby as he had before, but he was hungry. There was a delicatessen with a phone just three doors down the street. The deli served a delicious breakfast of eggs, bacon, toast, and the best home fries in the city. And he was still ravenously hungry. The bowl of Rice Krispies hadn't done the trick.

Carter Filipelli was dead, drowned in Montana, only days before the public announcement of the Penn-Mar takeover. It seemed so convenient. Perhaps he was just paranoid. Still, he wasn't going to make this phone call from the apartment. He was sniffing the five million now, and if Boreman and Barksdale found out that he was trying to track down the origin of the billion dollars the Germans were putting into the deal, they might fire him. Or worse. And there would go the Vermont farm, financial security, and everything else.

Falcon had checked both telephones in the apartment thoroughly for listening devices and found nothing, though he had to admit that he probably would not have recognized one if he had seen it. He knew so little about electronics, mechanics, engineering, and other real-world things. That was the curse of most investment bankers. They knew a little about a lot.

They could have put a bug into the computer or the Bloomberg terminal before delivering the equipment. It was even money they had some kind of listening device somewhere in the apartment. They didn't know him well and therefore didn't trust him. They had told him as much.

The Germans. Like the wire transfers, he had been trying to track them down too, but with no success. There was no record anywhere of a German-based investment firm called Westphalia Nord, Veens' supposed affiliate. His friends were still checking, but they did not anticipate finding anything. There was no record of a Werner Prausch either. Falcon had not seen or heard of him since the boardroom meeting Friday.

Veens & Company checked out, though it had not made the several acquisitions Chambers claimed. Veens had purchased only a tiny plastics manufacturer three months ago for six million dollars. And that was it. Not a stellar record.

Falcon moved through the door of the deli and out of the rain. The smell of frying bacon filled his nostrils, and his stomach gurgled. He shook the rain off the umbrella onto the floor, much to the consternation of the Mexican behind the counter.

"Two eggs over easy, bacon, toast, and home fries." Falcon called the order as he moved toward the counter. It was almost ten o'clock and the deli was quiet, catching its breath between the breakfast and lunch rushes.

The Mexican stared at him. "You want coffee?" The man spoke with a nasal twang. His expression remained impassive.

"Yes."

The man turned and screamed something in broken English which did not sound at all like what Falcon had just ordered. But that was how it always was, and somehow they got him the right food. The man behind the grill grunted, dropped his cigarette to the tile floor, removed a huge hunk of white lard from an ancient-looking silver-colored pot, and began to spread it over the cooking surface. Falcon looked away quickly. It was like what they always said about sausage—if you saw how it was made, you wouldn't want to eat it.

After ordering the meal, Falcon went to the phone booth. It was slippery with grease, and Falcon was suddenly sorry he had not used the phone in the lobby of the Portland. He dropped a quarter into the slot, punched the number, and listened to the ringing at the other end.

"Eddie Martinez, Funds Transfer."

"Eddie, it's Andrew Falcon."

"Hi, Mr. Falcon."

"Have you found the wires yet?"

"Nothing yet, and I been looking real good."

"Damn it." Falcon glanced around for anyone or anything that looked remotely suspicious. "Okay, but keep trying."

"Sure, sure. Uh, are you back in the bank yet from your seminar?"

"Not yet."

"Sure is a long seminar."

"Yeah. Listen, Eddie, please keep trying. It's very important."

"Okay."

Martinez hung up the phone. He liked Falcon. Not too many people in Falcon's position, the white-collar side of the bank, ever treated him with respect. But there was something going on which maybe he should not be a part of. He had a wife and kids to worry about. Perhaps it was time to talk to his boss about this.

18

PRESS RELEASE

Veens & Company, a New York investment firm specializing in strategic partnerships with plastics and chemicals firms, announced this morning, via a press release to all major wire and news services, that effective immediately it will begin a public-tender offer for all common shares of Penn-Mar Chemical Corporation (TICKER PMCC). The offer price is $75 dollars per share. A spokesman for Veens confirmed that the investment firm had bank debt, subordinated bonds, and equity in place to fund the acquisition, and therefore the tender offer is not contingent upon financing. Veens' lead adviser and co-investor in the transaction will be the National Southern Bank. The spokesman said that principals of the firm anticipate taking possession of the shares sometime in early August, once Williams Act requirements have been satisfied.

The New York Stock Exchange. The granddaddy of them all. Its existence enables corporate America to raise billions of dollars a year in equity funds to finance working capital needs, long-term capital projects, and acquisitions. It also provides millions of individuals with long-term investment returns well above those of bonds and money market funds—at least the savvy individuals. And it is the most prolific casino in the world. Though many other stock and commodity exchanges have developed over the years, none compares to the power, influence, and prestige of the Big Board.

Every investor reaches the floor of the exchange exactly the same way—through a broker. From middle managers with children about to enter college and blue-haired widows concerned with bequests to heirs, to pension fund managers entrusted with billions of dollars of retirement money and portfolio administrators handling the money of those too intimidated to handle their own. Of course, the pension fund manager and the portfolio administrator receive much greater attention and priority from brokers than the middle manager and the widow, because their orders are huge in comparison and the broker can make much more in commissions expending the same exact amount of energy as he or she would to complete a small trade. It isn't supposed to be that way. Everyone is supposed to be treated fairly. But life is rarely fair in the world of finance.

After the broker enters the orders onto the exchange's computer system, it is communicated to runners—low-paid stiffs hailing from a borough other than Manhattan who hope, though they are rarely successful, to learn the secrets of Wall Street by hanging around the Big Board. The runners man banks of brightly colored phones at the perimeter of the great room. Once a runner receives an order over one of the phones, he combs the floor until he locates the firm's trader, to whom he communicates the order. The floor trader then goes to the appropriate specialist and executes the order. Orders aren't always executed in the exact same sequence in which they are received. This casino caters to the big spender—as most do.

Specialists literally "make the market" for particular stocks. They are set up at specific locations, or "posts," in the huge room, much the same way merchants set up shop in the open-air agoras of ancient Greece. Whether a trader wants to buy or sell IBM, or any other security for that matter, he has to seek out the specific specialist responsible for IBM and test the market through open outcry. The specialist keeps a list of all those who want to transact—and at what price they will do so. That way, he knows both sides of the market. If there is a little room in the middle, he can pocket the difference. In finance parlance, this is known as an arbitrage. In the gambling world, it is known as a stacked deck. The specialist's activity is another of the Street's closely guarded secrets.

During summer months, runners and floor traders move across the paper-strewn floor with clear purpose but at a leisurely pace. The hectic trading of late spring tapers off from June to August as the world relaxes into summer vacations.

However, this June morning was different. There was a certain tension on the floor of the Big Board. As they moved about the floor, traders, runners, specialists, and regulators alike cast uneasy glances at the corner closest to the Wall Street entrance. This corner of the floor was home to Grumman Brothers, Incorporated, specialists for Penn-Mar Chemicals. Grumman employees were speaking to one another and exchange governors in hushed voices. Some traders, those who considered themselves good friends with someone at Grumman, were trying to pry information from these specialists. But no one was talking at Grumman.

Everyone at the exchange was aware of the press release of six o'clock that morning announcing what appeared to be the largest takeover of all time. And the rumor racing around the floor was that the opening volley by Veens, the seventy-five-dollars per share tender price, would be considered inadequate, and therefore hostile, by Penn-Mar's board. The board was supposedly meeting at this very moment in a conference room at the midtown offices of Morgan Stanley to assess the offer. Early indications were that management and the Morgan Stanley investment bankers were recommending to the full board, some attending by conference call, that Penn-Mar not accept the offer. How this sound bite had reached the floor no one knew—or no one was saying—but at this point it was being accepted as fact.

Also accepted as fact was that Morgan Stanley would be appointed by the board to seek a white knight—a friendly bidder. And that could mean only one thing: the stock might trade much higher than seventy-five dollars a share even before a competing offer emerged, if in fact it ever did.

A huge hostile acquisition of one of America's oldest and stodgiest industrial firms. It hadn't happened in quite some time, and suddenly here it was, dropped into everyone's lap like a bombshell from nowhere. Like a huge Christmas present. Though no one wanted to admit to it, everyone, from the most senior trader to the lowliest clerk, was excited. The smell of a quick profit was in the air, a scent which hadn't pervaded the Big Board in some time. Those on the floor of the exchange seemed almost intoxicated, as though under the influence of a drug. It was a drug called euphoria, and they were all on it.

New York Stock Exchange trading had started at nine-thirty that day, as it did every day. Now it was eleven o'clock, and still no Penn-Mar shares had traded hands. Exchange governors had held up, or "flagged," any trading in Penn-Mar shares until they could sort out what was happening. On a typical day, the total trading volume in Penn-Mar shares might be four hundred thousand shares. By this point, after just an hour and a half, traders had received over six million buy and sell orders.

The flag dropped, and bedlam erupted.

"Buy five thousand at seventy-four and a quarter!" Kent Howard, floor trader for Smith Barney, screamed at one of the Grumman Brothers specialists.

"I got nuthin' at your bid!" the specialist screamed back.

They could barely hear each other over the din. At least seventy traders had suddenly amassed before the Grumman specialists in a matter of seconds as trading began.

"Seventy-five flat!"

"Nuthin'! We're opening at seventy-six! People are convinced Penn-Mar's gonna fight this thing. It's a rocket!"

Howard glanced quickly at the penciled scribble in his book. As he looked back up from the notebook, he noticed one of his runners, dressed in a bright green exchange shirt, jumping up and down at the edge of the pack of traders. People on the floor communicated quickly by hand signals, there being no way for the runner to move into the mass of humanity and communicate the instructions verbally. Howard leaned over the shoulder of another trader and grabbed the specialist. "Give me twenty thousand at seventy-six! I need every share I can get." He muttered the last few words to himself.

The specialist nodded. "Twenty thousand at seventy-six! You're done!"

Howard felt a body tumble into him, then fall away. Jack Wagner, the grizzled PaineWebber broker, stared up at Howard from the floor, smiling. "Gonna be a helluva day, Kent! A helluva day!"

"Sure will be!" Howard held out a hand. "You'd better get up before you're trampled!"

Victor Farinholt leaned over his desk at Lodestar Investment Management and waved a piece of paper angrily at Peter Lane.

"How in God's name did you get the tip, Lane?" Farinholt roared.

Peter Lane shifted uncomfortably in the leather chair of Farinholt's office. "Huh?" Suddenly there was a ringing in Lane's ears, but he didn't know why.

"Then you haven't seen the announcement yet?"

"What are you talking about?" Lane contorted his face into a quizzical expression. "I read the *Financial Chronicle* this morning." He hadn't really. "I didn't see anything eye-opening in there."

"You didn't look very hard."

"What?"

"Then you haven't heard?"

"Heard what?" Lane was becoming exasperated.

"Some investment firm just announced that it's going to take a run at Penn-Mar Chemicals. They're going to pay seventy-five dollars a share for it."

Lane stared at Farinholt without seeing. The realization, one he should have come to long ago, hit him squarely in the face with the force of a sledgehammer. They were using him, and although he wasn't certain exactly how, he was certain that the implications for him weren't good.

He strained to keep his composure, to mask the chaos within. "Well . . . that's great. We more than doubled the President's money in a very short time." Lane needed time to think.

"Are you completely out of your mind? Do you know what's going to happen when the papers get a hold of what we did? With the fact that we invested in a stock on behalf of the President just a few weeks before the stock became a takeover target!"

"Nothing's going to happen. We haven't done anything wrong. And why do the papers have to know about our investment decisions anyway?"

Farinholt shook his head. "We have to report all trades made on behalf of public officials, and all the newspapers check those reports religiously. You should know that." His voice had suddenly dropped to a whisper. "I spent most of my adult life building this firm, and you are going to bring it down in the space of a few days."

"What's the big deal? Penn-Mar's a big American company. What's wrong with the President buying a few shares? I mean, it would almost be un-American for him to not have any shares in this company. Right?" Lane stood. "I think you're overreacting."

Farinholt slammed his fist on the desk. "I am not overreacting!" He took a deep breath. "They're going to accuse us of insider trading."

"Why the hell would they do that?"

Farinholt stared straight into Lane's eyes. "Because I'm convinced we did trade on inside information. I never trusted you. You're slimy, and I shouldn't have hired you. I should have listened to the people in the industry who told me to stay as far away from you as possible."

"I picked Penn-Mar after doing a butt-load of research, Victor, and I resent you assassinating my character that way!"

"You did lots of research, did you? Well, then, show it to me. Show me all of your calculations and your computer models that indicated to you that Penn-Mar was a good investment for the President."

Lane swallowed hard. He had no calculations or computer models, no real rationale for investing in Penn-Mar. He had simply taken money—four hundred thousand dollars of the original half million was sitting in a Grand Cayman account—in return for their request that Lodestar put the President into Penn-Mar. He had no idea who they were. In fact, he had met only the sexy young woman who had made both the initial contact and request and subsequently delivered the five hundred thousand dollars. But she maintained that she was representing significant interests. And she had the cash to back her claims.

Lane cursed himself. He should have been more careful. But he had needed to pay off the gambling debts badly because the loan sharks had given him a deadline. A deadline after which they had made it quite clear they would start breaking bones.

"Do you really have any research, Peter?"

"I've got it back in my office."

"Peter, you're lying to me. Who gave you the tip? I need to know. When this becomes public, I'm going to have a great deal of explaining to do. I'm not going to let this entire firm go down in flames because of you."

Lane moved to the door. He walked backward, pointing a finger at Farinholt. "Give me five minutes to put the information together. I need to print it off the computer."

"Five minutes, Lane!"

Lane turned and moved through the door, shutting it behind him. His office was down the hall to the left, but he turned right, toward the reception area. As he moved down the hallway toward the entrance to the firm, his walk became a jog and then a full sprint.

Falcon sat at a small desk positioned in one corner of the partners' conference room at the law offices of Dunlop & Latham, headquarters for the deal team. He stared at the Bloomberg terminal. It had been set up specifically at his request so that he could maintain constant contact with the market as the deal team strategized throughout the day. The only problem was, he didn't like what he was seeing on the screen.

The rest of the deal team—Chambers, Barksdale, and Scott Bartholemew, the transaction partner at Dunlop & Latham—sat at one end of the long table that dominated the room. They spoke in hushed voices, as they had all day. Periodically, young associates would move furtively into the room to deliver a message or request a signature. The men took the message or signed the form, usually without acknowledging the associate's presence. They were too engrossed in the deal. Because it totaled thirty-two billion dollars. That was *billion* with a *B*.

"Anything new on the screen, Falcon?" Barksdale had been asking this question every fifteen minutes. Exactly every fifteen minutes. It was his way of fighting a bad case of nerves. Chambers had vetoed Barksdale's signature Dunhill cigars, so he needed something else to cling to.

"Not a thing." Falcon glanced at his watch. It was 3:50, ten minutes until close. "I don't think we'll see anything until after the market shuts down at four o'clock. Typically that's what happens. The other side waits until the market closes before they make some sort of announcement. They don't want to release any information that will make the market any more unstable than it already is. Of course, it's pretty silly to take that attitude, because trading just keeps going in the shadow markets anyway."

"What's the price?" Bartholemew asked.

Falcon punched a few buttons. "Penn-Mar is now trading at eighty-one dollars a share."

"What's the high for the day so far?"

"Eighty-one and three quarters, which was around three o'clock. It's traded down a little bit in the last fifty minutes or so, but volume has been incredible since three o'clock, almost five million shares. For the day, almost twenty million shares have traded."

Bartholemew inhaled deeply. "The arbs that bought in where it opened this morning at seventy-five dollars are getting nervous because there's been no official announcement from Penn-Mar. They are thinking that Penn-Mar might accept our deal. At that point the share price would fall all the way back to seventy-five. Our bid. And they'd actually lose money."

Falcon looked over his shoulder and nodded at Bartholemew. "That's exactly right. They're saying, 'Hey, I've made five bucks a share in a few hours. Why should I risk losing that profit if no other bid surfaces?' " Bartholemew had surprised Falcon. He was far more knowledgeable about the takeover game than Falcon had anticipated. He had completed all of the required documentation correctly.

"But that price of eighty-one dollars a share is six bucks above our offer of seventy-five. People must think another offer is coming through." Barksdale tapped the table with a gaudy fountain pen.

"Of course they do." Chambers' voice was barely audible. He was irritated at Barksdale's statement of the obvious.

Cancer. That raspy voice had to be the result of cancer. Falcon stared at Chambers for a few moments. The older man looked worse than he had during their first meeting in NASO's boardroom. Falcon felt a sudden wave of sadness. Chambers wouldn't be around much longer. He didn't know the man that well, but he always felt sad when death's presence was obvious.

"Will Werner Prausch be joining us?"

Chambers' eyes narrowed as he turned toward Falcon. "No. He will stay in Germany. I will keep him informed."

"Andrew, do you think we ought to try to make contact with senior management at Penn-Mar yet?" Bartholemew asked.

Falcon's eyes moved from Chambers to Bartholemew. He noted that the transformation hadn't taken place yet. Bartholemew was still calling him Andrew. But it wouldn't be long. It never took long.

"Not yet, Scott," answered Falcon. "Let's wait a few more minutes, until after the market closes, to see what happens."

Bartholemew did not respond immediately. He sat low in the large chair, elbows resting on the chair's arms, hands together, fingertips resting on his lips as if he were praying. "Okay."

That was what Falcon liked about Bartholemew. He thought about things. He wasn't susceptible to knee-jerk reactions, and he didn't speak just to hear himself talk. When he spoke, Bartholemew had something important to say. There weren't many people like that around.

Falcon moved from the desk chair to a large leather chair next to Barksdale. "We know they're all camped out over at Morgan Stanley," Falcon said, glancing out of the large conference room window. Fifty-four floors above Fifth Avenue, it provided a spectacular late-afternoon view of midtown Manhattan. "And I guarantee they will be there for a while. A long while."

Suddenly, the panelled door of the conference room burst open, and a young female associate, Rachel Conway, rushed in. The four men sat up in their seats.

"I'm sorry to barge in this way, but . . ."

Falcon was already moving back to the Bloomberg terminal. He did not hear the rest of her sentence. He punched a sequence of numbers and letters into the keypad, and there it was. The official announcement. Short and sweet. Falcon read the words on the screen to the other three men.

"This afternoon the board of directors of Penn-Mar Chemical Corporation rejected as inadequate what they termed the 'hostile' tender offer made by Veens & Company earlier in the day. The board has determined that in the best interests of the shareholders they will seek other, higher offers. The board has directed its financial adviser, Morgan Stanley & Company, to contact other parties that might have a strategic interest in acquiring Penn-Mar."

Falcon turned to the men. "I don't think there's much of a need for us to try to contact senior management at Penn-Mar. We've been left at the altar. Now it's war."

Falcon moved back into the conference room, a steaming cup of black coffee in his hand. It was eleven o'clock at night. Chambers sat dozing in one of the chairs; Barksdale was in another office making telephone calls; and Bartholemew was off working on another deal.

Falcon walked quietly to the large window and gazed out at the blazing lights of Midtown. Perhaps he could get away for a few hours with Jenny. They had spoken often since their tryst three nights ago, but he hadn't been with her since. He laughed. She was so damn interested in what he was doing all of a sudden. Where he was every minute of the day. Andrew brought the mug to his lip. "Ouch!"

"Still hot?" Chambers asked.

Falcon turned quickly, almost spilling the coffee. "Yes. Yes, it is."

Chambers' eyes were just slits. He was obviously weak from the long day. "I should thank you for your help that day at NASO. But I'm not going to."

Falcon smiled and ran the thumb of his left hand up and down the underside of his bright-red suspenders. "That's fine." He moved to the table and sat in a chair near Chambers. "I do have one question though."

"What is that?" Chambers asked gruffly.

"When you were first starting to cough badly, you called out a name. You said, 'Katherine. Katherine, help me.' I checked out your bio. Your wife's name is not Katherine. Now, is there something we ought to know?" Falcon winked.

"What are you implying, Mr. Falcon?" Chambers hissed.

"Secretary, daughter's friend, I don't know." Falcon tried to smile innocently.

Chambers rose slowly. "I don't need to explain anything to you, Falcon. But I'll tell you anyway. Katherine is my sister's name." Chambers glared down at Falcon. "You sit there with that damn smirk on your face thinking you're so superior at thirty-five or whatever age you are. Try walking around with a diaper the size of a blanket stuffed into your suit pants because you have no idea when you're going to need to go. Try gumming a filet mignon. Try driving at night. Try any of these things and tell me you have any confidence in yourself. My only regret is that I won't be around to see you have all that fun. But I'll be happy then. I'll be dead." Chambers moved slowly from the room without another word.

Falcon sat staring at the steaming cup of coffee on the table before him. Chambers was right. Old age couldn't be a whole lot of fun. He had sympathy for that. There was just one problem with Chambers' diatribe. He had no sisters, just a brother in Florida. Falcon was betting on the fact that Katherine was a former secretary.

He put his head back and closed his eyes. He had made history today. He had engineered the opening bid for the largest takeover ever. Now the object was to protect his page in the history book. He shook his head and opened his eyes. Other bidders were out there. Prowling. He sensed them. Now he had to defend what was his. God, he wanted Penn-Mar.

19

The Dunlop & Latham conference room resembled a war zone. They had been at it for three days, and the big table was cluttered with old pizza boxes still containing cheese triangles; partially full cans of every soft drink known to humankind; SEC regulation manuals; and mountains of paper. The carpet and curtains smelled terribly of cigar smoke. Barksdale had been unable to keep himself from the four Dunhills he had smuggled in yesterday morning. Finally he had attacked one of the stogies this afternoon, when the other three men had moved to Bartholemew's office for a hastily arranged conference call with an antitrust specialist from the law firm of Davis, Polk. Chambers had erupted at Barksdale upon his return, but the damage was done. The room reeked of smoke.

Outside, thunder rumbled over Manhattan and lightning crackled between the skyscrapers.

"Damn it." Falcon glanced quickly away from the computer screen toward the window.

"What's the matter?" Barksdale did not bother to remove his hand from his face.

Falcon began to type more quickly at the computer. It had been set up at one end of the table only this morning. "If one of those lightning bolts knocks out the power to this building, and we have a power surge as the backup generator kicks in, I might lose this entire projection model." Frustrated, he began saving the file on a diskette.

"What are you doing?" Bartholemew asked. None of the men had gone home last night and therefore none had had the opportunity to shower or change clothes. But Bartholemew seemed as fresh as ever. The shirt remained unwrinkled, the pants were still finely creased, and the shadow on his face was very faint.

Falcon stopped working at the computer for a moment. He had decided around three o'clock this morning that Bartholemew's measured way of life was no act. "Do you ever get tired?" Bartholemew was the only one of the four who had not caught at least a few hours sleep last night on a couch somewhere in the offices of Dunlop & Latham.

Bartholemew smiled. He was a good guy. Quick with a cynical or sarcastic remark, as were most lawyers, he had added a good deal of levity to some otherwise boring hours. "Like my idol, Napoleon Bonaparte, I usually go on about five hours of sleep a night, and if I miss a night, it doesn't bother me," he said.

"What are you doing there?" Chambers asked. He said the words as if he were offended that Falcon had not yet responded to Bartholemew. But he used that tone each time he addressed Falcon now.

"I'm trying to analyze what Hoechst, the big German chemical company, might be able to pay for Penn-Mar."

"Forget Hoechst, they aren't doing well. Concentrate on DuPont," Chambers said.

"No, Hoechst isn't doing that well, but the thing is, the German mark has become very strong against the dollar. Penn-Mar could turn out to be pretty cheap for them in mark terms."

Chambers attempted to speak again, but one of several phones on the conference table screamed shrilly, cutting him off.

"Hello." Bartholemew was on it immediately. "Just a minute. Falcon, it's for you."

There it was. Bartholemew was now calling him by his last name.

Falcon moved to the telephone. "Hello . . . yes . . . Now? . . . Right now? . . . All right, we will." Falcon replaced the receiver.

"What's going on?" Barksdale leaned forward in his seat.

Falcon picked up the remote control and switched on the small television built into the wall. The television flickered as he switched the channel to CNN. "That was a friend of mine who is a trader on the floor of the exchange. He said we ought to be watching CNN. Something about an announcement."

"What kind of announcement? What the hell's going on?" Barksdale reached for another cigar.

"Please don't smoke that in here," Bartholemew said, obviously annoyed.

Falcon had not seen this emotion in Bartholemew before. Maybe he was losing his edge after all.

Barksdale gathered himself. "Shut the hell up. I'm paying your bill and—"

"Wrong! I'm paying his bill." Chambers glared at Barksdale. "Don't light that thing. Do you understand me?"

Barksdale stared at Chambers for a moment, then replaced the long Dunhill in its white case and screwed the top back on.

Falcon smiled as he turned up the volume of the television. Barksdale was the whipping boy, the dog to kick, someone Chambers could vent his frustrations upon. That was his role in the transaction.

The CNN announcer stared directly into the camera. "Repeating, E. I DuPont de Nemours and Company has just announced that it will tender for one hundred percent of the shares of Penn-Mar Chemicals at eighty-two dollars a share. The offer will be an all-cash offer. Just two days ago, Veens & Company, a New York investment firm, announced an all-cash offer at seventy-five dollars a share—"

"Damnit!" Barksdale threw a Pepsi can against the wall next to the television.

"Shut up, Phil!" At this point Falcon did not care what Barksdale thought of him. The world was blowing up, and he needed to hear what the reporter was saying. It was the nightmare scenario. Chambers had called it right on the button. Andrew shot a quick glance at Chambers. To his surprise the older man remained calm, almost serene.

"What the hell did you say to me, Falcon?" Barksdale barked the words.

"He told you to shut up so we could all hear. I think it was damn good advice." Chambers glared at NASO's vice chairman.

Falcon smiled at Chambers in disbelief. Where had that come from?

". . . the aggregate price for the equity at that price per share would be approximately thirty-three billion dollars. Adding the debt Penn-Mar has outstanding, the total amount of the deal exceeds thirty-five billion dollars, making it the largest tender offer in history. A DuPont spokesman stated that initially Penn-Mar would be left to operate independently, but that gradually, over time, Penn-Mar would be consolidated and absorbed into DuPont. The spokesman acknowledged that the Department of Justice might raise antitrust concerns with the merger of the two firms, which have many complementary lines of business, but said that at this point it was too preliminary to comment on exactly what the Department of Justice might decide."

A telephone in the conference room rang. Falcon turned down the television volume.

Bartholemew answered. "Hold on." He pointed at Falcon.

"Who?"

"Bhutto."

Kiran Bhutto was head of mergers and acquisitions at Morgan Stanley. His rise through Morgan, after graduating from the Wharton School twelve years before, was legendary. He was just thirty-eight. Falcon had worked with and against Bhutto several times during his years at Winthrop, Hawkins, but at that time Bhutto had been more junior.

Falcon grabbed the cordless receiver and moved to the window overlooking Fifth Avenue. "Hello, Kiran."

"Falcon, how are you?" Bhutto was always so goddamn friendly, like every other Indian Falcon had ever met. Friendly and brilliant.

"Fine, Kiran." He liked the accent and the way Kiran sometimes transposed the normal word order as he spoke. "How are you?"

"Fine. Falcon, I'm sure you are aware by now that DuPont has announced its intention to acquire Penn-Mar."

"We just saw the announcement on CNN. Congratulations. Didn't take much time for you guys to come up with the white knight, did it?"

"We try, we try. Anyway, I'm calling to tell you that my client, Penn-Mar, will not be unreasonable about the whole situation."

"Talk to me, Kiran. What do you mean by that?" Falcon glanced back at the table, at the other three men. They were watching him intently. He turned back toward the window. So the chess match was beginning. Bhutto couldn't even let the offer sit out there for five minutes. He had to know exactly how Falcon was reacting to the news so that he could judge the odds of a counterattack.

"They realize that you and your clients have put a great deal of effort into this thing. We want you to be treated fairly."

"Fine, then have DuPont rescind its offer."

"Falcon, you always were a funny guy."

"Tell me about fair, then."

"We will sell to you the operations of Penn-Mar that your clients most desire. Whatever those may be. I dunno, they want European operations, specific product operations? Again, I dunno.

But we sit down and talk about it next week. Monday, Tuesday, whenever you want, we talk about it."

"My clients want the whole thing."

"Falcon, you know how much firepower has DuPont. Why you want to make this thing so difficult? Take a piece and be happy. Then go home."

"We will bid higher for Penn-Mar."

"Senior management at DuPont want this thing real bad. You are not gonna win. They gonna go as high as you, plus one. They committed. You can go to eighty-nine, maybe ninety dollars a share. I been checking the last few days. I know the banks you got."

"Kiran, do you know where the equity money comes from in our deal?"

There was a momentary silence at the other end of the line. It told Falcon all he needed to know. Bhutto hadn't done all of his homework or perhaps had run into the same roadblocks as Falcon had during his due diligence.

"Of course I know."

"Where?"

"You think I'm stupid? You think I gonna show my hand?"

"Just the country. Just tell me the country where the equity money is coming from."

"Get out of here. Why would I tell you that?"

"All right, Kiran, my boy, I'll give you a little hint since you've got no idea whatsoever and I can tell that pretty easily. I'll give you the continent. Europe. The continent is Europe. And nobody, not you, not the *Wall Street Journal*, not the *Financial Chronicle*, and not CNN knows who the real money backing this deal is." Falcon glanced quickly at Chambers. The older man was smiling. "Do a little digging into the European chemical companies, and you might start coming a little closer. DuPont's big. Very big. But it won't stand up to the consortium we've put together." None of it was true, but what the hell, it was time to be a poker player. "Save yourself and DuPont some embarrassment. Don't go higher than our next bid. We'll sell DuPont some options so they don't look like total idiots. Then start whispering in the ears of senior management at Penn-Mar so you and the rest of Morgan Stanley don't look like idiots too. Start telling Penn-Mar management how we want to keep them around after the takeover. And tell them about how DuPont would kick them out on their asses about a month after the takeover is complete. Jesus Christ, did you see that report on CNN? Let me quote. 'Penn-Mar will be operated independently for a while, and gradually it will be absorbed into DuPont.' Or something like that. Let me put it succinctly. If DuPont wins, your guys are dead meat. Where do you think DuPont will look first to recoup some of its investment in this transaction if they win? They'll look at the guys who are probably sitting all around you right now with real smug looks on their faces watching you make this telephone call. Senior management. The guys with the big paychecks. And DuPont will chop them off at the knees. Why don't you put me on the speakerphone right now, and let me have a little talk with them?"

"That won't be necessary."

"Then you have a little talk with them, Kiran. Do them a favor. Show them the light. And let's all save ourselves a lot of money."

"I will get back to you, Falcon."

Falcon flipped off the cordless phone and turned toward the rest of the deal team. They were already on their feet, applauding. Even Chambers.

Rutherford did not want to stay on the line with the woman for very long. "You have been extremely helpful to us so far, extremely helpful, and I want to continue to receive this kind of information about Falcon."

"You will. I mean, I plan to continue to provide you with information. We have a deal."

Rutherford could hear the tension in her voice. She was scared out of her mind. That was what he wanted to hear. "Yes, we do, and we intend to stick to our side of the bargain. You keep taking care of us, and when this is all over, we'll take care of you." It was a bad choice of words. Immediately he wished he had said it some other way.

"That's what I'm sort of afraid of." The woman tried to make light of Rutherford's remark. She attempted to laugh as she finished the sentence, but she swallowed the last few words.

"We aren't that way. If you've gotten the wrong impression, I apologize."

She did not respond.

Well, the hell with her. She was right, wasn't she? When this was over, Phoenix would get his reward, and after a few hours of what Rutherford knew would be terribly painful torture, she would be taken care of. Grey would cut her into little pieces, stuff the remains in a fifty-five-gallon drum, and sink it in the middle of the ocean. They would never find even a trace of her body. Phoenix was nothing if not efficient.

He became impatient. "All right, thank you for your time, and I'm sure we'll be speaking again soon. Good-bye."

"Good-bye." Her voice was still shaking.

Rutherford put down the telephone. Things were going better than he could have possibly imagined they would.

20

It was nothing more than a small hole in the dense jungle, a place where the trees and the strangling vines from the huge overhanging limbs were only slightly less impenetrable. Overhead, the stars were obstructed by the thick foliage of the rain forest's canopy, which was good. It inhibited the view of prying eyes from passing airplanes.

Phoenix Grey glanced at the lighted dial of his digital watch. Seven minutes past two in the morning. It had been a long trip—six hours—but in the end it would be well worth the trouble.

From Santo Domingo, the Dominican Republic's capital, he and the other four men had been driven by limousine to San Cristóbal, forty miles west of Santo Domingo. The limousine had pulled into a warehouse on the outskirts of San Cristóbal, where the men were hustled out of the car and down a long set of stairs, through a tunnel, and into another warehouse. Here they waited for another forty-five minutes until they were led to a Land Rover, blindfolded, and helped into the back of the vehicle. For two hours they bounced over back roads of the Dominican jungle. The roads became worse with each passing minute, until the truck finally stopped, and they were helped from the vehicle and their blindfolds removed. Then they had walked an hour through the bug-infested rain forest.

Phoenix wiped a bead of perspiration from his brow, then

slapped at a blood-sucking mosquito. Six hours. A long, roundabout trip. But you couldn't be too careful. After all, he could not have Rutherford learn of this little excursion.

During the six hours, none of the men had spoken a word. There were no introductions, no pleasantries, and no idle conversation. There was no reason for any of that. Grey would never see any of these men again. They had each paid twenty-five thousand dollars for this evening, but it had nothing to do with camaraderie.

They sat in the folding chairs, arranged in a rough semicircle, in the darkness. They were just at the edge of the light that lapped at them from the two torches, alone with their thoughts.

Grey smelled the woman before he heard or saw her. The faint scent of perfume drifted through the night air, and he noted it immediately. He possessed tremendous senses and used them to his best advantage. He had trained for years not to rely exclusively on sight and sound, and it was his ability to use his body to its fullest capacity—as well as his absolute lack of remorse—that made him such a perfect killing machine.

Phoenix Grey was not a large man. In fact, he was quite average in stature, but that was how it had to be. A medium-size man could appear large through the use of certain cosmetic techniques. But a large man could not be made to appear of average build. Grey had no distinguishing marks: no scars, no blemishes. Again, that was how it had to be. They could be added cosmetically to disguise himself, as the wart on the outside of his left nostril had been tonight—along with the beard, the mustache, and the crow's feet around the eyes—but nothing could be real.

Despite his average build, Grey was immensely powerful. In addition, he knew and constantly practiced karate, so that no matter the size of his opponent, he could make useless whatever piece of anatomy was appropriate and render him helpless. He had killed many times with his bare hands in the past, but not recently. Perhaps it was time to do so again, simply to make certain that his skills had not diminished.

The five spectators watched as the two men, one white, one black, jostled the young woman into the light. Phoenix felt a slight anticipation, a quick uptick in his blood pressure, but he controlled it quickly. She was nude except for the high heels, but her nakedness was not what piqued his interest. He did not care that the entertainment was female. It could have just as easily been male, as it had been in Burma four months ago. What he cared about had nothing to do with the sex of the object.

The woman cried softly, but the men were indifferent to her fate. Grey appreciated the fact that the woman cried. It meant they had not drugged her, which could have made the experience less entertaining. He judged her to be twenty years old. Again he had to slow his heart rate.

The two men pushed the young woman face first against a tree and tied her hands behind her back with a pliant piece of white cord. She attempted to struggle, but to no avail. The men were too powerful.

A mammoth block of ice lay in a large plastic tub directly in front of the five chairs. Exactly thirty inches high, with a surface area six feet long by four feet wide, the ice stood waiting for the woman. It was already beginning to melt in the intense heat of the midsummer jungle night. Again Grey wiped perspiration from his brow. He wondered how in the hell they had transported such a huge chunk of ice into the deep jungle.

The two thugs forced the young woman up onto the ice, steadying her and themselves as they pushed and pulled her to the surface. With her hands tied securely behind her back and her feet deep in the spiked heels, her balance was precarious at best. Grey glanced to the right at the older man next to him. The man stared at the woman luridly as the thugs worked. Obviously he was not indifferent to the sex of the victim.

Suddenly the woman screamed and attempted to break free.

Momentarily it seemed that the two men must lose their balance. She had surprised them with her outburst. But before either of them fell from the ice, the men regained their balance and renewed their efforts. She continued to struggle, but they overpowered her. They were simply too strong. She was defenseless.

Phoenix Grey smiled. This one was a fighter. The evening could turn out to be very interesting, well worth the twenty-five thousand dollars. What would Rutherford say if he knew? Grey knew the answer to that question.

The noose hung ominously from the tall tree branch. The white man slipped it over the woman's head and pulled it down to her neck, tightening the loop so that it was snug about her throat. The rope hung loosely from the branch with several inches of play to its length. This play would give the audience more entertainment time. The black man whispered something into the woman's ear and then both men jumped carefully down from the ice.

The small audience watched. There was no sound in the jungle except for the girl's intermittent entreaties, which went unanswered.

After a short time, small puddles began to form on the ice's surface, and imperceptibly, the rope began to tighten, little by little. The woman pleaded with the men in Spanish as she felt the pressure grow against her throat. She screamed and sobbed, promising anything they wanted, but again, they did not care. She yelled the few words of English she knew—"Help me, help me, please!"—but the words had no effect. They were going to watch her die.

The men watched as she contemplated pulling her feet up, making herself slip so that her life could end quickly, mercifully. But she could not make herself do it. Her will to live was too strong. Her survival instinct merely prolonged her agony, while at the same time it increased the sordid pleasure of the audience.

Grey began to shake as he watched the death struggle. How

long had it lasted so far? He had no idea, which was one of the reasons he liked this so much. It caused him to forget everything else.

Slowly the woman's chin rose as the ice melted beneath her, tightening the rope about her throat. She fought the pressure by standing on her toes, but the soles of her shoes would slip out from under her, forcing the noose to tighten even more with each attempt. The end was drawing near, and they all sensed it.

The surface of the ice had receded so far now that the woman could no longer make contact. The long dark hair cascaded straight down her back, and her body began to twist and writhe at the end of the rope. From time to time her legs would kick wildly, searching for something on which to stand, but there was nothing, only air. She tried to scream, but the rope choked off the sound to a hideous gurgle.

Blood coursed through Phoenix Grey's body as he stared. This was it. Death was close. He was no longer able to control his racing heartbeat. He stood, as did the other men, and edged closer to the subject.

For another full minute the struggle continued, and then, with her chin skyward, the woman expired. Her body quivered spastically several times and finally was still. Slowly, the five men relaxed into their seats.

Grey stared straight ahead for several moments watching the body twist, then put his head back and stared up at the forest's canopy. Tomorrow he would buy a thousand dollars worth of very good cigars in downtown Santo Domingo, and after that he would be on to Antigua to continue his mission.

21

Byron Mitchell, vice chairman of the Fed, tapped the black gavel gently on the huge table. He was the acting chairman now and not particularly excited about his newly acquired duties. But the President's nominee to replace Carter Filipelli had not yet begun to negotiate the Senate confirmation hearings. "The meeting will come to order," Mitchell said. He was a quiet man whose voice faded at the end of his sentences.

Gradually, the FOMC members ended their conversations and straightened in their chairs. Without Filipelli the room seemed a great deal less intimidating.

"Let us observe a moment of silence for Governor Filipelli," Mitchell said, bowing his head.

Immediately, the other eighteen members bowed their heads also. For half a minute there was no sound in the well-insulated room.

Finally, Mitchell looked up from his respectful pose. He hadn't been very fond of Filipelli—none of them except Butler had—but he felt that the recognition was justified. And he wanted it in the official minutes, just in case President Warren had an aide check. "The first order of business this morning will be the bidding war for Penn-Mar Chemicals." There would be no further mention of Filipelli. "If that is all right with the rest of you." The members relaxed into their seats. Meetings were going to be very different—at least until the new chairman was confirmed.

"Personally, I believe the Penn-Mar situation is a good thing. A very good thing," Wendell Smith said, pulling his chair closer to the table. "It's what this country is all about. Competition. I know Governor Filipelli, God rest his soul, might not have agreed with that, but it's true. The shareholders will be rewarded, and Penn-Mar will become a more efficient entity."

"But if this investment firm, Veens & Company, wins the bidding, I understand that the National Southern Bank will be heavily involved," President Flynn said. "We can't have a bank as big as NASO committing too much capital and extending itself too far in a leveraged situation like this. We all know how big a player they are in the derivative and foreign exchange markets. A NASO hiccup could cause an earthquake in the marketplace."

"I hear your concern, President Flynn." Smith saw the opportunity to take control of the committee, and he would be painfully diplomatic to achieve this goal. "But Wallace Boreman, the chairman of NASO, is one of the most respected men in New York. I don't know him on a social basis, but his reputation in the financial community is one of prudence. I know he would not put the bank in a compromising position. I'm assured by my aides that he is monitoring this situation extremely closely."

"He's a gunslinger," Harold Butler interjected. He hadn't said a word since entering the room but now saw his chance to undermine Smith. "He cut his teeth at the North Carolina National Bank, what is now NationsBank, in the late seventies. I was there at the same time. He took an awful lot of risk in the mid-eighties at NCNB, as the senior vice president in charge of leveraged lending, to jump-start his career. I wouldn't call all the risks he took 'prudent.' I'm sure he's no different now. You need to go in there with your New York thugs and find out exactly what's going on at NASO. You need to stand up to that guy."

Smith gazed at each of the members in turn. He smiled wryly.

"You have all seen that I don't have a problem standing up to tyrants." Smith allowed the words to sink in.

The rest of the members turned toward Butler. He had been Filipelli's straight man, the lieutenant. But now Filipelli was gone. Smith was their man. Their eyes narrowed and Butler's head moved down between his shoulders like a turtle pulling in its neck. His clout had drowned in the Bighorn River.

"I can assure you that Mr. Boreman is no tyrant," continued Smith. "He is extremely competent. Plus, there are some very talented people reporting to him, and I am told he practices consensus management. He's a big believer in building a consensus. He wouldn't make unilateral decisions. It isn't a one-man show over there. Also, the board of directors is very active in the affairs of NASO. They would not allow the bank to take undue risks. But I will promise you that if I get even a whiff of anything amiss at NASO, my people will be in there like storm troopers." The other members nodded in agreement. Smith was beyond reproach now. He had emerged as de facto chairman. "Besides, at this point it looks as if DuPont will win the bidding for Penn-Mar anyway. If that happens, we won't have to worry about NASO."

"It would appear so," said President Flynn. "My God, what's the total value of the deal now, over thirty-five billion dollars?"

The rest of the committee shook their heads. It was unbelievable.

Wendell Smith leaned over the table. "How about some discussion on interest rates?" He wanted to change the topic quickly.

"I believe we should lower the fed funds rate fifty basis points," Flynn piped up quickly.

Byron Mitchell laid the gavel on the tabletop and leaned back into his seat. Let Smith take control. It was all right with him. He didn't enjoy chairing meetings anyway.

"I'm glad you could get away from the deal for a while. And it was very romantic of you to arrange for the same room as last time." Jenny ran her fingers along Falcon's chest as they lay together on the king-size bed of the Four Seasons Hotel.

Falcon kissed her forehead. "Thanks for coming into the city at such short notice. I missed you." He rose to a sitting position.

"What's the matter?" Jenny asked. "Why are you getting up?" She rose to a sitting position also, not bothering to pull the sheet up around her breasts.

"I need to get back to Dunlop & Latham."

"No, Andrew." She clasped both hands around his neck. "I won't let you go. It's two-thirty in the morning for crying out loud. What can you possibly do at this hour that's so important?"

"Can you keep a secret?" he asked.

"Of course."

Falcon stared at her. It wasn't smart to convey this kind of information to anyone, but she was trustworthy and interested, and he felt like talking. "We're going to top DuPont's bid."

Jenny brought both hands to her mouth. "You're kidding!"

Falcon shook his head. "No, I'm not. Tomorrow we'll announce a bid of eighty-five dollars for Penn-Mar. That beats DuPont by three bucks a share. I convinced the last bank to approve the price increase just before I came over here. It's a thirty-eight-billion-dollar deal now with the fees included."

Jenny kissed him on the neck, then on the cheek. "Well, well, Mr. Finance. Thirty-eight billion dollars. How do you know how to put together a deal like that?"

Falcon flashed his crooked smile. "It's all in the wrist." He pulled away gently, stood, and moved from the bed to the window. He should be exhausted. He had slept only two hours in each of the last three nights, and Jenny had kept him busy since nine o'clock. But he wasn't tired at all. "Jenny, you can't use the information I just gave you to profit yourself. The government has strict rules about that." He glanced at her and raised an eyebrow.

Jenny smiled at him devilishly. "Are you kidding? I'm going to call my broker and wake him up as soon as you're gone." She thought briefly on the irony embedded in that comment as she followed him to the window and wrapped her arms around his torso. "Please stay."

"I really can't."

She stared out the window over his shoulder and whispered into his ear. "You were going to tell me something before."

"What?"

"You were going to tell me something about the deal. I can't remember exactly. Was it the new bid? It seemed as if it was something you were worried about. Maybe it was just the new bid."

"Oh." Falcon hesitated. "It was just silly paranoia. It always happens to me in the middle of a deal. It's my way of dealing with the stress."

"I'm glad to know you actually do feel stress sometimes, because you certainly don't show it." She hugged him tightly. "Tell me about your paranoia. I want to hear." She laughed.

Falcon turned from the window, took her in his arms, and kissed her. "Just some things that either don't add up or are strange coincidences."

"Such as?"

Falcon hesitated. Like the bid increase, it wasn't a good idea to tell her this. "Veens & Company, the investment firm that is trying to buy Penn-Mar, supposedly has a German parent. I know the name of it, but it doesn't show up on any of the information services. I have some friends in Düsseldorf who have been looking."

"Germany is a big country," Jenny said. She kissed his shoulder.

"Not the business community. It's very tight. If there was a Westphalia Nord, my friends would either know of it or be able to find out everything about it in a matter of hours."

"Don't take offense, but that doesn't sound like a very big deal to me. Will that affect the Penn-Mar transaction? I thought you already had the money."

"We do."

"So what's the problem?"

Falcon pushed out his lower lip.

"There's more?" Jenny asked. She had seen that look before.

"Two senior executives at Penn-Mar have died under strange circumstances recently. Both murdered. One death was officially listed as an accident, but it wasn't. Both of them held the same exact job."

"So after the deal is over, if they ask you to take the job those people had at Penn-Mar, turn it down quickly. And watch your back." She giggled.

Falcon did not smile. "There's one other thing."

"What?"

Falcon paused. "I know this is crazy to think. It's probably just a huge coincidence."

"What?"

"One of the people in Washington who could have really shut us down, really gotten in the way of Veens effecting this takeover, was Carter Filipelli, chairman of the Federal Reserve. Last week he drowned on a fishing trip in Montana. The timing is unbelievable. And the top guy from Veens never worried about Filipelli. Never once. I kept telling him it could be a problem, but he never acknowledged it."

Jenny stared into Falcon's eyes and began to laugh. "You think that . . . he didn't really drown. That somebody killed him?"

"I don't know."

She put her arms around him again and kissed him deeply. "Go take a shower. And make it a cold one. Perhaps that will wake you up and bring you back to reality."

Falcon laughed. "I suppose you're right. That is kind of a wild thought. It's just the deal. My imagination's playing with my mind because I'm tired even though I don't think I am," he said. "I should get going. But I will take that shower first." He began to move toward the bathroom.

Jenny caught him by the arm. "Do you mind if I use the bathroom first?"

"Not at all." Falcon watched her until she closed the door. He breathed deeply. She was incredible.

Falcon stretched and as he did, he knocked Jenny's purse from where it lay on the small mahogany desk below the window, to the floor. Its contents—lipstick, mascara, crumpled tissues, tons of change, and Jenny's wallet—spilled onto the thick carpet. "Damn it." Immediately he bent down to put the articles back into the purse. As he picked up the wallet, a small piece of paper floated lazily to the floor. He retrieved it, and when he began to put it back in the wallet, he noticed that the wallet was stuffed with hundred-dollar bills. He counted them. Eight. "Jesus!" Falcon glanced at the paper he had picked up from the floor. On it were ten digits. No name, just the numbers. A telephone number. A 617 area code. Boston. Who did Jenny know in Boston?

The toilet began to flush. Hurriedly Falcon inserted the piece of paper into the wallet, then carefully put the wallet and the rest of the articles back into Jenny's pocketbook. He placed the pocketbook back onto the desk and then stretched out on the bed.

The bathroom door opened, and Jenny moved back to the bed. She lay down on top of him, kissed his chest, then gazed into his eyes. She hoped they wouldn't try to reach her tonight.

The halls of Dunlop & Latham were quiet as Falcon moved down the dimly lit office-lined corridor. It was three-thirty. Even the cleaning staff had finished for the night. He should have been home in bed, but this was the biggest deal of his life, and he wanted to read the new offer to purchase one more time before they sent it to the three papers for publication. He wanted to make certain it was perfect. It was going to shock the arbitrageurs, who were convinced that DuPont's bid of eighty-two a share was going to win Penn-Mar.

Falcon stopped abruptly when he spotted a tiny shaft of light emanating from an office ahead. He laughed to himself. It was probably some hungry associate burning the midnight oil. Firms that constantly catered to the biggest U.S. corporations, firms such as Davis, Polk or Shearman & Sterling, went all night, every night. It would have seemed like the middle of the day at those places right now. Not at Dunlop & Latham, though. Dunlop & Latham was a quiet labor-relations practice where people sacrificed some level of compensation for quality of life. Bartholemew was the only hard charger at the entire firm. Except for this associate.

Falcon resumed his footsteps over the thick carpet. As he neared the door he recognized the whispery voice. Chambers. What the hell was he doing here? He had left at eight o'clock this evening, before Falcon had gone to the Four Seasons to meet Jenny.

"Yes, I know. You're certain Rutherford has completed his task? No more interference from them? Good. Yes, you were correct. He was a valuable addition to the team. You are always right."

Falcon strained to hear the words, but Chambers was barely audible from behind the slightly open door.

"What did Smith tell you? What was the reaction from the rest of the FOMC? They bashed Butler. Good. I suppose we're on our way. Yes. Yes, poor Mr. Filipelli. May he rest in hell. Right, I need to go too. All right."

The phone clicked.

Falcon slipped inside the darkened office next to the one Chambers was using. He left the door open a crack and listened, trying not to breathe. Chambers exited the office, moved down the corridor toward the reception area, and pushed through the glass doors into the elevator waiting area. Falcon heard the elevator bell ring but waited a full three minutes before moving.

Finally, Falcon moved stealthily out of the pitch-black office and to the doorway of the office Chambers had just exited. He flipped off the office's overhead lights, allowing himself to be guided only by the dim glow from the hallway. His heart was in his throat as he stared at the telephone. He picked up the receiver and then pressed the automatic redial button. Immediately the line clicked and began to dial. He stared at the numbers lighting up on the phone's display. Area code 516. It couldn't be.

"Hello."

Falcon gazed at the phone. His hands began to shake.

"Hello! Devon, is that you again?"

Falcon put down the phone slowly. This was getting crazy. Why would Devon Chambers be talking to Granville Winthrop? And what was all of that stuff about Filipelli resting in hell?

22

The phone in front of them whistled shrilly. "Bartholemew. Yeah, wait a minute." Bartholemew glanced at Falcon. "For you. It's Bhutto."

Falcon felt his pulse quicken instantly. "Here we go. At least he's calling to let us know what DuPont's next offer price is going to be." He shook his head. "God, we only increased the bid to eighty-five dollars a share at nine o'clock this morning. You would think Bhutto would have waited a couple of days to raise the ante." Falcon took the telephone from the lawyer. "Hello."

"Falcon, Kiran Bhutto calling."

"Hello, Kiran. Listen, would you mind if I put you on the speakerphone? Our attorney here at Dunlop & Latham, Scott Bartholemew, is in the room, as are Devon Chambers, the senior executive from Veens & Company, and Phil Barksdale, vice chairman of NASO. I'd like them to hear what you have to say."

Bhutto paused. "I suppose I have no problem with that."

Falcon switched on the speakerphone and replaced the receiver. "Go ahead, Kiran."

"Okay. So you want to buy Penn-Mar. Well, I got news for you. If we can work out a few things, I think you may have a deal." Bhutto's voice was loud and clear.

A tremendous rush of adrenaline coursed through Falcon's entire body as he felt Bartholemew grab his arm. Penn-Mar management was conceding defeat. Bhutto was calling to make a deal. This was an incredible development. DuPont was out at eighty-five. It didn't mean the fight was over. In this game the battle was never over until the requisite number of shares had been duly tendered *and* paid for. After all, someone could come up with another hostile, unsolicited bid for the company, just as Veens had done. But this telephone call did mean two very important things. First, Penn-Mar management was going to embrace or endorse Veens's higher bid, which would significantly lower the odds of success of any other competing bid. Second, it meant that DuPont was backing out, and they were the only real competition.

"Are you telling me that Penn-Mar management is endorsing the Veens offer?" Falcon's voice was controlled. He glanced at Chambers, who sat serenely across the table.

"That is exactly what I am telling you."

"Are you also telling me that DuPont is out of the bidding?"

"Yes."

"Why, Kiran? Why is DuPont dropping out of this? They have a lot more dynamite in their keg. They could keep going."

"I dunno, Falcon. Honestly. They said something over the phone about the price being way out of hand."

"But we only upped the bid three dollars from their first offer. . . ."

Chambers reached across the table and turned on the mute button. "Are you out of your mind, Falcon? The man just said DuPont wasn't going to bid any further. Leave it at that. Don't try to convince Bhutto he ought to push DuPont harder. Let it go. We won. Who the hell cares why DuPont decided not to bid higher? Just accept it." Chambers turned off the mute button.

Falcon stared at Chambers for a moment. He wanted to ask Chambers how he knew Winthrop; why they had been talking about Filipelli so early this morning; what had happened to those two senior executives at Penn-Mar; and why there was no

Westphalia Nord anywhere in Germany. All of these things he wanted to ask but didn't. Five million dollars were almost in his grasp.

"Falcon, we need to put this deal together." Bhutto's voice crackled through the speaker.

"The deal's already together, Kiran. Once we've closed on the tender offer, we'll meet with Penn-Mar management out in Toledo. Until then, tell them to manage the company as if nothing was going on. Got that, Kiran?"

"What about DuPont? We gotta give them something."

"I'm sure they own a few shares of Penn-Mar, right?"

"Probably."

"Then they're doing fine. They've already made some good money. You keep them at bay. You got it?"

"Sure, I got it." Kiran was resigned to the directive.

"One more thing, Kiran. Let me write the press release announcing that Penn-Mar has accepted our offer. You can look at it before it goes out."

"No problem."

"Good. I'll be in touch later on." Falcon switched off the telephone. It was done. They had Penn-Mar. Another bidder might crawl out of the woodwork, but, as he thought about it further, that development would be unlikely at this late juncture. He had his spies out there listening, and they had heard nothing.

It was incredible news, but now the work began all over again. NASO had committed thirteen billion dollars to the deal, and he had to get rid of most of that commitment at supersonic speed. That or risk the bank's collapse if Penn-Mar had a problem before he could sell the paper to other institutions. At least now he could get some help. The takeover was official, and he could physically return to the bank and not have to use his apartment as an office. He would be able to bring others onto the team to help him sell the notes and the bonds. Selling eleven billion dollars, the amount Boreman and Barksdale had determined that they wanted to get rid of, by himself, and quickly no less, would have been impossible.

He should have been ecstatic. They had Penn-Mar. Once the tender was closed and the commitments sold, NASO would deposit five million dollars into his account. But he was uncomfortable. Something was wrong. DuPont should not have given up so easily. In his years as a merger-and-acquisition specialist, he had never seen a deal go this way. He had never seen a huge multinational corporation back out of a hostile-bidding situation so meekly.

Falcon stared at the other three men seriously, then broke into a wry smile as he focused on Devon Chambers. "Mr. Chambers, may I present you the keys to Penn-Mar Chemicals!"

The other three men rose to their feet instantly and began to yell, shake hands, and pound the table. Even Chambers. Falcon sat quietly watching them. He could not show that kind of excitement. It was not in him.

Alexis danced effortlessly to the music booming from the speakers in the upstairs room of Club Tatou. Falcon sat at a booth table and watched her move as he sipped on a martini. She danced with several men, keeping perfect rhythm to the bass. They rubbed themselves lewdly against her in time with the Spanish beat. Two weeks ago he would have been insanely jealous. Now he didn't care.

She glanced at him every so often through the dancing bodies, aware that he was watching, but also aware that he seemed indifferent to her escapades. Falcon was able to mask every emotion but one, jealousy. Had he been jealous, he would have pulled her firmly from the dance floor and taken her home as he had done before. But tonight something was wrong. He sat calmly in the chair as the men groped her. She glanced at him again. Something was definitely wrong, and it hurt her deeply, more deeply than she could have imagined it would at the beginning of all of this.

Falcon looked away from the dance floor and scanned the room. He didn't like this place. It had been hot in the early nineties when it first opened, but now it was full of greaseballs and low-level professionals. And the music was fringe stuff, nothing he recognized, much less liked. But Alexis was wild about Tatou, so of course they came here.

He was getting drunk, very drunk. And why shouldn't he? He had managed to put together the biggest takeover in history in less than three weeks. He had delivered Penn-Mar Chemicals to Chambers and Veens & Company on the proverbial silver platter. He had done what even he had not thought possible. He deserved to get drunk.

Barksdale had been ecstatic, unable to control himself. They had spoken several times after the conversation with Bhutto, and each time Barksdale reminded Falcon of a child. He actually giggled on the other end of the line. Boreman must be throwing him a big bonus for this one, Falcon thought. He had to kowtow to Barksdale for a few more weeks, until the five million dollars had been deposited into his account at NASO and then subsequently spirited away across the wire to an account he had set up at J. P. Morgan this afternoon.

After the initial jubilance, Chambers had seemed almost sad at the news of the victory, as if he were sorry to see the battle end so quickly. Perhaps it was the fact that the man did not have long to live, and the end of the bidding for Penn-Mar probably marked the last major accomplishment of his life. He did not want to let go of life yet, but there was no choice, and the completion of the takeover would give his last few days little meaning. There was nothing left to drive him on.

Falcon looked up to find Alexis standing directly in front of him. She was wearing a low-cut evening dress which had shifted to one side as a result of her gyrations on the floor. Her right nipple was almost exposed.

"Fix your dress." Falcon nodded at Alexis's chest.

"What's the matter, don't you like what you see anymore?" She was giving him her vulture stare. Her head was tilted down so that her dark eyes gazed at him from just beneath her eyebrows, and her mouth was slightly open. "I thought maybe it might turn you on to see me exposed in public."

"What?" Falcon could not suppress a smile. This was a side of Alexis he had never seen before.

She sat in his lap and put her arms around his neck. "Why don't you take me home and show me some things?"

"Things?"

"Yes, you've told me that you wished I would be more passionate in your bed."

"It's your bed too."

"No. You're the man of the house. It's your bed and I'm only there because you want me to be. If I haven't been satisfying you, then I need to fix the problem. If you're willing to teach me, then I'm willing to learn." Alexis brought both of her hands to Falcon's face and kissed him deeply.

Jenny stared at them from the other side of the room. Her eyes narrowed as she watched Falcon respond to Alexis.

23

The air was stifling in New York City. It had been hot as hell all summer and this was the worst day yet—at least ninety-five degrees, with the humidity close to a hundred percent. And it was only eight o'clock in the morning.

Falcon emerged from the subway, dripping with perspiration. It was unbearable down in the hole, at least ten degrees hotter than street level. And it was made worse by the fact that he was slightly hungover from the late night at Tatou. He tugged at his dress shirt several times. "Jesus Christ, this is ridiculous." The temperature at street level actually seemed refreshing. What was he thinking about? He should have taken a cab. He was going to be a millionaire soon, and he ought to start living like one.

Five minutes later, after a short walk through Midtown, Falcon negotiated Fifth Avenue and moved over the open courtyard before NASO's headquarters. He had not been here since the day Barksdale had recruited his help on the Penn-Mar transaction. It was nice to be back. Working at home was all right for a short while, but he wouldn't want to make a habit of it. At least not until "home" meant a farmhouse in Vermont.

"Mr. Falcon!"

Falcon turned in the direction of the voice as he was about to enter the revolving doors of the NASO building. An attractive black woman sat on the four-foot wall of the huge flower garden that ran the length of the NASO building. Falcon removed his sunglasses and moved slowly toward the woman. "Yes, can I help you?"

The woman slid gracefully down the face of the granite wall. "I hope so." She smiled, and suddenly Falcon forgot the heat for a moment.

He smiled back. "What can I do for you?"

The woman moved smoothly toward him, hand outstretched. As Falcon was about to take it, he could not help but notice the fresh scent which reached his nostrils. It was not perfume, just a clean, natural smell, and it was pleasing.

"My name is Cassandra Stone. I'm a reporter for the *Financial Chronicle.*"

"Whoa." Falcon's hand recoiled as if shocked.

"What's the matter with you?" Stone looked at him curiously.

Falcon replaced the sunglasses on his face. "My mama told me never to talk to reporters, especially attractive ones."

"Your *mother* never met me."

"No, I guess she didn't." Slowly, beneath the sunglasses, Falcon's eyes covered her body. Her skin was a rich brown and her hair shoulder-length and wavy. Her face was thin, accented by huge, dark eyes that were surrounded by long, curving lashes. She was dressed sharply in a light blue sweater, white blouse, pleated pants, and half heels. Falcon decided that beneath the loose-fitting clothes was probably an extremely attractive body.

"Have you finished ogling me yet?" Stone smiled again. Evidently she had been through this before.

"Almost."

"And how do I stack up?"

"Very well." Falcon ran his fingers through his hair. "And how about me? What do you think of me?"

Stone rubbed her lips for a moment. "Well, I don't really go for white men, but I suppose one of those prissy preppy girls might find you acceptable, in a pinch." She winked at him.

"Well, thank you so much." Falcon spoke sarcastically, as though hurt by her barb, but he was enjoying himself immensely. The woman was easy to talk to and, somehow, instantly trustworthy, which, of course, was one of the reasons she was a reporter. She could probably draw a story out of anyone, he thought. Falcon drew back slightly, then shook her hand in earnest. "Andrew Falcon. I'm sorry for all of that."

Stone smiled widely and waved the hand she withdrew from Falcon's. "Are you kidding? I enjoy that kind of stuff. Most of the people I deal with are pretty stiff."

"I can imagine." Falcon glanced at his watch. "So, what can I do for you?"

"The *Financial Chronicle* wants to run an article on you, front page, left column."

"Why?"

"Aren't you running the Penn-Mar deal for NASO? Aren't you the investment banker advising Veens & Company?"

Falcon hesitated. "Maybe."

Stone laughed. "You act as if you've seen *All the President's Men* one too many times. You really don't have to be afraid of the press, at least not me. There are lots of aggressive types in the business, but I'm not one of them."

Falcon smiled. "How do I know? You could be a shark."

"I'm not trying to expose anything deep and dark about you. Promise. I just want to do a story on the man behind the biggest corporate takeover in history. I don't think you should have a problem with that. In fact, you should be flattered. I could give you the names of people on whom I've done stories. You could talk to them. That would probably help."

"I'd want to be able to edit it before it went out."

"You know I can't let you do that."

Falcon stared up the side of the NASO Building to the sky beyond. A front page *Financial Chronicle* story. There could be no more effective way than that to flaunt his success in Granville

Winthrop's face. He might even be able to get in a few digs at Granville through the article without Stone realizing. He turned his gaze back to Stone. "Day after tomorrow."

"Where?"

"Sparks."

"I'll make the reservation and meet you there at noon." She turned and moved away without another word.

Falcon's gaze followed her until she reached the corner of the building. She had a nice walk.

24

Peter Lane tried to calm his nerves as he lay beneath the palm trees of the deserted St. Croix beach. But he hadn't been able to completely relax since Veens & Company had announced its takeover offer for Penn-Mar only a few days after he had convinced Farinholt to put twenty thousand dollars of the President's money into the chemical company. He had been looking over his shoulder ever since. St. Croix was his third island hideout in the last two weeks.

He gazed at the huge palm tree swaying rhythmically above him in the midafternoon breeze. He should never have listened to that woman who had so smoothly approached him in Georgetown's River Club that Friday evening. But she had been so beautiful. He had been unable to resist her offer to buy him a drink or her offer of money. He had desperately needed that money, especially the amount she was talking about. And her request had seemed so simple.

After running from Victor Farinholt's office, Lane had driven straight from Washington to the Philadelphia airport. He hadn't bothered to return to his sparsely furnished apartment in Southeast because it would have been too risky. Within ten minutes, Farinholt would have realized that he wasn't coming back with the research data. Farinholt would have erupted into a rage and sent someone to Lane's home. Fortunately, he had been prepared for such an emergency. The suitcase had been packed and stowed in the BMW's trunk for weeks.

He had driven all the way to Philadelphia for two reasons. First, National, Dulles, or BWI would have been too obvious. After posting a man at his apartment, Farinholt would have sent people to the Washington airports, and probably Amtrak's Union Station as well, to stop him. Second, Lane knew that there was a direct flight from Philadelphia to St. Thomas every day at four in the afternoon. It was his flight to freedom.

Farinholt didn't really have anything on him, not yet anyway. But Lane knew that Farinholt would have tried to stop him any way he could, because somehow the old man had sensed that something was amiss. Farinholt wouldn't have been able to detain him legally, but the old man's friends could be very convincing. Or so he had heard.

The worst part about the situation was that Lane didn't know why the people from whom he had taken the five hundred thousand dollars wanted him to put Lodestar into Penn-Mar. Perhaps the loan sharks had somehow learned of the takeover and concocted the scheme to destroy him. But that seemed highly unlikely because it didn't achieve their ultimate goal—recouping their money. More plausible was the possibility that Farinholt had an enemy who saw an opportunity to settle an old score. And Lane was the pawn. But why had the woman specified that it should be the President's money that went into Penn-Mar? And how would the enemy have known of the takeover?

He hadn't known much at that point. But standing outside Farinholt's office he had known two things for certain. One, there was almost four hundred thousand dollars sitting in the Caymans waiting for him. And two, he wanted to stay a free man. That freedom would have been seriously endangered if he had stuck around Washington too much longer and become embroiled in some sort of scandal. Or worse, taken a long ride with Farinholt's friends before the scandal ever got started.

Lane had moved the money eight times since fleeing from Washington. It cost him three thousand dollars in total to do it, but it was worth every penny. The money *had* to be clean by now. Still, he had less than four hundred thousand dollars already. If he lived like a pauper, that amount might buy him ten years of anonymity. Could he have been more stupid?

Lane stared up at the large leaves. They seemed somehow to resemble elephant ears as they moved in the soft breeze. Back and forth, back and forth. God, he was tired. He listened to the aqua blue water rolling constantly into the beach against the white sand, hissing benignly as it receded to the sea. He allowed his eyes to close momentarily, then snapped back to consciousness. He could not allow himself to fall asleep. There was no telling who might be trying to find him.

Lane propped himself up on one elbow and gazed out over the lonely beach. He squinted against the brightness of the sun's rays. There was nothing in sight except for a catamaran sailing far offshore. Lane squinted harder, trying to focus on the craft. There appeared to be only one person aboard, but he could make out no details with the boat so far away. He lay back on the sand. He had to stay awake. It was too dangerous to fall asleep.

Phoenix Grey moved stealthily through the palm trees until he reached a point directly behind the sleeping Peter Lane. Grey glanced back to see if he could see the catamaran pulled up on the shore several hundred feet up the beach. Good. It was out of sight.

Grey had been following Lane since flying from the Dominican Republic to Antigua, where he picked up the man's trail. Now it was time to act.

There was no danger that Lane would awaken—the man hadn't slept in forty-eight hours—but Grey worked quickly and purposefully anyway. He bent down next to Lane and delivered a quick chop to the side of the man's neck. It paralyzed Lane but did not kill him, just as Phoenix wanted.

Lane's eyes flew open immediately. He began to scream at the pain surging through his body. Unceremoniously, Grey inserted a large, spongy rubber ball into Lane's mouth. The brute strength with which he accomplished the maneuver dislocated Lane's jaw, causing him even greater pain, but Grey had no sympathy. The ball effectively muffled Lane's cries and would not leave residue in the throat and lungs as a cloth gag would. There probably would be nothing left of either the throat or lungs when it was over, but you could never be too careful. It had to look natural.

Phoenix removed latex gloves from a dark blue waterproof backpack he had carried with him from the catamaran. He donned the gloves, then removed a clear plastic bag from which he painstakingly extracted several pieces of paper. He first moved to Lane's right hand, carefully pressing the limp fingertips against the paper in many places, and then to the left hand, repeating the procedure. When he had finished with the left hand, Grey replaced the papers into the plastic bag, sealed the bag shut, and placed it into the backpack. He removed the latex gloves from his hands, stuffed them into the backpack, and zipped the backpack closed.

Lane moved his head from side to side because it was all he could do. The pain was unbearable.

Grey stood and gazed down at Peter Lane. "I thought you would have passed out by now, you dumb bastard." He curled his lip and kicked the paralyzed man in the side of the head. The kick had no purpose except to deliver pain.

Grey glanced up and down the beach. There was no sign of anyone. He slung the backpack on his shoulder and then stooped over to pick up Lane. "Come on, old man." With ease he flipped Lane over the same shoulder that supported the backpack.

Within minutes the catamaran was heading back out into the ocean. Peter Lane lay sprawled across the tarpaulin deck of the craft, barely conscious. Grey searched the waves for the chum slick, and what he saw made him smile. Shark fins. Lots of them. The sea vultures had taken less time than he had anticipated to gather in the mess of fish blood and guts he had meted out during the last hour. He sailed into the middle of the feeding frenzy and allowed the large sail to go slack.

With precision Grey made several deep incisions in Lane's arms and legs to entice the sharks, incisions that could still be mistaken for bites were the coroner's office to perform its work too diligently. There was no reason to believe the coroner would be that diligent. After all, this was St. Croix. But he had to be careful anyway. Blood pulsed from the incisions.

Phoenix moved up the tarp to Lane's head and pried the rubber ball from the man's mouth with an ice pick. Lane could no longer even move his head. He simply stared at Grey sadly.

"Over you go!" With one great push Phoenix Grey dumped Lane's body into the sea. The sharks moved to the man immediately as he floated faceup on the surface. Grey had been careful to dump Lane overboard so that he would float faceup, aware that it might take the sharks some time to become bold enough to begin ripping his body apart. And he did not want the coroner to determine that Lane's death had been a result of drowning, just in case the sharks did not shred him too badly.

But there was no reason to worry. The sharks butted Lane's body with their snouts several times, and then the gaping mouth of a large blue closed over Lane's head and began shaking it violently. Others quickly joined in the attack, and Lane's body was ripped to pieces in a matter of minutes. Grey scanned the water. Nothing remained on the surface but a bloody hand with just two fingers still attached.

25

Sparks Steak House was a man's place if there ever was one. From the obligatory premeal drinks at the stained wood bar and the all-male Sicilian staff, to the checkerboard tablecloths and the mammoth, bloody portions of beef, it screamed machismo. Sports celebrities frequented the establishment—their autographed pictures adorned the walls. The three-martini lunch guild came here to impress only their heartiest business clients. And the Cosa Nostra, the toughest of any secret New York fraternity, regularly accounted for half of the occupied tables. A godfather had died on the front steps, his belly full of Sparks steak and an assassin's bullets.

It was one of Falcon's favorite places in the world. The food was incomparable, the wine list long and delectable, and the maître d' an old friend.

He was purposely thirty minutes late, and as he moved through the foyer, the bright sunshine faded to a comforting darkness. He could not restrain a slight smile as he considered what Cassandra Stone had endured in the last half hour.

Cabrelli, the dictatorlike maître d', met Falcon at the door. They shook hands firmly, and a ten-dollar bill passed subtly from one hand to the other. Cabrelli then stepped back and jerked his head to the right, in the direction of the bar. A strange expression clouded his face, but Falcon disregarded it.

"Whenever you're ready, Andrew, my boy," he said in a deep, guttural tone.

"Thanks, Pauly." Falcon smiled at the older man, recalling the many closing dinners he had hosted at this restaurant to celebrate the execution of wildly profitable transactions for Winthrop, Hawkins. Those had been the days. Now it seemed they were back. Better than before.

Falcon turned toward the bar, expecting to see a helpless soul, one Cassandra Stone, who, after dealing with the loud and pushy male crowd at the bar for the last thirty minutes, would see him as a lighthouse beacon in the storm. His expectations were quickly shattered.

Cassandra sat on a stool in the middle of the bar, smiling broadly as she concentrated on something in her hand. She was surrounded closely by four large men. That inner circle of four men was wrapped by a more loosely packed outer layer of individuals who were intently watching the inner circle and Cassandra. Both the audience and the inner group alternately cheered and groaned as they witnessed the proceedings and consumed their prelunch cocktail. The bartenders too were engrossed in whatever was going on. Falcon gazed for a moment at the scene but could discern nothing. He glanced back at Cabrelli, but Cabrelli only shrugged his shoulders.

Falcon moved into the bar area, pushed his way through the audience, and then through the inner circle. "Cassandra!" He grabbed her forearm.

"Andrew! How are you?"

"Fine. What the heck are you doing?"

"Just playing a little liar's poker." She gestured at the inner circle of men.

By using the serial numbers of dollar bills—the eight green-colored numbers on the face of the bill, bounded at either end by a capital letter—players could create crude poker hands: a pair of sevens, three fours, et cetera. By including and guessing at the serial numbers of the other players' bills, which were kept hidden from view, hands people claimed to have could become quite large, depending on the total number of people playing. Play moved clockwise until someone was "called." The player who had been called then discreetly checked all of the other bills. If by aggregating the serial numbers on all of the bills, the player actually had the hand he claimed to possess—say, ten eights—then he took all of the players' bills, and another hand began with fresh cash. If the player was short, he put his bill on the bar for the eventual winner, and play began again without him, with the same bills.

Falcon glanced down and spotted a twenty-dollar bill in Cassandra's hand. He noticed that the four men also held twenty-dollar bills. So she was a gambler. And she played for pretty high stakes, even in a casual game of liar's poker. This woman would have to be monitored closely. "Come on." He pulled her gently.

"I'm in the middle of a hand." But she did not resist Falcon and followed easily as he pulled, laughing as she slid from the barstool.

A chorus of boos arose from the other players.

"Sorry, fellas." Cassandra waved as she moved away.

"How much did you lose?" Falcon asked as he led her away from the bar, toward the restaurant.

"I won three hundred dollars. I figured you'd make me wait, so I came prepared. You can always get a bunch of men interested in liar's poker if you're a woman. They assume you're easy money. I went down early with ones and fives, as the ante to get them overconfident. After a few hands they were hooked. Then we started playing for some serious money."

"You think that's pretty good, don't you?"

Cassandra removed a wad of bills from her purse and waved it at him. "Yup."

He glanced at her and shook his head. "Serious gamblers play with and for their credit cards."

She tossed her head back and laughed. Wall Streeters. They always had another angle to one-up you.

They reached the maître d' podium.

"Andrew, you're not gonna have a drink before lunch?" Cabrelli seemed concerned.

"No, Pauly, I think we'll just sit down."

"Okay. This way." Cabrelli moved into the maze of tables. "Hey, Andrew, I thought you said I might need to take care of her when you called this morning," he said over his shoulder.

Falcon attempted to cough loudly to drown out Cabrelli's words, but Cassandra heard the remark. Solemnly, she raised her eyebrows at Falcon as she sat in the seat Cabrelli held out for her.

Cabrelli moved off to alert their waiter. Falcon turned toward Cassandra, ready to receive questions about the takeover he knew would come, or at least a rebuke for having intentionally left her at the bar for a half hour. But he received neither. Instead, he was treated to nothing but an enjoyable meal. For an hour they ate, drank, and talked about world events, sports, fashion, and places they had each visited. Falcon was impressed with her. Definitely impressed.

"Cassandra, would you care for dessert?" The waiters had descended upon the table at Cabrelli's signal and quickly cleared the remains of the main course. "They have a great *tiramisu* here."

Cassandra breathed deeply. "I couldn't." She looked up at the waiter. "Just some espresso, please."

"Make that two."

The waiter nodded at Falcon and was gone.

"Okay, Andrew, now it's time for you to earn your meal. There's no free lunch at the *Financial Chronicle.*"

Falcon leaned back in the padded chair. "Here we go. Now I get peppered."

Cassandra ignored the remark. "Tell me something about yourself. Something unrelated to the Penn-Mar takeover, or business, or even New York."

"Is this a technique you use to pry the pearl from the oyster?"

"Of course, one of the most basic techniques. So go for it. Tell me something. A secret for instance."

Falcon grinned. "What?" He stared at her. She had kept pace with him, drinking the wine, glass for glass.

"You strike me as someone who probably has a few secrets. Tell me one."

"You know, you make me laugh. That's one thing I'll say about you." Falcon took the last sip of wine from his glass. "Let's say I had a few secrets, which I'm not saying I do. Why would I tell them to a newspaper reporter I just met?"

"Because you trust me. You probably don't have too many people you feel you can confide in, and you need one. I can tell. So you can confide in me. You'll feel better when you do. I know it. Trust me," Cassandra said matter-of-factly.

"You win three hundred dollars in twenty minutes at a game called liar's poker, plus you're a newspaper reporter digging for a story, and I should trust you? I don't think so. The only thing I should do is go to Atlantic City with you."

Cassandra smiled. "You're right, you should. I do very well there."

"Let's go the other way. You tell me something about yourself."

Falcon wasn't going to be easy to crack. She could see that. "Fine. I was born in the Rose Hill Projects of downtown Atlanta thirty-four years ago. I went to Emory on a journalism scholarship. I started working at the *Chronicle* four years ago after seven years at the *Minneapolis Star Tribune*. My favorite sports team is the Los Angeles Raiders, although I liked them better when they were the Oakland Raiders. And I don't invest in equities. I'm strictly a fixed-income investor. How about that?"

Falcon's eyes danced. This woman could cover all the topics. And she was as sharp as a tack. She ought to be an investment banker, he thought. "Are you married?"

"I got married when I was young. It didn't work."

"Divorced?"

"Uh-huh."

"Children?"

Cassandra turned toward the bar. "Yes. A boy."

"How old?"

"He would be eighteen by now."

"I'm sorry." Falcon's eyes dropped to the tablecloth.

"For what?"

"I just assumed when you said 'would,' you meant he had died."

Cassandra hesitated. "No. I put him up for adoption." She stared at him, trying to tell if he had become suddenly judgmental, as so many others did when they heard that little item. But there was none of that from Falcon.

The waiter returned with the espresso. They sat in silence as the man put down and arranged the saucers, cups, and a small pot of the rich coffee. He departed quickly, sensing that his presence was not appreciated.

"So, you want to know something about me?" Falcon began, breaking the silence. Somehow he knew Cassandra was not lying about her past to engender confidence in her subject. He knew she was telling the absolute truth. He could read a face, and he had seen the pain in the corners of her mouth at the thought of the son she hadn't seen in so long.

"Don't feel sorry for me, Andrew. It's okay. I made a mistake when I was a kid. But I'm all right."

Falcon waved a hand. "Hey, I don't feel sorry for anyone who wins three hundred dollars in a half hour of gambling. And we're supposed to be talking about me here anyway, right?"

"Yes." She laughed as she poured espresso for both of them.

"Don't you need to pull out a notepad or something?"

"Oh, right, you civilians think all reporters wear brown fedoras and carry notepads, and you don't feel comfortable talking to us unless the notepad is in full view. Kind of like the psychiatrist and the couch thing. Jesus, I would think you wouldn't want me to write anything down."

"Enough." Falcon held up his hands. "I'm from eastern Pennsylvania. I attended the University of Pennsylvania and then Harvard Business School, after which I went directly to Winthrop, Hawkins. I left Winthrop, Hawkins—"

"—to start MD Link with Reid Bernstein," Cassandra interrupted him. "I knew that. I knew about Winthrop, Hawkins too. As a matter of fact, I can even get as far back as your second year at the University of Pennsylvania. But I don't get anything before that. Not on any of the information systems I have. It's as if you started life in that year."

"You'll have to dig deeper."

"What about your family?"

"When I left home for college, I left for good."

"What happened?"

"I had an argument with my father."

"Lots of eighteen-year-old boys have arguments with their fathers."

"That's all I'm saying."

"Not going to make this easy for me?"

"I just don't think there's any reason to include background on me in this article. People won't be that interested."

"I think if we include a sketch, you might get some fan mail from a few women."

Falcon smiled at her.

"So, do I get my story?" Cassandra asked.

"Let's go for a walk in Central Park. I'll tell you everything you want to know about the Penn-Mar deal and Wall Street in general. It will make for a very good article. There's lots of good scoop."

Cassandra smiled and nodded. "Great, let's go."

Falcon rose from the table and helped her from the chair. "And we can finish it up over a nice dinner."

Cassandra shook her head, still smiling. "Oh, Andrew," she sighed.

"What?" His face looked like that of a young boy with his hand caught squarely in the cookie jar.

"You've got those thoughts of interracial sex dancing in your head."

"I do not!" Falcon protested vehemently.

"Besides, I already have a dinner date tonight with my lover."

"Cancel it. I'm much more interesting."

"Really?" She smiled at his bravado.

"Absolutely."

Cassandra laughed. "She'll be surprised to hear that."

26

"Andrew Falcon, this is Henry Landon, president of Penn-Mar Chemicals," Chambers said, making the introduction.

Falcon glanced at Chambers. The man looked a good deal better than he had in New York. There was actually a bit of color to his hollow cheeks. Perhaps a few days as the new Penn-Mar chairman and the lack of stress from the takeover were the prescription he needed. Falcon still had been unable to determine exactly what was wrong with Chambers. He had asked Barksdale on the flight out from New York that morning, but Barksdale didn't know or wasn't saying.

Landon shook Falcon's hand. Falcon could feel the perspiration in his hand. Chambers had already been out here for a week. What the heck was this guy so nervous about?

"A pleasure to meet you, Mr. Falcon. Call me Dutch." He spoke with perfect diction, enunciating each syllable.

"Okay, Dutch." Falcon judged Landon to be about sixty. He was of medium height, balding on top, and his stomach was creeping over the wide belt holding up his brown polyester pants. Landon had clearly come up through the engineering side of the company. Falcon already knew Landon's background from reading the company's annual 10-K report as well as articles off Bloomberg and Lexis/Nexis. But you could tell so much more by meeting a man than by reading about him.

Landon wore a yellow, short-sleeved, blend shirt—the tiny balls of material around the neckline alerted Falcon to the fact that the shirt was not all cotton. The plastic protector inserted into the shirt pocket was filled with different colored pens and a small calculator. Landon's glasses were thick, smudged, and dusted with dandruff. Physically, he was about as impressive as a ladybug. He must have known the hell out of engineering.

"And this is Lex Sotos, chief financial officer."

Falcon's focus shifted. Sotos did not speak as they shook hands. His palm was completely dry, devoid of perspiration. And it was cold.

So here was the spit and polish of Penn-Mar Chemicals. If Landon was Mr. Inside, then clearly this was Mr. Outside. Sotos was tall, almost six four, and in excellent physical condition. He could have been anywhere from forty-five to sixty-five. The dark, faint chalk-striped suit fit perfectly in all the right places. The white pima dress shirt was crisply starched, and he wore a startlingly red tie, decorated with blue giraffes. The suit coat was buttoned and the pants were cuffed. His face and hands were deeply tanned. Clearly this man did not miss many opportunities to play the company golf course, which surrounded Penn-Mar's headquarters building.

Sotos quickly withdrew his hand from Falcon's. He was arrogant to the point of being insolent. Obviously, in his position as CFO, he believed that NASO needed him more than he needed NASO. Because he knew where every nut was stored and every mine was buried. He knew everything about the firm's financials, things no one could discern from the public statements. He could make life very difficult for NASO if the bank and Veens weren't accommodating. That was his view.

"And this is Phil Barksdale, vice chairman of the National Southern Bank." Chambers completed the introductions.

Barksdale shook hands with both Penn-Mar officers. Sotos was only slightly less condescending to Barksdale than he had been to Falcon.

Pleasantries completed, the five men took seats at the plain boardroom table. Landon and Sotos sat on one side, while Chambers, Barksdale, and Falcon sat on the other. They weren't all on the same team yet. It would take some time. It always did, Falcon thought.

Falcon watched as Landon and Sotos took their seats. Landon's eyes moved constantly as he leaned forward over the Formica-topped table, hands clenched before him. Sotos leaned back and stared at something on the wall above Falcon's head. Falcon smiled. This was going to be fun.

"We certainly appreciate you two gentlemen taking the time to meet with Falcon and myself today." Barksdale's deep voice rumbled throughout the room. "And I want to thank my friend Devon Chambers for setting this up." Barksdale gestured toward Chambers.

"Let me tell you, Lex and I have had a wonderful opportunity to get to know Devon over the past few days," said Landon, "and we certainly think he and Veens will bring a great deal of knowledge and experience to Penn-Mar. We look forward to our association with Veens, as well as with the National Southern Bank."

It was all Falcon could do to suppress a smile. The guy was so stressed he was almost spitting on himself to get the words out. He wanted to make certain they liked him. Bhutto had really misjudged this one. When the hostile bid had first been announced, he must have told these guys all kinds of crap. Falcon pictured the Indian convincing Landon and Sotos that there was no chance Veens would win the battle and how they didn't have to worry about sucking up to some clowns from an obscure investment boutique. They had probably all laughed long and hard. In their wildest dreams, these two men had never believed that this meeting would ever take place. Falcon sensed it. Now they were being hit over the head with the fact that they no longer controlled Penn-Mar. They were coming to the realization that they had bosses again—Chambers and Barksdale. They could no longer run the company as their own empire, disregarding the public shareholders as they probably had for so long. It was interesting to see the different reactions. Landon was worried about his job, Sotos about his pride.

Barksdale coughed. "As you both are well aware, National Southern is not only a coequity investor with Veens in the transaction. We are also the agent for the consortium of domestic and international banks that provided twenty-eight billion dollars for the deal. We felt it was important to get out here and meet face-to-face as quickly as possible. So, here we are."

"Yes, here you are." Sotos's tone was sarcastic. "What percentage of the shares did you get in the tender?"

"Ninety-eight point six percent." Falcon offered the detail. "We closed out the other one point four percent with a back-end merger yesterday."

"That's an appropriate term." Sotos laughed caustically. "Back-end merger." His tone was bitter.

"Easy, Lex." Landon smiled nervously at the men across the table.

"Anyway, we are planning on having a meeting here in Toledo for all of the banks next week. Andrew will be in charge of that." Barksdale waved a hand in Falcon's direction. "And the week after that, we will have a meeting for potential junk-bond investors."

"How much does NASO have in this deal, Barksdale?" For the first time Sotos leaned forward in his seat.

Barksdale took a quick look at Chambers, who nodded subtly. "At this point, thirteen billion. Three in equity from funds we control, six in subordinated junk bonds, and four in senior bank debt."

"So Veens is a front. You guys are the real owners."

"Veens owns seventy-five percent of the voting shares. Most of the securities we bought do not allow us to vote."

"That's a pretty good deal for your friend over there." Sotos nodded at Chambers.

"We believe this is a good deal for all of us," Barksdale said.

"Okay, what's in it for management here at Penn-Mar?" Sotos asked, his tone becoming confrontational.

"Lex, please." Landon was visibly shaken.

"That's all right, Dutch." Chambers' breathing was labored, but he still managed to smile evilly at Sotos.

It was the second time Falcon had seen that look. It was a look he did not care for.

Chambers continued. "Dutch, we're going to offer you a rather nice employment package, one which we will go over with you in detail later this afternoon. We are excited about having you stay on."

The room was quiet for a few moments.

Sotos glanced around. "And me?"

"Falcon." Chambers pointed at him.

Falcon did not hesitate. "Lex, my boy, are you a golfer?"

Sotos' eyes shot to Falcon. His eyes were filled with disdain. Falcon was going to enjoy this.

"Yes." Sotos' voice was suddenly rough. The cool had melted like an ice cube in an inferno. He suddenly realized that he had misjudged everything.

"Well, good. Because you're going to have lots of time to play. But you won't be playing on the Penn-Mar course. You're fired," Falcon said coolly.

Barksdale had informed him on the plane that he would be firing Sotos. Chambers found him arrogant and incompetent. Falcon had protested. It would make selling the bank debt and the bonds more difficult. You didn't fire the CFO and expect to excite potential investors. But Barksdale didn't care. He had his orders from Chambers. Chambers was the general and Barksdale just a sergeant. But it was a chore Barksdale did not relish. Down deep, he hated confrontation. So he was going to pass the buck to Falcon. Because he could. Because he was the vice chairman.

"What?" Sotos stood, a look of disbelief consuming his face instantly.

"Fired." Falcon didn't mind the chore now. This guy was an asshole. He wouldn't have gone over very well with investors anyway. "You have a half hour to clear out. You will be monitored by a security guard while you are packing your possessions."

Sotos stared openmouthed down at Falcon. "You're out of your fucking mind!" he screamed.

"Probably, but that's the deal." Falcon smiled at Sotos. He had been right. It was fun.

Sotos turned toward Landon for help, but Landon refused to make eye contact with what had just become his former partner.

Penn-Mar's headquarters reminded Falcon of the Goodyear Tire & Rubber Company, across the state in Akron—he had been close to Goodyear when he was with Winthrop, Hawkins. The Penn-Mar building was just four stories high, but it was long and wide and had hundreds of thousands of square feet of office space. Like so many midwestern manufacturing headquarters, it had been constructed in the 1950s, when largesse was in vogue and efficiency and downsizing were not part of a CEO's vocabulary. Now Penn-Mar needed only half the space. A result of several rounds of "synergy layoffs" over the past few years. The entire wing he was now exploring was all but empty.

The long, tiled corridors stretched on endlessly, leading to hundreds of offices, only a few of which seemed to be occupied. The corridor was faintly lit by gaudy chandeliers burning low-wattage bulbs. The walls were lined with long glass cases framed by dark wood. The cases contained black-and-white photographs of old manufacturing sites, replicas of early products, trophies of winning company bowling teams, and awards for outstanding corporate citizenship.

Falcon stared at a picture of a softball team, one member of which held a plaque inscribed 1964 Champions—Indianwood Summer League. He smiled. The men all sported crew cuts. He breathed deeply. The venerable hallway was musty. It reminded him of his old public high school in Philadelphia.

Falcon turned from the picture and walked slowly down the corridor. His steps echoed in the lonely hallway as he walked. Sotos' dismissal had turned ugly. He had started screaming about suing Veens, and they had called a security guard to escort him out immediately. They hadn't even given him the time to gather his belongings. Falcon knew how that felt, but he had no sympathy for Sotos.

Chambers had suggested that they take a break once Sotos was gone, and everyone quickly agreed. So Falcon had gone for a walk. He enjoyed architecture and old buildings and he needed to relax, to work off some excess energy. And he wanted to find Chambers' office.

Falcon moved farther down the long, shadowy hallway. Cassandra's *Financial Chronicle* article was due out soon. He had spent three hours with her in Central Park after lunch. During that time he had recounted the takeover in detail. He had given her an inside look at the biggest takeover ever, and at Wall Street. She had been appreciative, as she should have been, and against her better judgment had promised to show him a draft of the article just prior to publication.

He had called her references yesterday, people she had worked with, and as he had anticipated, she checked out. People had nothing but good things to say about her: honest, trustworthy, fair, thorough.

Falcon stopped to look at another photo. He did not want to seem too purposeful and arouse the suspicion of anyone who might see him. Occasionally someone would come out of what looked like an abandoned office. He stared at the picture in the case without seeing. There were so many questions. He ought to leave it alone. Forget about it. But he couldn't. It wasn't his nature. And he knew of only one place to start looking for answers without raising red flags. But he had to be so careful.

Chambers' office wasn't listed on the corporate directory yet. Falcon had checked with the receptionist on the way in. So he would have to find it himself. He had followed Chambers at a safe distance after the boardroom meeting had broken up, but, not wanting to make his objective obvious, he had turned off into a rest room the second time Chambers had looked over his shoulder. Now he was lost in the labyrinth of the mammoth building.

A tapping sound emanated from the office at the far end of the waxed hallway. It was like a flashing beacon in the dead of night, and he headed for it.

"Hello."

The middle-aged secretary stopped typing and looked up at him over horn-rimmed glasses.

"How are you?" He tried to play the nonthreatening, hometown boy, but the power tie was a dead giveaway. She knew that no Toledo native would have the gall to wear that.

"May I help you?"

"Yes. I'm looking for a rest room."

"You're a little off the beaten track, aren't you?" She was suspicious. This part of the building was abandoned for all intents and purposes. People didn't look for rest rooms here.

"I suppose." He paused. "Actually, I was also looking for Mr. Chambers' office. We need him back at the boardroom meeting."

"Why didn't you just call him?"

Falcon smiled at her. He was close. This had to be Chambers' secretary. Why else would she be so protective? "Just wanted a little exercise. I must say this is a beautiful building. Was that you I saw in the picture at the other end of the hallway? The one holding the bowling trophy for last year's team."

Suddenly her face changed, as if someone had thrown a switch. "Why, yes, it is."

Thirty seconds later he knew the exact location of Chambers' office.

Falcon peered through the darkness toward the Penn-Mar building. It loomed in the night like a ship drifting silently on a dead-calm sea. Amiable and unthreatening, it seemed almost to beckon to him. Falcon pushed a button on his digital wristwatch. The liquid crystal display glowed a bluish-green color: 10:15. A pair of headlights moved up the long driveway that meandered through the golf course surrounding the building. Falcon crawled farther beneath the huge boxwood bush. The car moved slowly around the circle before the main entrance and stopped in front of the huge pair of double doors. Falcon was fifty yards from the doorway but was able to see the faces of the two security guards in the arc of the main entrance light as they emerged from the sedan. One man leaned back against the car and lit a cigarette as the other began to walk hurriedly around the building, shining a powerful flashlight before him. The beam of light bobbed to the rhythm of his gait.

Several minutes later, the man who had set off into the darkness reappeared in the main entrance light from the other side of the building. Falcon checked his watch again, careful to cup one hand over the display so as not to chance detection. The man had taken just over eight minutes to circle the building, just as he had a half hour ago. There was no way the guard could have entered the building during this round. If he had, he would have taken much more than eight minutes to complete the inspection.

The men got back into the car and drove away, toward the guardhouse at the bottom of the hill. The guardhouse was approximately half a mile from the headquarters building, located at the intersection of the Penn-Mar driveway and the main road. A huge hedge growing on the chain-link fence surrounding and protecting the entire property rendered traffic on the main road nearly inaudible. The hedge and fence had proven quite an obstacle for Falcon nearly two hours before.

The red taillights of the sedan disappeared into the distance. If he was really going to do this, it had to be now. He had a little more than twenty minutes before the guards would be back, provided they kept the same schedule they had since eight-thirty this evening.

Falcon crawled out from beneath the boxwood bush, stood, and began running along a curved line of maple trees growing parallel to the long fairway. He ran for several hundred yards, until he had maneuvered to the structure's east side—the side of the building opposite the front entrance. It was pitch black on this side, making it the safest point of entry. Falcon moved behind a large oak tree, hesitated as he glanced about, and then sprinted across the closely cropped lawn to the brick wall of the building, a distance of a hundred feet or so.

He was in excellent shape but found himself breathing hard. The night was hot and fortunately overcast—there was a full moon. He knew about the full moon because he had checked with the Washington office of the National Weather Service. To some it might seem a silly detail. But Falcon knew the value of covering all the details. Diligence could be the difference between winning a deal and losing it. This was not a deal he wanted to lose. This was a deal he couldn't lose.

Falcon had called the National Weather Service from a pay phone at a nearby strip mall, where he had also procured the dark jeans, shirt, and boots he was now wearing. He had donated his suit, dress shirt, and shoes to a Goodwill office at the end of the mall. The Hermès tie that had overpowered Chambers' secretary was stuffed in his back pocket. It was one of his favorites, and what the hell did the Goodwill need with a tie anyway?

Falcon hesitated for a few moments to allow his breathing to become regular. He was perspiring heavily in the humid air. After thirty seconds, he withdrew a small flashlight from his pocket and began sliding between the dark wall and the perfectly manicured bushes that surrounded the building. Finally, in the dim light, he located the large piece of wadded paper he had dropped that afternoon to mark the window he had unlocked. By stepping onto the thick limbs of the bushes, Falcon was able to boost himself to the old window. The bottoms of the first-floor windows were high up, at least ten feet off the ground. He reached and pushed. It opened easily. No one had checked. Thank God.

Falcon pulled himself through the aperture and tumbled onto the carpeted office floor of the building. He picked himself up and closed the window. Quickly, he moved out of the office, into the dark hallway, and toward Chambers' office. He didn't know what, if anything, he would find there, but he knew that it was the only place to start looking for explanations.

Barksdale was already back in New York. Or so Falcon hoped. The flight had departed exactly on time, at four-thirty that afternoon. Barring any major problems at La Guardia, Barksdale was at this very moment reclining in his Park Avenue apartment watching his beloved Yankees.

At the last minute, as the plane had been about to board, Falcon had rushed up to Barksdale from the pay phones to tell him that he had generated another potential acquisition deal in Dallas and that he was going to go directly to Dallas from Toledo. He would be in touch in the morning. At that point it was obvious that Barksdale's primary concern was getting home as quickly as possible, and he voiced no dissent.

Falcon didn't leave the boarding area until the plane had rolled back from the gate, taxied to the runway, and taken off. He didn't leave until he was certain Barksdale was airborne and unable to contact anyone. The plane was small, a puddle jumper, and would connect with another flight in Cleveland. Because it was an older, smaller plane, there were no phones on board. Barksdale might have conveyed a message to someone on the outside from the cockpit, but that seemed unlikely.

At the airport, Falcon rented a car using his personal credit card and then drove all over Toledo to make certain that he was not being followed. It was cloak-and-daggerish, and at times he felt foolish, but he wasn't going to take any chances.

Before leaving the airport, he called Jenny to have her make reservations at the Dallas Hilton, stressing that he had passed the trip by Barksdale. She complained about not seeing him for another day but promised to make the reservations immediately. Then he called Alexis to tell her that he wouldn't be home, that he was going to Dallas. She seemed indifferent.

Falcon moved quickly and quietly up a stairway to the second floor. He had been all over the building during the afternoon break in the meeting with Landon, searching for cameras, infrared alarm systems, and other detection equipment in the halls and offices. But there weren't any. After all, this was Toledo and Penn-Mar was just a chemical company. The research-and-development center, the only potential target of corporate espionage, was located in Seattle. Besides, the facility was protected by the fifteen-foot fence and the guardhouse. What else did they need? Falcon's hands were perspiring heavily inside the work gloves he had purchased at the strip mall's hardware store. The gloves were hot, but they would mask his fingerprints.

Falcon reached Chambers' office. The door was locked, as he had anticipated, so from his belt he removed a long, industrial-strength screwdriver, purchased from the same store as the gloves. The lock popped easily, and the aging doorknob crashed to the tile floor.

"Shhhh! Jesus Christ!" His nerves were on fire.

He pushed the door, and it gave way. He moved into the dusty outer office to the inner office door. The inner door was also locked, and again he used the long screwdriver; however, this lock did not yield quite so easily. He leaned against it heavily. Finally it gave way. He checked his watch. It had been twelve minutes since the guards had guided the sedan back down the driveway.

There was no way he was going to make it out before the next check. When the timer on his wristwatch read eighteen minutes, he would have to turn the flashlight off and sit tight.

The whole thing was idiotic. If he was caught in here, it would be difficult—if not impossible—to explain. He would probably be fired and forfeit the five million. And for what? Because he had some silly, unfounded suspicions. Maybe he should get out of here as quickly as possible. Falcon glanced around the office. No way. He had come this far. He wasn't turning back now.

He moved to the old metal desk. What was he looking for? He had no idea. He pried the desk open with the screwdriver and checked the drawers. And in the lower right-hand drawer he found it. He knew immediately it was something he needed to inspect.

He placed the wooden box on the desktop. It looked to be an antique in the dim glow of the small flashlight. The edges were beveled and the joints dovetailed. On top of the box was a gold plate inscribed with initials—DCC—which Falcon assumed were Chambers'. The box's latch was secured by a tiny silver padlock. He found a large stapler on the credenza behind the desk and smashed the lock as he held the box down on the desk's blotter. The lid popped open immediately. He peered inside and removed four legal-size manila folders.

The first folder was marked "the Sevens." Falcon caught his breath. The Sevens were a clandestine society at Harvard University. Of all of the university's secret groups, they were the oldest, most powerful, and most revered. In the school library he had read about them—their fabulous gifts to the school, their secrecy, and their history. He had seen the seven painted on the business school's wall in white paint every day for two years. But could this be the same group?

His heart was in his throat as he pulled the folder from the box. Inside the folder was a single piece of paper and on the paper was simply a list of names with several ten-digit numbers opposite each name. A flash of heat whipped through his body as he saw the first name: Granville Winthrop. And there was Chambers' name, and Boreman's, and Wendell Smith's, whom he recognized immediately as the president of the New York Federal Reserve. My God! What was this? And then he remembered the brand on Boreman's inner forearm. It was the Sevens. It had to be.

He gazed at the last three names on the list but did not recognize them, then scanned the ten-digit numbers. Phone numbers. That's what they were. They had to be. Falcon stared at the number opposite the last name: William Rutherford. He could not place the name, but the number seemed very familiar.

Falcon dropped the file on the desk and moved to the second folder, marked "PM—Environment Information." It was thick, and he leafed through the pages quickly. Suddenly a handwritten note on one page caught his attention. "J. Case, Crossings Strip Mall, 10/18." His eyes widened.

Falcon flashed the light on the tabs of the other two folders. They were marked "Real Estate" and "Lodestar." What the hell had he found?

Suddenly, the door of the office burst open and the overhead lights flashed on.

"Hold it right there!"

Falcon froze, paralyzed by the sight of the security guard's pistol pointed at him.

"Get your hands up where I can see them!" The guard moved slowly into the office, both hands on his gun.

The desk stood between Falcon and the guard, and he was able to drop the flashlight and the work gloves to the carpet without the guard noticing before he raised his hands above his head. How could he have been so stupid? The guard was early, but he should have anticipated this possibility. The man must have seen the flashlight through the window.

"Officer, I'm working on a project that Mr. Chambers wants out by tomorrow morning." The man wasn't a police officer.

That was clear. But he wanted the guard to think that the intruder felt inferior. So he addressed the man as "officer." "You do know who Devon Chambers is?"

The guard nodded but seemed unimpressed.

"Good. I'm a representative of Veens & Company, the firm that just bought Penn-Mar. The firm Devon belongs to also." Falcon attempted to make his voice stern but not overly so. He stared straight into the other man's eyes.

"We have no record of anyone checking into the building late. Everyone who had checked into our logbook today was out of the complex at seven forty-seven this evening. This building is supposed to be empty."

"Look, I'm—"

"Quiet!"

Falcon could see that the guard was nervous. The man had probably never before confronted an intruder at Penn-Mar. Falcon glanced toward the door to see if the other guard was in the vicinity, but he saw nothing. If this inspection was running like the others, the second guard was standing next to the sedan, smoking a cigarette, waiting for this man to return. But in a few minutes the other guard was going to realize that his partner was late.

Falcon searched for a two-way radio on the guard's belt but did not see one. That was good.

"Name, please."

"What?"

"What is your name?"

Falcon stared at the guard. There was no reason to give his real name yet. "Frank Scudder." He said the words quickly and convincingly.

"All right, Mr. Scudder, although I'm not certain why you would be sneaking around Mr. Chambers' office in the dark if you are who you say you are, I'll give you the benefit of the doubt. But you have to appreciate my position."

"Of course." Falcon smiled smoothly. Experience. There was nothing like it. He wasn't glad to have been held at gunpoint before, not glad that Bernstein had burst into his office, waved the shotgun at him, and killed Froworth and Hudson in cold blood; but that experience was enabling him to remain calm instead of panicking. He had seen the eye of a wild man who didn't care whom he killed. This man didn't have that look. Far from it. In fact, it was obvious to Falcon that this man would do anything he could to avoid firing the pistol.

"I'm going to call the guardhouse and tell my men what's going on."

Falcon and the guard glanced simultaneously at the telephone on the desk. The guard would have to come quite close to where Falcon stood to use it. With a little luck he might be able to get the gun away from the other man. It was a ridiculous notion, but Falcon was desperate. He could be killed, easily. But if the guards detained him, Chambers and the rest of the Sevens would know that he had seen these files. And then he might be a dead man anyway.

The guard realized how close together they would come also. "Move back a bit, Mr. Scudder."

"Certainly." Falcon smiled and took a step back.

The guard moved toward the desk, eyes glued to Falcon, and reached for the receiver.

At the exact instant the guard's hand touched the telephone, Falcon kicked the flashlight on the floor behind the desk as hard as he could. It flew across the aging gray carpet and smashed into the far wall. The guard turned toward the sound, and in a fraction of a second Falcon was over the desk and on the man. They crashed to the floor together, and as they did, the gun exploded.

Falcon jumped to his feet immediately. He stared down at the guard. Blood was already oozing from a hole in the white shirt. The bullet had passed through the guard's upper chest.

"Help me," the man whispered. A small stream of blood began to drip from one side of his mouth.

Falcon shook violently. The man had taken the bullet in his lung. It was a serious wound but might not be fatal. Falcon stared at the man through widening eyes. If he lived, he would be able to identify Falcon. He needed this man to die. It was an awful thought. In a split second it had come to that, and his life had changed forever.

"Please help me." The man reached up toward Falcon with both hands. Blood began pouring down both sides of his mouth. He began to cough, spitting red liquid on the floor.

Falcon moved backward instinctively. The gun lay beside the guard. Falcon spotted it, moved quickly to where it lay, and kicked it out of the guard's reach. As Falcon kicked the gun, the guard reached for his leg and grabbed hold. "Jesus Christ!" Falcon shook his leg but the man would not let go. "Get off me. Get the hell off me!" Falcon reached down and tried to pry the guard's fingers from his leg, but they were locked in place.

Wrenching spasms began to rack the guard's body. He dug his fingers deeply into Falcon's calf as he convulsed. Suddenly, he rolled to one side, pulling Andrew to the floor. They struggled desperately, tumbling into a floor lamp, which crashed to the carpet. The bulb exploded on impact, sending blue sparks shooting across the room.

For an instant Falcon felt the guard's fingers relax. Quickly, as the guard grasped his own chest, Falcon scrambled away. He crawled to the wall and watched in horror as the convulsions intensified. Falcon's chest heaved. The guard was going to die. Falcon had no medical training, but judging from the amount of blood pouring from the wound and his mouth, it would not be long. But how long would it be? That was critical. The other guard had to know something was wrong by now. He might even have heard the gunshot and already be running this way. Falcon could probably still escape, but the man might hold on long enough to give the other guard a description of him. How the hell had this happened?

The guard's body was racked by another huge spasm, causing the man to grab his chest again. He groaned loudly, ripping at the shirt and the black uniform tie. He tried to rise to his feet but only reached his knees. The veins of his forehead throbbed as he struggled, and then a huge vein of his neck began to pulsate rapidly. There was a gurgling sound in the man's throat, and he fell backward onto the floor. He gazed at Falcon for several seconds, and then, slowly, his eyes rolled back into his head.

Falcon's breathing was labored. He was covered with perspiration and there was blood on his dark jeans. He fell onto his knees beside the man, reaching for the man's wrist, searching for a pulse. But there was none. The guard was dead.

Quickly, Falcon shoved his flashlight and the work gloves into his pocket. He grabbed the four manila folders, turned out the office lights with his palm, and ran down the hallway. He just wanted to make it back to New York now. Never in his life had he thought he would want to see the city so badly. Suddenly the timer on his wristwatch began to beep loudly.

The small twelve-seater rose steeply away from the Toledo airfield. Falcon stared out the small window at the green and blue ground lights that gleamed eerily in the pitch-black night. The lights grew small quickly as the plane gained altitude. His nerves were balanced on the razor's edge. The plane could turn around at any second. The cockpit door might swing open suddenly. Or most likely, they would arrest him at the Pittsburgh airport as he changed planes for New York. The whole thing was crazy. Absolutely insane.

Falcon glanced up the aisle suspiciously at the only other passenger, a woman in her mid-forties who was already asleep. There was no reason at all to be suspicious of her, but he was not rational at this point.

A small bag, which he had purchased at the all-night airport store, lay between his feet on the floor of the plane. The obese woman behind the counter, who barely fit in her state-issue blue pants, had looked at him strangely even though he had tried to straighten his appearance in the rest room before buying the bag. He had tried to wash the blood from his jeans, but is seemed to Falcon that she stared at the dark water stains too long as she made change for the ten-dollar bill.

The bag zipped down the middle and was decorated on both sides with the Cleveland Indian baseball logo. He reached down slowly and removed the manila folder marked "the Sevens." He opened it, and in the dim cabin lights he stared long and hard at the telephone number opposite William Rutherford's name. Suddenly he made the connection. It was the same number that was on the paper that had floated from Jenny's purse to the floor of the Four Seasons Hotel room.

27

"This is good. Right here," Falcon said as the taxi rolled to a stop on 82nd Street, several hundred feet east of the entrance to his apartment building. He did not want to get out directly in front of the building. He wanted time to check the street before he committed himself to the high-rise and its limited escape routes.

"Thanks." Falcon groaned as he lifted himself out of the cab. He was tired and hot. The four cups of coffee he had consumed on the flight from Pittsburgh were wearing off, and despite the fact that it was only 7:45, the temperature had already reached ninety degrees. The ride in from La Guardia Airport had been miserable because the cab's air conditioner didn't work.

Falcon reached back into the taxi and picked up the nylon traveling bag that held the four manila folders. "Here." Falcon threw a twenty and a ten through the open passenger's side window onto the front seat beside the sullen Arab. The cabbie grunted and squealed off without offering change.

Falcon glanced up and down the street and then at the building's entrance. No one had followed him from La Guardia, he was certain of that. And he saw nothing suspicious on the street, although it would have been difficult to identify anyone focused on him through the hundreds of commuters already heading toward the subway. He looked around once again and began moving carefully toward the entrance.

They knew by now. They must. The dead guard had probably been discovered no more than ten minutes after Falcon had raced from the Penn-Mar building with the manila folders under his arm. By the time he had reached the airport, the police had been probably already crawling all over the building and the grounds looking for clues. And by the time the tiny plane had taken off from Toledo, Landon and Chambers had probably reached Penn-Mar to assist in the investigation. Chambers would have realized immediately that the files were gone. Falcon had half expected to be met by a group of police officers as he deplaned in New York. But La Guardia had been quiet, just revving up for the morning rush of lawyers, bankers, and corporate executives screaming off to far-flung destinations.

He was being paranoid. He knew that. The authorities would have called Landon first. He was still the president of Penn-Mar, so that was probably procedure. Landon would have been the first member of senior management at the scene. That gave Falcon some time. There was no way Landon would come to the conclusion on his own that Falcon was the perpetrator of this crime. No way. The accident had occurred in Chambers' office, so it would have been logical for Landon to call Chambers immediately, but so what? Why would Chambers automatically assume that Falcon was responsible? Chambers had walked both Barksdale and him to the car after the meeting had ended at Penn-Mar. As far as Chambers knew, they were both going directly back to New York on the same flight. Chambers might have spoken to Barksdale after he reached New York, but that seemed unlikely. Barksdale wasn't a Seven—at least he wasn't on the list—so there was no reason to think Barksdale would have called Chambers after arriving in New York, or vice versa.

And if they had spoken, so what? Barksdale might relay—and then again he might not—the news of Falcon's trip to Dallas, and that would be that. There would be no reason for Chambers to become suspicious at the news of Falcon's spur-of-the-moment jaunt to Texas. He was definitely being paranoid, but it was safer to be paranoid. It kept your mind in high gear.

Falcon reached the steps of his apartment building. He tried to peer into the lobby through the glass, but the morning sunlight was bright, creating a nasty glare.

The door popped open suddenly. "Jesus Christ! What the . . ."

"Morning, Mr. Falcon!"

"Oh, hi, Johnnie." Falcon was breathing hard and his heart was suddenly racing madly. He was going to be dead of a coronary before the police or the Sevens ever found him.

"Everything okay? You're looking a little out of sorts this morning." The doorman allowed the glass door to close as Falcon moved into the building.

"Fine, Johnnie. I'm fine." The air-conditioning was refreshing. Suddenly Falcon felt as if he could lie down on the lobby carpet and go to sleep. He was utterly exhausted. Falcon turned back toward the doorman. "I was expecting a friend this morning. Anybody come for me yet?"

"Nobody's come in yet. Lots of people have gone out, to go to work, you know. But nobody's come in."

"Nobody's been around asking for me either?"

"No." Johnnie shook his head.

"When did you get in?"

"I got the graveyard shift this week. I was in at midnight. Only got another five minutes or so before Carmine gets here." Johnnie held up a fat wrist and gazed at his Rolex watch.

Falcon glanced at the Rolex. It was an imitation. The second hand did not sweep but ticked. "What time did Alexis get in last night?"

Johnnie's face broke into a huge grin. "Checking up on her, Mr. Falcon? I'd marry that woman quick if I were you, before someone else does."

Falcon forced a smile. "Yeah, I'm checking up on her. What time did she get in?"

The doorman's grin faded. "It was pretty late. Maybe three o'clock." He hesitated.

"What is it, Johnnie?"

"Well, I shouldn't say this I guess, but . . ."

"But you will because I'm the one who'll write your Christmas bonus check."

"Right." The doorman lowered his voice. "I think she had a little bit to drink."

Falcon nodded and tried to appear disgruntled. "Thanks, Johnnie." He patted the man on the shoulder, then moved toward the elevator.

"Don't tell her I told you that, Mr. Falcon," Johnnie called after him.

"I won't," Falcon said under his breath as he moved into the waiting car. He pushed the button for the tenth floor. Immediately the doors closed and the elevator began to ascend.

Falcon glanced down at the nylon bag under his arm. He had read and reread each of the four files on the flight from Pittsburgh to New York in his seat at the deserted back of the plane, covering the papers anytime a flight attendant neared. The contents of the file marked the Sevens were self-evident—a list of the men who were members of the society. It could be nothing else. Falcon laughed as he stared at his reflection in the chrome elevator doors. Granville was a Seven. Chambers was a Seven. Boreman and Wendell Smith were Sevens. It was incredible. Of course, Boreman could do anything he wanted with NASO. The New York Fed was the law and the sheriff was on the take. And Barksdale would do anything Boreman told him to do. He owed his career to Boreman.

The file marked PM—Environmental Information was the thickest. It detailed the extent of Penn-Mar's massive environmental liabilities as well as a senior management conspiracy to dump waste illegally. It described how Jeremy Case and Tom West had fed the Sevens information and ultimately paid for it with their lives.

Falcon glanced at the bag again. The file marked Real Estate simply listed properties around the United States and what must have been their aggregate purchase value—almost six billion dollars. The Lodestar file was even less helpful. It simply contained an article about the investment management firm and its list of high-profile clients. And there was one name in the file: Peter Lane.

But what did it all mean? What were they trying to do? Was there anything at all to what he had found? Or was the box just an innocent collection of information? He shook his head. There were too many coincidences now.

The elevator began to slow its ascent. Why did Jenny have Rutherford's number? He shook his head again. There was only one conclusion. And it was a conclusion he didn't want to come to. She was working with them. They wanted to keep an eye on him and they were using her to do so. No wonder her attitude had changed so dramatically. He thought of the eight hundred-dollar bills he had counted in her wallet at the Four Seasons.

The doors opened and Falcon moved into the hallway. Suddenly he stopped short. Alexis might be working with them too. Why not? In retrospect their meeting at the club had seemed too scripted. She had fallen in love with him too quickly. He might be walking right into the spider's wed. But Johnnie had said there had been no visitors since Alexis had come home. None at all. And it was a secure building. He would be careful. And he wouldn't stay long.

Falcon slipped the key into the lock and entered the apartment quietly. He moved silently to the bedroom. Alexis was asleep, passed out as Falcon had expected. He could tell that she had imbibed a great deal of alcohol last night. Her clothes were strewn over the bed and on the floor. Her mouth was wide open and a drool spot was growing in circumference on the pillow. Only when she drank did she breathe so heavily through her mouth. The room actually smelled of alcohol. She would be out for a while. That was good.

The computer and the Bloomberg terminal flickered to life. He didn't have enough yet to go to the authorities. He could probably interest a couple of Fed examiners in what he had found and have Boreman suspended, but he couldn't actually prove anything about the Sevens. He couldn't really even prove they existed yet. He had the files, but he needed more. He needed to connect the Sevens concretely to Jeremy Case's murder. He needed telephone records. He needed to find the billion dollars of equity money that had come into NASO a month ago, money that was supposed to have come from Germany but that he now knew had come from the Sevens. Most of all, he needed to figure out the puzzle.

And how was he going to go to the authorities anyway? There was a dead Penn-Mar security guard in Toledo, Ohio. If he went to the authorities with the files from Chambers's office, it wouldn't take them long to figure out that he was connected to the guard's death. Falcon caught his breath. The guard was dead. Because of him. He had watched the blood pour from the man's mouth. And prayed for him to die. He shook his head. There was no way he could think of that now. But he would have to come to terms with it later.

Falcon punched Penn-Mar's ticket into the Bloomberg terminal. He moved through the system to the news section and found the lawsuit article. He scanned the print quickly. And there it was. The name of the law firm. Cleveland, Miller & Prescott. And the lead attorney for the plaintiffs was Turner Prescott. The same Turner Prescott on the list in the file. Falcon had no doubt of that. He stared at the screen for several minutes. And then the enormity of the whole scheme hit him.

Suddenly the telephone screamed. He heard Alexis groan. Jesus! He should have pulled the phone wire from the wall. But it was too late now. Falcon stared at the screen. He needed to check out Rutherford and Henderson. But it was too late. He flicked off the terminal and bolted for the door.

"Boreman?"

"Yes?"

"It's Winthrop."

"What is it?" Boreman asked.

"How are you?"

"Well, I'd say I'm doing pretty well, given that I'm about to die."

Winthrop wasn't amused at Boreman's reference to the accident Phoenix Grey was about to stage.

"Is Prescott still going to deliver the shocker to the Baltimore courtroom tomorrow?"

"Yes."

Boreman laughed. "I can't believe the Pleiade Project is almost over."

"We're getting there. Listen, I want you out of New York City and with Grey by three this afternoon. Once Prescott lays the environmental information out to that jury tomorrow, you are going to be a hot item."

"I'll be out. Don't worry. I'm going to go into the bank this morning, and then I'm to leave at one to get to a two o'clock flight departing from La Guardia for Los Angeles. Or that's where people will think I'm going. I'm supposed to be visiting our L.A. office. But of course I won't ever show up."

"Good. And you have left the keys to your car where Grey can get to them?"

"Easy, Granville. I spoke to Phoenix. Everything is taken care of."

"Boreman, I've been living and breathing this project for four years now. Humor me."

"Has Phoenix procured the body yet? When I spoke to him Monday, he still hadn't gotten it."

"He's gotten it." Winthrop paused. "How did Barksdale and Falcon's visit in Toledo go yesterday?"

"Fine, I suppose. I spoke to Barksdale last night after he got home. They fired Sotos and went over a great deal of other information. It seemed like a lot to go through just for appearance's sake, given that Prescott's going to release the information tomorrow. But it would be natural for NASO to want to get out there quickly, so I guess it's best that they went. And of course Barksdale and Falcon don't know what's going on."

"How is Falcon?"

"Okay. He went to Dallas directly from Toledo at the last minute yesterday. He's generated another M&A transaction and wanted to get right on it."

An alarm went off in Winthrop's mind. "Really?" It was probably nothing.

"Yeah. By the way, when are we going to release the information about Falcon's supposed insider trading?" Boreman asked.

"Not until next week. Bailey Henderson will disclose Lodestar's trades in the *Financial Chronicle* tomorrow, and then print Lane's memo on Friday or maybe Saturday. We don't want to release too much at one time."

"Yeah, I agree . . ."

"Boreman, I've got another call coming in. I don't know who the hell this could be, but I'd better take it. How much longer will you be there?"

"Ten minutes."

"I might call you back. If I can't get back to you before you leave, I may call you at NASO."

"I thought you weren't ever going to call me at NASO."

"I probably won't, but we're close enough to zero hour now that I don't think it matters too much. After tomorrow they'll think you're dead. Look, I've got to go."

"Bye, Granville."

Winthrop switched lines without saying good-bye. "Yes?" He could hear the caller breathing. "Hello? Who is this?"

"It's Chambers."

Instantly, Winthrop knew something was wrong. He didn't bother to chastise the man for calling him at this number, as he had explicitly instructed Chambers and the other five not to do. "Devon, what is it?"

"Something very . . . very bad has happened." Chambers could barely speak.

"What?"

"I can't believe it." His voice shook terribly. "I'm so sorry."

"What?"

"There was a break-in."

"A break-in? Where?"

"Yes . . . yes. Here at Penn-Mar."

"Devon, tell me what's happened. Just tell me. I don't have time to screw around."

"I just found out myself. They called Landon first. Landon didn't even know I was using it as my office. He didn't know. I believe him."

Chambers was babbling, to the point of being incoherent, but Winthrop understood enough to feel the tiny hairs on the back of his neck beginning to stand on end. "The office you were using. Was that the office that was broken into?" he asked, coaxing Chambers. He had to. The man was barely able to speak.

"Yes."

"Did the intruders get anything?"

"A security guard was killed. The police believe he must have surprised whoever did this. He was shot with his own gun. And a few of my files . . . they're missing."

"What files?"

Chambers was silent.

"What files, Devon?" Winthrop was losing control.

"The Sevens, the environmental information on Penn-Mar, the real estate partnerships, Lodestar." His voice was barely a whisper. "Everything."

"Are you kidding me? Tell me you aren't that stupid, Devon! Tell me this is a horrible joke you have all decided to play on me at the last minute. Tell me that's what is going on!" This was potentially devastating.

There was no answer from the other end of the phone.

A flash of heat passed through Winthrop's body. Oh, God. Falcon!

"Funds Transfer."

"Eddie?" Falcon spoke in a low voice.

"Yeah."

"Eddie, it's Andrew Falcon." He could have called from the apartment. After this morning he wasn't going to be back there for a long time. But if they were listening, if they had the apartment tapped, which, now knowing who "they" were, he had no doubt but that they did, they would be able to track down Martinez. And that couldn't happen. He had to have Martinez.

"Oh, hey, Mr. Falcon. I'm glad to hear from you."

But Falcon could tell from Martinez's voice that he was definitely not glad to hear from him. "Anything yet?"

"You mean on the wires?" he asked.

"Yes." Of course that was what he meant. Martinez was stalling.

"No." Martinez did not want to tell Falcon that he hadn't even attempted to locate the transfers since the last time they had spoken.

"It is of the utmost importance that you find the money and then find where it came from. I can't impress upon you how important it is."

"Maybe you could just tell me what this is all about, Mr. Falcon."

"No! I mean it wouldn't be a good idea. It's just routine, I promise you."

"Uh-huh."

Falcon could hear the hesitance in Martinez's tone. "Eddie, it's worth two thousand dollars to you. Cash, my friend."

Martinez held the phone away from his ear and stared at it. Two thousand dollars! There was definitely something going on here that wasn't on the up-and-up. And he shouldn't be a part of it. All the same, he could use that money. Martinez's eyesight blurred. He shouldn't even be thinking this. But they didn't pay him very much for his long hours at the bank, and the station wagon was on its last wheels. The engine and the transmission were shot. Beyond repair. He'd have to put down just about that amount for the replacement car they were going to have to buy very soon. And he didn't have any savings. None. He, his wife, and the four children lived paycheck to paycheck. Martinez brought the phone back to his ear.

"Five thousand dollars, Eddie," Falcon said, becoming impatient. He was negotiating against himself, but time was of the essence.

Martinez swallowed. "Five thousand?" His voice cracked.

"Yes. In cash."

Martinez looked around the room. Was anyone watching him?

"Going once, Eddie!"

"Okay, okay." The woman at the next desk glanced at him. Martinez turned away. "Okay."

Falcon took a deep breath. Everyone had his price. Eddie's was five thousand. His had been five million. And both of them would probably pay for accepting that price. "Transfers have to be identified, don't they, Eddie?"

"Of course. Otherwise nobody would know where they came from."

"All right, then look for transfers which have a notation on them about Penn-Mar. You know, Penn, PM, or something like that." Falcon paused and looked around the lobby. "Or maybe they have a seven as a notation."

"A seven?"

"Yeah."

"You're saying they're coded. That the notations are a code."

"Yes."

"What's going on here?" His voice was filled with self-doubt.

"Don't ask, Eddie. It isn't worth knowing about. Don't worry. Just find the transfers."

But Martinez was still worried. He had a family to think about. On the other hand, there was five thousand dollars on the line too.

Falcon sensed Martinez second-guessing his decision. "Look, Eddie, nobody's ever going to give you a hard time about this. But on the off chance they do, you know I'm an officer of the bank. I can request an inquiry into a transfer anytime. I mean, it isn't as if you're doing anything wrong."

"Yeah, sure," Martinez said, unconvinced.

"So you'll do it, Eddie? For five thousand, you'll do it? Right?"

There was a long pause. "I want the money this afternoon."

"Half this afternoon. Half if you find the wires."

There was another long pause. "Okay."

"Just one more thing, Eddie. Don't tell anyone about this, you got that?"

"Yeah."

"I'll call you later to set up a time to give you the money."

"Okay."

"Bye." Falcon hung up the phone. Martinez had to come through. It was the link he had to have to nail these people.

"Hello."

"Do you know who this is?" Rutherford spoke slowly so the woman would recognize his voice.

"Yes." He had a distinctive voice, and she had heard it a great deal lately.

"Good."

She was nervous.

"Is Falcon in New York?"

There was an edge to the man's voice she had not heard before. "No, he's in Dallas. He called yesterday to say that he was going to go straight from Toledo to Dallas. It was a last-minute thing."

"Are you sure that he actually went to Dallas?"

"I think so." She hesitated. "I haven't heard from him since yesterday. I expect him to call me at some point this morning."

"Where was he going to stay?"

"At the Dallas Hilton."

"Give me the number there."

She hesitated, wondering if this was information she ought to give. The voice at the other end of the line sounded strange today.

"Give it to me!"

She did but transposed two numbers. Perhaps Falcon would need the few seconds it would take the man to find the correct number.

"I'll be back in touch within the hour."

"Okay." She replaced the telephone. Something terrible had happened.

Falcon dialed Cassandra's number.

"Hello."

"Cassandra?"

"Yes?"

"It's me." He looked out of the boardinghouse window at the bodega across 132nd Street. A large cockroach crawled along the windowsill. He flicked it off, then leaned out of the open window and watched it fall to the pavement three stories below.

"Hi, there. Listen, Andrew, I tried to call you at the office about an hour ago. I had a few more questions regarding the article. . . ."

"Forget the article."

"What?" She laughed. "What are you talking about?"

"Things have happened."

"What kind of things?"

"I need your help. Do I get it?"

She was silent.

"Do I?" He raised his voice.

"Of course, of course. But why? Andrew, what's wrong?" Cassandra's voice became serious.

"I don't want to tell you over the phone. I need to meet with you."

"When?"

"Probably tomorrow."

"Where?"

"I'll let you know. I'll call you in the morning."

"Fine. But what's this all about?"

"I'll tell you tomorrow. Just keep watching the screens. Penn-Mar and NASO will be front and center. Not in a positive light either." He paused. "I need a favor."

"What?"

"I need you to do a little research."

"Okay."

"Two names. William Rutherford and Bailey Henderson. I need to know everything about them."

There was a silence as she wrote down the names. "Well, I can tell you who—"

"I don't have time now," Falcon interrupted her. "I've got to get going. I'll call you. Oh, by the way, you can't run the article."

"What?" She was instantly upset. She had deadlines. "But you gave your word that I could."

"I know, but I care about you. Running the article might get you killed."

28

The loud banging continued relentlessly. For several moments Turner Prescott believed he was dreaming, and then suddenly he realized he wasn't. Immediately he swung his feet over the side of the bed and grabbed for the pistol in the middle drawer of the nightstand. He glanced at the clock on top of the table. Four in the morning. What the hell was going on?

Prescott quickly moved out into the hallway and down the long stairway. He reached the foyer, flicked on the outside lights, and pulled aside the curtains. "Christ Almighty!" Prescott rushed to the door and yanked it open.

Granville Winthrop pushed past Prescott into the foyer of the opulent home. "Is your wife here?" Winthrop did not bother with pleasantries.

"No. She's in Martha's Vineyard. Look, why didn't you call to tell me you were coming?"

"I tried. There was no answer."

"Oh, Jesus, I'm sorry. I disconnected the phone because I was working. We're really coming down to it in the trial. I was just doing some last-minute prep for tomorrow." Prescott paused. "Well, come in. Would you like something to eat or drink?"

"No."

The two men moved into Prescott's living room. It reminded

Winthrop of the Harvard Club. Lots of horse prints and antiques. Winthrop and Prescott sat at opposite ends of a long couch.

"What the hell are you doing here, Granville?"

"We have a problem." Winthrop wasted no time in getting to the point. "A serious problem." Winthrop's voice was determined, and there was an atypical strain to it.

Prescott heard the strain. He scanned Winthrop's face for further clues, but there was nothing. "What is it?"

"Chambers had several files stolen from his office at Penn-Mar." Winthrop's eyes narrowed as he gauged Prescott's reaction.

"What! What files?"

"Files relating to the Sevens, to the environmental information you are supposed to present to the court today, to our real estate partnerships, and to Lodestar. Everything."

Prescott felt a burst of heat flash through his entire body. Perspiration began to form on his forehead immediately. "Are you kidding me?" He rose and moved to the large fireplace which dominated the room, placing his hands on the mantel to steady himself.

"Do I sound as if I'm kidding?"

"Well, how the hell did this happen?" Prescott's temper exploded to the surface.

"Easy, Turner. Easy . . ." Winthrop had known Prescott for thirty years and had never encountered an eruption like this before. He had always known Prescott to remain as calm as he in the face of anything. It was what he valued most about Turner.

"Was there enough in those files to take us down? To prove conspiracy? We're talking about my career. My life! Jesus Christ Almighty!" Prescott picked up a vase from the mantel and hurled it into the hearth. "That guy Chambers is an idiot! How could he let this happen? What kind of moron keeps files as sensitive as those where someone can get to them? Granville, I'm not going down for this! I'm not going to see my career and my life destroyed because of his stupidity!"

"Calm down. Nobody's career is going to be destroyed. Nobody is going down." Winthrop was as steady as ever. "Look, there's nothing we can do about it now. We need to go forward. We need to proceed as if nothing happened while we reacquire the documents."

"My God!" Prescott took a series of short breaths. He felt a pain in his chest. This couldn't be happening. Not in a million years could this be happening. "They broke into Chambers' office at Penn-Mar, is that right?"

"Yes."

"And whoever broke in took Chambers' files." He was beginning to regain his composure. "I mean, is Chambers certain he didn't take them back to his hotel in Toledo?"

"Chambers is certain the files were not and are not at the hotel. He was keeping them at the company because he didn't want them at the hotel. He was afraid one of the cleaning people might discover them while he wasn't there. And he didn't want to keep transporting them back and forth each day. He figured that would be an easy way to lose them. And he was occupying an office in a wing of the Penn-Mar building that was not being used, so he figured they'd be safe there." Winthrop spotted the wet bar in the corner of the room next to a walnut corner cabinet. "Maybe I will take that drink now." Winthrop stood and moved toward the bottles.

"Did whoever broke in take anything besides the files?" Prescott moved behind the bar to fix the drink. "Scotch mist?"

Winthrop nodded. "No, that was it. It was as if he knew what he was looking for. The intruder was interrupted by one of the security guards, so I suppose that the person might have taken other things if he had had time. But I think the intruder got what he came for."

"But the guard must have stopped what was happening. How did the intruder get away?" Prescott handed the glass to Winthrop.

"The guard was killed."

"Killed?" Prescott looked up from the drink he was pouring for himself.

"Yes. Killed with his own gun. So we can assume that whoever broke in was not armed but somehow managed to take the guard's gun away and kill him with it."

"This all happened last night?"

Winthrop hesitated. "The night before last. I've been trying to recover the files since then. I didn't want to alarm you, which is why I didn't contact you right away. I had hoped that we would have recovered them by now. But we haven't, and I know you are planning to present the new environmental evidence today."

"The night before last. Tuesday . . . That was the day Barksdale and Falcon were in Toledo," Prescott said.

"That's correct." Granville sipped the drink as he sat on a barstool.

"Do you think that's a coincidence? That Barksdale and Falcon were out there the same day?"

"I don't think it's a coincidence at all."

A shooting pain seared through Prescott's chest. "Jesus!" He bent over slightly.

"What's the matter?" Winthrop rose to his feet.

"Nothing." Prescott breathed deeply, then waved a hand at Winthrop. "Look, you said you thought it wasn't a coincidence. What are you saying? That Barksdale and/or Falcon is involved?"

"Not Barksdale. He's too stupid. It's Falcon."

"I can't believe that. Damn it, I knew that guy was bad news. I told you that a long time ago. If he is involved, and this whole thing somehow unravels, it's going to be your . . ." Prescott didn't finish. He glanced away from Granville and out a window into the darkness beyond. Even at this point he wasn't willing to confront Winthrop.

"What are you saying?" Winthrop's voice rose noticeably.

"Nothing."

"That's what I thought, Turner." Winthrop took a huge gulp of the drink. "It's done. There's nothing we can do now. We have to move forward." He was angry.

"How do you know it was Falcon?"

Winthrop did not respond. He was concentrating on a painting behind Prescott, trying to control his outward emotion. Inside he was seething. Not at Prescott—though Prescott would bear the brunt of Winthrop's temper if the man pushed any further—but at himself. Suddenly, he sensed that Falcon was more formidable and resourceful than he had ever given him credit for. And for the first time in as long as he could remember, Granville felt panic. Only a hint of it, but unmistakable just the same. They had been right. He shouldn't have combined the project and his personal vendetta. But he had disregarded their advice. Because he felt himself beyond reproach. He was Granville Winthrop. Worth over three billion dollars. A man of supreme power. Able to make or break Fortune 500 companies at will. He needn't heed anyone's advice. But now he was paying the price for that attitude. And because of him, they might all pay. So the hell with the insider-trading charge and a slow death in prison for Andrew Falcon. The hell with the painful revenge for Falcon turning his back on Winthrop, Hawkins and him. It was time for Phoenix Grey to use his deadly talent to its utmost.

"Granville?"

"Yes, yes . . . what?"

"You were saying, about Falcon."

"I know I was. You don't have to tell me." Winthrop's eyes bored into Prescott.

"All right." Prescott breathed deeply. Winthrop was distracted. This was bad. Very bad. He had never seen this anger.

"Chambers said good-bye to Barksdale and Falcon Tuesday afternoon at Penn-Mar. After that Barksdale and Falcon drove to the Toledo airport. At the last minute, just as they were boarding the plane, Falcon tells Barksdale he's going to Dallas to work on a deal he has just originated. Barksdale thinks nothing of it because he's an idiot. He just says okay and gets on the flight. But Falcon never goes to Dallas. He stays in Toledo. He has his secretary make a reservation at the Dallas Hilton, and he buys a ticket on a flight for Dallas that was scheduled to leave at seven-thirty Tuesday evening. It connected with another flight in Memphis. He also makes a reservation on a flight out of Dallas that was to leave for New York at six o'clock yesterday evening. He was very careful."

"But how do you know he didn't go to Dallas?"

"The reservation at the hotel wasn't used. He never checked in."

"Maybe he stayed in another hotel. Was the ticket to Dallas used?"

"It was."

"So then he did go to Dallas, and we've got nothing."

"Not quite nothing. At seven twenty-four Falcon used his corporate AT&T card to call the National Weather Service in Washington, D.C."

"The National Weather Service?"

"Yeah, I haven't figured that out yet."

"Maybe he was concerned about thunderstorms on the way to Dallas."

"Maybe, except he made the call from a strip mall very close to Penn-Mar's headquarters. And Penn-Mar is at least a half hour drive from the Toledo airport."

"Then the plane left Toledo late."

"It pushed back from the gate at seven thirty-eight, eight minutes late. That left him eleven minutes to get from that strip mall to the plane because the call lasted three minutes. It doesn't work. He couldn't have made the plane from where he made the call in that amount of time. There wasn't another flight to Dallas until eight o'clock the next morning. But there was a New York flight at eleven-thirty that evening. That would have given him plenty of time to break into Chambers' office and then get to the airport."

"But you said he used the ticket to Dallas."

"No, I said the ticket was used. He probably sold it to someone at the airport. Which would also explain why there's no record of him renting a car or buying a ticket for another flight out of Toledo. Look at it this way. He took only a hundred dollars in cash with him to Toledo for expenses, at least according to NASO's records. So, after he waves good-bye to the idiot Phil Barksdale, Falcon goes to the counter, buys the ticket to Dallas with his corporate credit card for five hundred thirty-five dollars, and then sells it to someone at the airport for, say, three hundred. The ticket shows up as used, and he's got cash."

"Was his ticket to New York used?"

"No."

"But if he rented a car, wouldn't he have to use a credit card? Don't they require that?"

"Yes. But if you pay the bill with cash, they rip up the credit card slip. Just as they do at hotels."

Turner groaned. "Anything else?"

"Yes. There were only two people on the first leg of the flight from Toledo to New York that night, the Toledo-to-Pittsburgh flight. A Mabel Taylor and a John Richards. Phoenix talked to the stewardess about John Richards. She described Falcon to a tee. Said she could never forget a face like that. She also said that the man seemed distracted. And by the way, the second ticket, the ticket for the Dallas to New York flight, wasn't used."

The pain in Prescott's chest was subsiding. He took a long gulp of the bourbon he had fixed for himself. He felt better as they talked it through and the liquor began to pervade his system. "You're right. He's our man. Do we know where he is now?"

"He's back in New York."

"How do we know? Maybe he stayed in Pittsburgh."

"We know he's in New York. We have our contacts."

"Of course." Prescott hesitated before asking the next question. "You don't think Chambers is involved, do you? It's awfully coincidental that Falcon, if it really was Falcon, would have been able to get to those files like that. How would he even know to look, let alone know where to look?"

"I thought of that. I'm going to get Rutherford to administer a polygraph test to Devon this evening. Devon has volunteered to go to Boston. I asked him to take it, and he agreed right away. If he doesn't show up tonight, I'll have Phoenix pick him up." Winthrop's voice softened. "I don't think Devon would sabotage this project at the last minute. We've all worked too hard."

"I'm sure you're right."

"Turner, I need you to hold off disclosing that information to the court today."

"I can't do that!" Prescott became agitated again. He slammed his fist on the bar. "This is a multimillion-dollar federal court trial! This isn't exactly a traffic violation we're trying here. These federal judges don't fool around!"

Winthrop sensed the volcano beginning to erupt again. "You have to delay the trial. We have to find Falcon first. We can't disclose until we have Falcon. He can link every one of us to the whole thing. Look, Turner, it's as simple as this. We've got to stop Falcon before he can put all this together and ruin us. I mean, as it stands right now, we haven't done anything wrong. We've stretched a few Federal Reserve rules, but Wendell can take care of that problem. But once you disclose the information, Falcon could prove a conspiracy and a whole lot of other things."

"We've killed Jeremy Case and the other guy at Penn-Mar before him. Then there's Peter Lane and the little matter of Filipelli's 'drowning.' "

"No one can prove those things."

"Never assume that." Prescott was nervous again as he swallowed the rest of the bourbon. "Look, I can't put off conveying the information to the jury. At some point today, the judge is going to look at me and ask me if we have any more evidence to present. I don't have anything else."

"Can't you stall for a day or two? Ask for a continuance or something."

"I can try. But if the judge says no, I'm up shit's creek. I've got to be able to pull the trigger today!"

"If you have no choice, if you have to disclose, then do it," Granville said quietly.

The men were silent for several moments, staring at each other. It was an impossible situation.

"What do you think Falcon will do with this stuff? Do you think he's just waiting until we disclose all of the environmental crap so that he can get us on the conspiracy charge?" Prescott asked.

"I don't know. He's killed a man or is somehow connected with his death, so in a way he's in as bad a position as we are. I doubt he's chomping at the bit to deal with the authorities."

"He could send it to them anonymously."

"He could, but I'm not sure what that would accomplish for him."

"Chambers didn't tell the police it was Falcon, did he?"

"Of course not. He's not that stupid."

Prescott bit his lip. "But why the hell would Falcon steal the information? Why would he risk everything to break into Chambers' office? What's his motive?"

"I've thought a lot about that. I don't know. I thought for five million he'd sit tight and just get us Penn-Mar, but I guess I was . . ." Winthrop did not finish the sentence.

Prescott began to fix himself another drink. "Do you think he found the account and the wire transfer linking him to the purchase of Penn-Mar shares? Do you think somehow he figured out that we were setting him up for an insider-trading charge?"

"Maybe."

"Clearly he intends to use whatever he found. Otherwise he wouldn't have risked the break-in."

"You're right," Winthrop said. "So I think it's safe to say that we are very lucky that guard surprised him and that subsequently the guard was killed."

"So what do we do?"

"We sit tight, stay calm, and let Phoenix Grey go to work."

The two men gazed at each other. This was real trouble, and though they both tried to convince themselves otherwise, there was no denying it.

Sharon Cruz stared at the jury. They were bored to tears. The fat man in the second row of the jury box was falling asleep. His head bobbed farther and farther back as he fought the inevitable, until finally it lay still against the dark wood panelling of the courtroom wall. For three or four seconds the fat man sat balanced in this position with his arms folded across his chest and his mouth wide open. Then his head began to roll slowly to one side. He awoke with a start, so that he kicked the tiny Chinese woman in the pink dress sitting directly before him in the front row of the jury box. She squealed, but no one took notice.

The fat man looked around for a moment, silently pursing his lips, afraid that someone had noticed him dozing. But no one except Sharon had. He coughed twice, took on a very serious face, and attempted to concentrate on what was transpiring. It was a losing battle. Within two minutes his head was bobbing back again. This was bad, Sharon thought. Very bad.

Prescott was way off today. The steel-trap mind that had so mesmerized Sharon Cruz and the rest of the courtroom since the opening statements of the trial had suddenly taken a holiday. In contrast to his former wizardry, Prescott was now plodding and dull in his interrogation of the University of Maryland toxicologist. At times the questions were irrelevant or disconnected. And the sudden slouch and deep bags under his eyes gave him the appearance of a beaten man.

Sharon glanced at the legion of Penn-Mar attorneys. They were sitting up in their chairs, no doubt taking notice of the legendary attorney's sudden ineptitude. They smelled an opportunity, though of course they were as baffled as the rest as to what was happening.

What was wrong with him? The toxicologist was their final witness before they would rest and the defense would begin its case. Besides the truck driver, the toxicologist was Prescott's star witness. He was the man who would link the poison in the cattle's blood and the water supply to the poison in the drums marked Penn-Mar recovered from the Parker farm. And here was Prescott, stumbling, rambling, asking all the wrong questions, apparently paying more attention to a manila folder on the plaintiff's table than he was to the witness.

Come on, Turner, get it together. We are losing all the ground we gained in the last three weeks. Sharon glanced first at the Bradlees, who seemed agitated and worried, and then again at the Penn-Mar attorneys. They were suddenly sensing a settlement. A very small settlement.

"Mr. Prescott!" The judge interrupted Prescott's last question of the little man with the thick glasses.

"Yes, Your Honor?" Prescott asked.

"Is this going anywhere? The good people of the jury have real jobs, you know. At some point we need to send them back to those jobs. Preferably before Christmas."

"Yes . . . they do have real jobs. And we do need to send them back before Christmas . . ." Prescott spoke slowly, mechanically.

Sharon noticed Prescott glance at his watch. He was stalling. She looked down at hers—eleven o'clock. An hour until lunch.

Prescott stared at the toxicologist for a few moments, considering whether or not to ask another question. He decided against it and walked slowly toward the bench. He stopped directly before the judge and began in a loud, clear voice. "Judge Thomas, new evidence has just come to light that we believe will significantly impact this case. However, we have not had time—"

Judge Thomas held up a large, gnarled hand. "Are you through with this witness, Mr. Prescott?"

Sharon Cruz blinked. What the heck was Prescott talking about? Was there really new information he had not told her about, or was this simply a case of theatrics of the sort Prescott had been famous for in his younger days?

Prescott considered the question for a moment. "Yes, I am finished with Mr. Koric."

"Good."

Sharon took a deep breath. Prescott hadn't gotten through half the questions they had decided to ask Koric today. She fought the urge to stand and ask the questions herself.

"Mr. Jordan, you may cross." The judge pointed a long finger at Penn-Mar's lead attorney.

Jordan rose. "Um, at this time we have no questions for Mr. Koric, Your Honor."

Judge Thomas beamed. "Good! Now we're getting somewhere. Progress. I just love progress." He looked down at the witness. "Mr. Koric, thank you for your testimony. You may step down."

The toxicologist nodded at the judge, rose from the witness box, and returned quickly to his seat in the courtroom. He and everyone else suddenly sensed that something significant was about to occur. Even the fat man of the jury was wide awake.

The judge followed the toxicologist until he was seated, then leaned far over the bench and peered down at Prescott from eyes which seemed much too small for his gigantic head. "So, you have new evidence, do you?" The judge used a mocking tone. "You wouldn't be about to ask me for a continuance, would you?" The judge smiled a sarcastic smile. "Or at least a few days to try to put this evidence together?" The judge knew of Prescott's theatrics.

Prescott nodded. Somehow he felt like a man stringing the noose for his own hanging.

"What was that?" Judge Thomas cupped a hand to his ear. "I didn't hear you."

"Yes. We request two days to put the new evidence together."

The judge leaned back in the leather chair, which squeaked beneath his great weight. He shook his huge head slowly. "I can't do that. I've got another trial, which has already been delayed two weeks because of this one. The dockets are overflowing as it is. You know that. I'm sorry. I really am. But you had months to put together your evidence. Two days now isn't going to make a difference."

"It could make a big difference, Your Honor." Prescott took a step toward the bench so that he and Judge Thomas were very close. Prescott needed time and he needed it badly. They had to find Falcon before Prescott could bring forth the evidence in the manila folder on the plaintiff's table. There could be no doubt now that it was indeed Falcon who had broken into Chambers' office at Penn-Mar and taken the files. Falcon hadn't shown up for work at NASO yesterday or this morning. He hadn't gone back to his apartment either. And Phoenix Grey hadn't found him. "Please give us just a two-day recess. Please . . ."

Sharon stared at Prescott. He was begging. Her senior partner was begging. It couldn't be. Prescott wouldn't beg for anything.

"No!" The judge was becoming irritated. "Get on with this thing."

The Penn-Mar attorneys smiled at one another. Judge Thomas was suddenly on their side. Thomas could have easily given Prescott two days. It wasn't an outrageous request.

Prescott turned and stared at the folder on the table where Sharon Cruz sat. With Falcon running around out there in possession of all that information, to present this evidence now might be tantamount to signing his own death warrant. If the authorities could link the Sevens to the deaths of Case, Filipelli, or Peter Lane, they might all be prosecuted for murder. If they got to Phoenix Grey and were able to get Grey to talk, they would be able to prove anything they wanted.

They would never get to Phoenix. That was Rutherford's claim. He was too clever. But even if, by some stroke of dumb luck, the police or the FBI did detain Grey, they would get nothing out of him. Rutherford had assured them of that at the beginning of this thing. Over and over.

But how the hell could he be sure? He didn't know Phoenix Grey. Prescott felt perspiration pouring from his forehead.

Prescott moved to the table on which the file lay. His steps on the hardwood floor echoed heavily in the hushed courtroom. The only other sound in the room was Jordan rustling papers as he prepared to begin the defense of his client in the case of *Bradlee Company v. Penn-Mar.*

If he didn't present the evidence now, the Pleiade Project was dead. The window of opportunity was here. Now. It was wide open. But it would slam shut in seconds. Forever. Prescott stared down at Sharon Cruz. It was now or never.

Sharon gazed back at Prescott. There was a sadness to his face. The face of a condemned man. What the hell was wrong with him?

Prescott shifted his gaze to the file. Everything the Sevens had worked for hung in the balance. It was a mammoth decision. Prescott took a deep breath. No wonder he had babbled on all morning. He picked up the file and began to put it into his briefcase standing open atop the long table.

"Have you any more evidence, Mr. Prescott?" the judge asked.

Prescott did not answer as he put the file in his case.

"Mr. Prescott!"

"No." Prescott whispered the word into his bow tie.

"I couldn't hear you!"

"No!" Prescott said the word loudly over his shoulder.

"All right then." Judge Thomas seemed very satisfied. "Attorneys for Penn-Mar. Mr. Jordan, have you any motions for me to consider at this time before you present your defense?"

"Yes, Your Honor."

"Please proceed."

Prescott glanced into the crowd toward the back of the courtroom. He knew exactly where Granville was sitting. He had glanced back there a hundred times this morning, so that if this moment came, he would know exactly where to look. Prescott stared at Winthrop. Finally, Winthrop nodded solemnly.

"Wait!" Prescott pulled the file from the briefcase.

Judge Thomas glanced at Prescott for a moment and then rolled his eyes. "Approach the bench, Mr. Prescott!" Thomas could see something coming, and he wanted to head it off.

Prescott ignored Judge Thomas. He lifted the file high above his head for all in the courtroom to see. "In this file is irrefutable proof of a conspiracy at the highest level of management at Penn-Mar Chemicals!"

"Mr. Prescott!" Thomas began to scream. He rose from his chair and towered over the courtroom. "I'll hit you with contempt, so help me God, Prescott!"

"A conspiracy to cover up a pattern of illegal dumping of toxic chemicals! Illegal dumping that has been going on for years and years!" Prescott used the most dramatic voice he could find.

"Approach the bench, Mr. Prescott!" Veins in the judge's forehead bulged as he yelled above the growing din of the courtroom.

"Dumping from seventeen plants in this country and Europe, including the Wilmington plant!" Prescott turned to gaze at the audience as he shouted. He continued to hold the file aloft. "This file will destroy Penn-Mar Chemicals. The amount of damage to the environment from Penn-Mar's illegal disposal of toxic waste is staggering. When the cleanup is over and the fines have been tallied, Penn-Mar will be insolvent. Therefore, we fully intend to go after the company's secured lenders under Section 2-a3, paragraph four of the Federal Environmental Responsibility Act of 1995. People, after this is over, the company, its management, and its banks will be in ruin. I guarantee it!"

The courtroom exploded.

Chairs crashed to the floor.

Reporters streamed for the exits, pushing past the guards, who attempted in vain to keep the doors closed to maintain order. But order could not be maintained. It was too late.

The Penn-Mar attorneys, all five of them, stood and gaped at the chaos. Jordan rushed to the judge's bench, arms flailing. He screamed at the judge, but his shouting was drowned out by the bedlam of the courtroom. Judge Thomas simply stared at Jordan and shook his head. There was nothing he could do. Turner Prescott had played the courtroom perfectly. He was the master.

Winthrop watched the hysteria, arms folded across his chest. He breathed deeply. He had been hunting Falcon. Now Falcon was hunting him. He could feel it. Somehow the man had turned the tables.

"Alexis?"

"Andrew! Where are you?"

"I'm in New York."

"Where? Tell me where."

"I'm staying at a boardinghouse on 132nd Street in Manhattan. But I won't be here for long. Just tonight." He heard her committing the street number to memory.

"Isn't that Harlem?"

"Yes."

"What in God's name are you doing there?" she asked.

"Some things have happened."

"What things?"

"I can't tell you. I've got to go. I'll call you later."

"Andrew!"

Falcon cut off the call, waited for the tone, and dialed the second number.

"Hello."

"Jenny?"

"Andrew?"

"Yes."

"Are you still in Dallas?"

"No. I'm back in New York."

"Jesus, Barksdale and his secretary have been calling all morning. He really needs to speak to you."

Falcon laughed. "I'm sure he does. Listen, Jenny. I'm staying in a boardinghouse on 132nd Street in Manhattan. I'm just here for the night. But don't tell anyone. Not a soul. Do you understand?"

"Yes, but what's going on?"

"I can't tell you. I'll call you later."

"Andrew—"

He cut off the call again. Coincidences were no longer coincidence. Friends were enemies until proven otherwise. Lovers might be carrying poison. And survival was the name of the game now.

29

"Hello, pretty lady. What you like today?"

"I'd like a soft cone, please."

"And what flavor you want?"

"Vanilla."

"Sure, sure. You got it."

Cassandra Stone smiled. Here was a man who was happy with life. He dipped ice cream for a living and probably didn't make much doing it. But the money didn't matter to him. He got to work outdoors all day and put smiles on people's faces. She would like to do that someday. Just hand out smiles for a living.

"Here you go, nice lady."

"Thanks." She took the cone in exchange for several dollars.

"Have a good day. Come back and see me again, okay?"

"I will. You have a good day too." Cassandra turned away from the ice-cream stand, took a long, delicious lick from the cone, and then checked her watch. Three-thirty. Falcon was a half hour late. He had called her at five of three and told her to come here immediately, saying that if she wasn't here by three, he was leaving. So she had sprinted from the *Chronicle*'s Water Street headquarters. And now he wasn't here. After all that. Maybe he just liked to jerk people around. Some people were that way. It was a power thing. Maybe she had misjudged him.

She walked down the cement path to the water and leaned

against the retaining wall overlooking New York Harbor. Battery Park. It was a lovely nook of greenery tucked into the very southern tip of Manhattan. Trees, grass, and flowers surrounded the old fort, which had guarded the island in the very early days of the great city. The breeze coming up from Staten Island to Battery Park smelled wonderful in the afternoon sunshine. She took a deep breath. For the first time in several weeks the oppressive midsummer humidity had broken and the air was fresh and clear.

"Hello, Cassandra."

Cassandra turned. Falcon stood twenty feet away, leaning against the wall, staring down into the water. She barely recognized him with the dark blue windbreaker zipped up about his neck and the Australian outback hat pulled down over his face. His beard was rough. "Hello, yourself. Why are you always late for our appointments?" She began to move toward him.

"I have to be kind of careful all of a sudden."

"Would you mind telling me why?"

"Don't come any closer."

Cassandra stopped ten feet from where Falcon stood. "What?"

"Look out into the harbor. Don't look at me when you speak to me." He was nervous.

"Andrew, aren't you—"

"Do as I ask!"

"Okay." Cassandra turned toward the harbor and gazed at the Verrazano Bridge in the distance. She was becoming irritated at his inane demands.

Falcon rotated his body so that his back rested against the retaining wall. He folded his arms across his chest and from behind the dark glasses searched the park for any sign of someone watching them. There were only a few people in the park now. A few hours ago, during lunchtime, it had been jammed with bankers and secretaries.

He had been watching Cassandra for thirty minutes, searching for any indication that she was being followed. Or that she was working with someone. He could trust no one now. That was why he had called her by surprise and told her to come immediately—because that way she would have less time to alert anyone. Less time to set him up if she were a plant. He had seen her running from a quarter of a mile away. He had watched her fall onto the bench and clutch her chest after running all the way from the *Chronicle*. And he felt bad for putting her through all this. But he couldn't be too careful at this point.

Just like Alexis, Cassandra had come into his life suddenly, though not quite as coincidentally. Falcon had confirmed for certain that Cassandra was a *Financial Chronicle* reporter. He had spoken to her senior editor to be sure that the *Chronicle* was really running the story on him. He had gone to the midtown library to read stories of hers in the back issues of the *Chronicle*. He had found her work in the *Minneapolis Star Tribune*. He had even found her picture in the 1984 Emory University yearbook he had sent for by Federal Express. Everything she had told him checked out.

But they could have arranged for Cassandra too. They were very powerful. Falcon was convinced of that.

"I'm sorry to put you through all this, but I think I'm involved in something that's, well, pretty bad. I know that sounds crazy, but I have to be very careful."

"It would if I hadn't been watching the screens all afternoon, as you told me to do."

"What do you mean?" he asked.

"Haven't you heard?"

"No."

"There was a bombshell dropped in Baltimore federal court this morning."

Falcon smiled. "Let me guess who dropped it. Turner Prescott, of the law firm of Cleveland, Miller & Prescott."

"Yes. So you've heard?"

Falcon shook his head. "No." He pointed to the bag at his feet. "It's all in there. Have they released the information about the real estate partnerships yet? About NASO's thirteen billion dollars in bad loans and investments in Penn-Mar and the six billion dollars of bad loans to certain real estate partnerships? About how nineteen billion dollars of bad investments completely wipes out NASO's capital?"

Cassandra stared at Falcon.

"I told you not to look directly at me."

Cassandra's gaze snapped back toward the harbor.

"Has all of that information been released?"

"Yes, but how did you know?"

"And NASO is going down, isn't it?" Andrew ignored her.

"That's the rumor."

"I bet the financial markets are going nuts."

"The Dow Jones industrial average was off seven hundred points at two o'clock. It's the biggest single one-day decline in the Dow, ever. They were talking about shutting the exchange down early when I ran over here. All the other markets are off too. People are talking about a crash of the entire U.S. financial system. NASO can't cover its foreign-exchange positions, its swap obligations, or its deposits. People are trying to pull money out of NASO like there's no tomorrow. But they can't get it. NASO doesn't have any. And other institutions are rumored to be in trouble too. The ones with big exposures to NASO. It's surreal. The reporters on CNN can't even keep up with the developments. Everyone's crowded around TV sets. Nobody's working. It's incredible. The next sound you hear is going to be people hitting the pavements as they throw themselves out of windows. The President is supposed to make an announcement at four-thirty."

Andrew stared at her. "The Fed isn't stepping up to stabilize the system, is it?"

"No. CNN is screaming about how the Fed's been invisible. The rumor is that the New York Fed is crawling all over NASO, but they haven't said anything about stabilizing the bank or the market. It's crazy."

"Of course, they haven't." Falcon thought about Filipelli drowning in the Bighorn River.

"What?"

"Nothing." Falcon searched the trees of the park for anyone lurking in the shadows. "My God, they are sharp."

"Excuse me? 'They,' Andrew? Who are 'they'?"

Falcon stared at Cassandra. "A group called the Sevens."

"The Sevens."

"Yes."

"Who exactly are the Sevens?" Cassandra asked cynically.

"Forget the details at this point. Suffice it to say they are a small group of very powerful men with some very important connections."

"Are you talking about the mob?"

"No. I'm talking blue bloods."

"What?"

"Yes."

"How powerful are these people?" she asked.

"Do you think the president of the New York Federal Reserve is a powerful man? Or how about the senior partner of Winthrop, Hawkins?"

"Of course." Cassandra stopped short. She realized what he was saying. "You must be joking."

"No. I'm not."

They stood in silence for a few moments. Falcon continued to check the shadows of the park for anything suspicious. But he saw only a pair of lovers walking slowly through the trees.

"Did you check out those two names, Rutherford and Henderson?"

Cassandra nodded. "I'm still checking on Rutherford. Henderson was easy."

"What do you mean?" His eyes moved quickly from the trees to her. There was something strange in her voice.

"Henderson's my boss. He's the president and CEO of the *Chronicle.*"

Falcon stared at Cassandra Stone, trying to understand the implications of what she had just said. "What!" He swallowed hard. Death could be very close. They might be using her and she wouldn't even know it. Her line could be tapped. Worse still, she might be part of the scheme. But he dismissed that quickly. If she were, he would probably already be dead. "Will you help me, Cassandra?" Falcon glanced through the trees again.

"Of course."

"You could be putting yourself in great danger by helping me."

"Why?"

"I think these men know that I am aware of what they are trying to do."

"Why do you think that?"

Falcon turned toward Cassandra Stone. "Look at me, Cassandra."

"I thought I wasn't supposed to look at you."

"Look at me!"

"All right!" She turned.

Falcon stared at the dark brown eyes. "I have to be able to trust someone. Are you involved with them?"

"What? With whom?"

"The Sevens." It was stupid to ask her this way, but he had absolute faith in his ability to read a face. And she was still calling him Andrew, not Falcon.

"Are you out of your mind?"

It wasn't the words which convinced him that she was telling the truth. It was the eyes. She hadn't once looked away from him.

"I can't believe you would think that of me!"

"Okay, okay. I'm sorry. Will you help me?"

Cassandra stared at Falcon for a moment. "It is very dangerous, isn't it?"

"Yes."

"How did you get the information you have in that bag?" Her face showed fear.

"I broke into one of the Sevens' offices at Penn-Mar's headquarters building in Toledo, Ohio, while I was out there two days ago. I already had information that made me suspicious, and when I got into this office I sort of hit the mother lode." Falcon did not tell her about the guard.

"All of what you have told me is in there?"

"And more."

"Am I going to regret this?"

"Probably." He paused. "So, will you help me?"

"Why don't you go to the authorities?"

"Not yet. I don't have enough information, and I can't get to it. I need you to help me get that information." He scanned the park quickly.

"You can't go to your office to use the systems, can you? You're afraid they'll find you."

"No and yes to those two questions."

"What do you need?"

From his pocket Falcon removed a folded piece of paper. He moved the short distance to Cassandra, took her by the arm, and pressed the paper into her open palm. "First, I need you to get the telephone bills for the last six months for each of the men on that list I just gave you. Second, I need to know who William Rutherford is. He's the only name on that list I can't place. I need to know everything about him. I think you have his phone number, the number next to his name. Third, I need to know what the hell Lodestar Investment Management is. I need to know if a guy named Peter Lane works there or is somehow associated with it. And fourth, I need you to contact Jeremy Case's widow. Case is the man I think the Sevens paid off for the environmental information before they killed him. Call his wife and see if there is anything you can get out of her about his death. You can get the background of his death from Nexis."

"What am I supposed to get out of her?"

"I don't know. I honestly don't know. I'm grabbing at straws at this point."

"I've got to write all this down."

"No. It's all written on the paper I gave you. The four things I need you to follow up on."

"I hope I live to regret this."

"I hope you do too." Falcon searched the park one more time. "I've got to get going. I need to make a twenty-five-hundred-dollar down payment on some information."

"What?"

"Don't worry about it. Wait for my call, Cassandra. Oh, and one other thing."

"What is it?" she asked.

"One of the names on that list I just gave you is Bailey Henderson, the chief executive of your *Financial Chronicle.*"

Cassandra gaped at Falcon, not fully comprehending what he had just said, unable to believe it.

"By the way, you're going to need a napkin." Falcon nodded downward.

Cassandra looked at her right hand. "Oh, God." She had completely forgotten about the ice-cream cone. It had melted all over her wrist. She looked up again, but Falcon was already moving into the shadows of the park.

She glanced at the stand where she had purchased the cone. A man stood leaning against the structure, reading a paper. Was he really reading the paper, or was he watching her? She took a deep breath. Paranoia was already setting in.

"*¿Dónde está el gringo?*"

The swarthy man behind the counter of the bodega grinned slyly at Phoenix Grey, exposing a gold tooth. He said nothing.

"*¿Dónde está el gringo?*" Phoenix asked impatiently. He glanced at his watch: 8:20. Rutherford's female contact here in New York had been specific. Falcon would only be at the boardinghouse tonight, and then he was leaving. Moving to a new location because he was nervous sleeping in the same place more than one night. "*Por favor.*"

The Puerto Rican shopkeeper smiled triumphantly. The white man was no longer so condescending. "*Yo sé dónde el ésta.*"

Phoenix breathed deeply. So the man knew where Falcon was. Now they were making progress. "*Diga me. Por favor.*" Phoenix said "please" dutifully. He would say "please" all day to the old man to get this information.

"*¡Dinero!*"

Phoenix reached quickly into his boot for the wad of cash. The information he was about to receive could easily be false, but he had no time to argue. Time was running out. He threw a fifty-dollar bill on the counter next to the huge jar of pickles. "*Diga me!*"

The Puerto Rican's eyes grew wide. He reached for the cash, but Phoenix caught the man's wrist before his fingers could scoop up the money.

"*¡Diga me!*"

The shopkeeper could feel the strength of the white man, and he was surprised. The white man did not appear to be that strong.

"*Uno tres dos.*" The Puerto Rican jerked his head backward. "*Entre Avenidas Segunda y Tercera.*"

"*Bueno.*" Phoenix released the man's wrist.

The shopkeeper scooped up the fifty-dollar bill and stuffed it into his pocket.

"You'd better be sure."

The man gestured obscenely at Grey, who did not see the motion. He was already moving out the creaky door of the small shop.

Though he wanted to, Phoenix did not run as he moved east along the south side of 132nd Street. He walked slowly and carefully. This was a Puerto Rican stronghold of New York City, and whites were not welcome here. He did not want to attract any more attention than he had to. Phoenix had no doubt that he could handle four or five at a time—unless they had weapons. There was no defense in the world against an AK-47 or Black Rhinos, no defense at all against the firepower that the gangs and the drug merchants carried these days in this part of New York City.

Grey crossed Fifth Avenue. The question had been where on 132nd. Falcon hadn't been specific, and the woman had not wanted to push, for fear of causing suspicion. So Phoenix had had to search for Falcon. He had been to four bodegas, where no one would help him, before he found the swarthy shopkeeper. The others all knew where Falcon was staying, as surely as they knew their own names, because Falcon would stick out like a sore thumb in this neighborhood. But they wouldn't help. Not even at the offer of money. Because you didn't rat on people in this hell. By ratting, you aligned yourself with one side. If your side lost, you paid dearly, because word always got back. It was just better to say you didn't know.

But there was always one who would risk life and limb for the almighty dollar. Always one. Phoenix smiled. People were so weak.

The building was nothing but a shell, an abandoned brick carcass. But it provided perfect cover to observe the boardinghouse directly across the street. Falcon kicked a pile of rusty syringes across the floor. He had time. The crackheads wouldn't be moving in for another two hours or so.

Falcon turned and checked 132nd Street from the glassless basement window. Nothing. Just a few children playing noisily with a broken toy wagon. The daylight was beginning to fade as the sun set. Falcon checked the street again. Still nothing. He glanced at his watch: 8:35. If the Sevens were using Jenny or Alexis, or worse, if Jenny or Alexis were working for the Sevens, someone would be by soon to look for him. He was certain of that.

He glanced back against the far wall and noticed the outline of a huge rat crawling along the base of the brick. This neighborhood was active at night.

The other white man moved slowly but with purpose down 132nd Street toward the boardinghouse. He passed the children, who stopped to look at him. They so rarely saw a white person. The man did not acknowledge them. Falcon's eyes narrowed. This man was coming for him. He sensed it immediately. The man quickly climbed the four cement steps leading to the boardinghouse and disappeared inside. Falcon shifted his attention to a window on the third floor. He waited for what seemed like forever, but he knew that it was only a matter of minutes. Finally, a woman leaned out of the window and waved a bandanna.

Falcon glanced back at the front door of the boardinghouse. The man reappeared almost instantly and took a long look around the street. Falcon moved back behind the edge of the window, his heart pounding. With one eye, he watched the man from around the edge of the window. After a few moments the man shrugged his shoulders and began to walk back the way he had come.

The prostitute had thought at first that Falcon wanted a "roll" this morning when he offered her the hundred dollars. She laughed when all he asked was for her to watch his door that evening and then wave the bandanna out the window if anyone came to or tried to enter his room. She had taken the money, but Falcon was afraid she wouldn't come through.

There were only two people in the world he had told of his whereabouts, only two people who could have given the information to the man who had come to his room: Jenny and Alexis. At least one of them was working with the Sevens. There was no doubt now. Falcon breathed hard and allowed his heart rate to return to normal—or at least as normal as could be expected under the circumstances.

Falcon leaned out of the burned-out building's window and looked up the street. The man was gone. He waited another five minutes just to be certain, then picked up the bag containing the four files, moved out of an open back door, walked across a vacant lot, and started off down the sidewalk in the opposite direction from which the man had gone.

Darkness had almost befallen the city, and there were no working streetlights in this part of town. They had all been shot out. The street was dark and intimidating. He wanted to get out of here quickly. Somehow the sight of the man they had sent had unnerved him. The man was not physically imposing, but there was something evil about the way he moved. As if he had been moving in the shadows all of his life.

Falcon turned the corner at 132nd Street and Second Avenue and saw the man immediately. He stopped short. The man stood in the doorway of a pizzeria, chewing on a slice. Recognition was immediate. Falcon saw it in the man's eyes. The man had probably been given photographs. Those pictures could have come from myriad sources, including Jenny or Alexis. They gazed at each other momentarily. Falcon bolted first, across Second Avenue, through the traffic. Then the man dropped his pizza on the filthy sidewalk and sprinted after him.

A city bus swerved to avoid Falcon. The driver leaned on his horn, but the warning was not enough for a red Ford next to the bus. Falcon heard the impact but did not see it. He tucked the bag tightly in the crook of his arm like a football, dodged a cab, and crossed the last two lanes of the avenue. He glanced over his shoulder and in the headlights of the cars could see the man in pursuit.

The man might not be physically imposing, but they wouldn't have sent an amateur. He would fight the man if it came to that, if he were caught, but he did not expect to survive a struggle.

A thought rushed into Falcon's brain as he tore up the sidewalk. The man probably had a gun. Immediately, he began to swerve from side to side to make himself a more elusive target, just in case. It cost him valuable time, but it might save his life. He wondered how bullets would feel ripping through his body. He had seen the shotgun pellets burst out the back of Froworth's body. He had seen the damage a shotgun shell could do. But what would a bullet feel like when it hit? He put his head down and ran faster than he ever had in his life.

At 134th Street, Falcon moved back out into the traffic. He could hear the man breathing heavily in pursuit. The man couldn't be more than twenty feet behind. When would the bullets hit? Maybe they already had but he didn't realize.

The car horns screamed. He waved frantically for a cab as he ran, but there was no way any halfway savvy New York cabbie was going to pick him up. He was being chased. There was only one chance now.

Falcon bolted through the gleam of the headlights to the west side of Second Avenue, aware that he had been able to put some distance between himself and his pursuer by zigzagging through traffic. To the shouts of *Andale! Andale!* from the onlookers he leaped over the curve and raced west on 135th Street. Adrenaline pumped through Falcon's body. He sprinted across Third Avenue. Lexington was next. If he could only last.

Phoenix Grey churned after Falcon. He was in excellent physical condition, but he was not fast afoot. Never had been. And Falcon was faster than Phoenix had expected. Phoenix felt the gun in the shoulder holster beneath his light jacket banging against his chest. That was only the last resort, per Rutherford's orders. But if he had to shoot to bring Falcon down, he would. He wasn't going to let him escape. That message from Rutherford had been loud and clear.

Another half a block, if he remembered his subway map correctly. Falcon sucked in air. 135th and Lex. There was a subway station entrance at that corner. Thank God for his memory.

He tried to place the man's face as he ran. He had seen it somewhere before. He knew it. But where? And then he remembered. God! The Portland Hotel. The first time he had called Martinez. They had been watching him since the outset. He would never worry about being paranoid again.

Grey felt his lungs beginning to burn. The prey always had the advantage in these situations. It was do or die for the quarry. For the predator it simply meant going hungry. He felt the heavy gun against his chest. It was almost time to bring it out. He was perhaps twenty-five feet behind Falcon. By the time he could remove the gun from the holster and aim, Falcon would have gained another twenty-five to fifty feet. Phoenix was extremely accurate at seventy-five feet. At fifty feet he didn't miss.

Falcon was gaining ground. There was no choice now. Phoenix stopped, whipped the gun from the holster, and aimed. But as he pulled the trigger of the .38-caliber pistol, Falcon disappeared.

Falcon heard the report of the gun as he ducked down into the subway station. He heard the bullet ricochet off the yellow metal banister and carom away with a scream. Falcon leaped three of the grimy stairs at a time, narrowly avoiding several people coming up the steps.

Grey bolted forward, stuffing the piece back in its holster as he moved. He reached the stairway and scrambled down to the platform, knocking over an elderly black lady wearing a floral-patterned hat as he descended. The woman cursed him, but Phoenix paid no attention. He was losing vital seconds and the prey was escaping. He could feel it.

Grey jumped the last four steps to the platform level and hurdled the turnstile. He reached the edge of the tracks. There was no train in the station and only ten or fifteen people milling about, waiting for the next train. Phoenix looked to the left and right, but Falcon was not on this side of the platform. He ran the length of the platform, staring at the downtown side in case Falcon had hopped down onto the tracks, jumped the live rail, and pulled himself up on the opposite side. But he wasn't there. Phoenix could sense Falcon slipping away. These were vital seconds. Where could he have gone? Phoenix Grey began to panic. What was he going to tell Rutherford? He could lie, but then he would have to get to Falcon before Rutherford did.

Nothing. Falcon was not in the station. Grey trotted to the other end of the platform. There was nowhere else to hide. He must have made it to the other side, pulled himself up onto the other platform, and headed up the stairs back to the street. He would be long gone by now.

Phoenix turned. Three young black men stood just ten feet away. Despite the heat, each man wore a wool ski hat and a sweatshirt, as well as a nasty expression.

"We ain't too happy about the way you treated Mrs. Jones on the stairway there." The one in the middle, the big one, spoke in a heavy ghetto accent. He was huge, over six feet four and well over two hundred pounds.

"Well, I'll just go apologize to her." Phoenix checked the waists of their pants. No guns. Perhaps he wouldn't have to use his.

"Oh, man, white boy, what's up with that? It's a little late for apologies." The man to the right of the huge man spoke. He had a squeaky voice, but a cool delivery.

"Gentlemen, I suggest you leave before you get hurt."

The three men laughed and gave each other high fives, then turned suddenly serious.

The huge man made his move. Instantly, Phoenix came down with a devastating chop kick directly to his attacker's left knee. The man doubled over, and as he did, Phoenix reached for his neck. Taking time to find the softest flesh, he grabbed the man's windpipe and ripped. It was a perfect counter. Part of the throat came away in his hand. The huge man went down hard on the cement, gasping for air, which now had no way of getting to his lungs. Phoenix held the bleeding flesh before the other two men's faces.

Without a word, they turned and bolted for the stairs.

Falcon pulled himself up onto the platform at 126th Street and lay on the cement. He was sweating heavily, not only from the heat, fear, and physical exertion, but also because he was slightly claustrophobic. It had taken all of his intestinal fortitude to run through the tunnel. But he'd done it because there was no other choice.

A kind-faced Hispanic woman knelt down beside him. "Are you okay?"

Falcon smiled up at her, still breathing hard. "Yes, thank you." He pulled himself up to one elbow, took her hand, and kissed it, then lay back down on the cement.

So at least one of them was feeding the Sevens information. Jenny or Alexis. It couldn't be Cassandra. He hadn't told her where he was staying. And he hadn't been followed from Battery Park. He had made certain of that. It was Alexis or Jenny. One of them had sacrificed her soul. And for what? Money? Revenge? Falcon rolled to his stomach and then made it to his knees. He had to get going. Phoenix Grey might come running out of that tunnel any second. He shook his head. It didn't matter why one of them had done it now, only that she had. And it was imperative to find out which one.

30

Falcon lay on the bed and scanned the crisp copy of the *Financial Chronicle* he had just purchased downstairs in the lobby of the Princeton Hyatt Hotel. On the nightstand were unopened editions of the day's *New York Times* and *Wall Street Journal.* The headlines were all the same, screaming about Penn-Mar, NASO, and the imminent collapse of the country's financial system. He read the *Chronicle* first. He would pore over the others afterward.

Falcon was about to begin the article concerning yesterday's twelve-hundred-point crash of the Dow Jones industrial average when another headline caught his eye: PRESIDENT LINKED TO INSIDER ACTIVITY AT LODESTAR.

Falcon froze. "What the . . . ?" His focus moved immediately to the text of the article.

By R. Walker Davis
Staff Writer for the *Financial Chronicle*

Washington, D.C., August 16.—Early this morning, officials of the Securities and Exchange Commission, the Department of Justice, and the Federal Bureau of Investigation stormed the Washington offices of Lodestar Investment Management. Lodestar is a high-profile investment-management firm known primarily for working with some of Washington's most influential figures, including the President himself.

Details remain sketchy, but apparently the authorities were tipped off that Lodestar was guilty of insider-trading violations related to the July takeover battle for Penn-Mar Chemicals, ultimately won by Veens & Company, a New York investment firm. Records indicate that Lodestar purchased 645 shares of Penn-Mar at $31 a share on July 2, little more than a week before Veens announced its tender offer for Penn-Mar at $75. Veens' final tender price was $85 a share, netting a one-month profit of approximately $35,000 on a $20,000 investment. In addition, the firm bought call options on Penn-Mar stock, which netted another $143,000 profit. Records also indicate that these trades were made on behalf of and for the account of the President of the United States, Buford Warren.

The early-morning raid, carried out by more than 100 officers of the three government agencies, apparently yielded significant information, including a confidential internal memorandum that indicated the President had personally instructed Victor Farinholt to make the investment in Penn-Mar.

Through his press secretary, Peter Arland, the President has officially denied direct contact with Farinholt or any other employee of Lodestar since depositing money in a blind trust with the firm four years ago. The President has scheduled a press conference for today at 4:00 P.M. EST to discuss the situation. The press conference will be carried live by all four major networks, CNN, and Bloomberg Television News.

A senior White House official, speaking on the condition of anonymity, admitted that the situation could prove extremely damaging unless addressed immediately. Unfortunately, the President has been completely distracted by the national banking crisis brought about by the NASO–Penn-Mar debacle and the continuing Wall Street meltdown, the source said.

Falcon allowed the *Chronicle* to fall to his chest. Lodestar Investment Management. The fourth file. He gazed at the gray bag sitting on a table next to the remnants of the room service and laughed. Incredible. It was all about taking down an administration. Penn-Mar, NASO, the Sevens, the real estate, and Lodestar. All of it. It was about seven Yankee conservatives destroying one southern liberal. About sending Buford Warren back to Alabama in disgrace. About restoring their people to power. And they were succeeding. The bastards were winning.

Falcon picked up the paper from his chest and skimmed the article about the free fall of the Dow and the collapse of the banking system. Not only did the article relate the events of the previous day, but it also outlined, in detail, the failures of the President with respect to the situation—a front-page editorial within a news story. The article screamed that by appointing the autocratic Carter Filipelli to head the Federal Reserve, the President had actually created a situation whereby this kind of meltdown could occur. Filipelli had taken away the power of the Federal Reserve field examiners to act independently. Filipelli and his personal staff had been so dictatorial over the past four years that the people in the field, the people monitoring the national banking system on a day-to-day basis, had become confused about how much flexibility they were to give to the member institutions and about their role in safeguarding the system. As a result, abuses had occurred. Testimonials to this effect were given by high-ranking Republicans on the Senate and House banking committees. It had been a time bomb waiting to explode, but they had been powerless to do anything because of their minority status on the committees.

Now the President wasn't reacting quickly enough to the crisis situation. He was focusing on the revelation of his involvement with Lodestar and his long relationship with Victor Farinholt, on the insider-trading charge, which was rumored to be imminent, and on the Lane Memo, as it was being called. The President was completely preoccupied with personal damage control, and the rest of his staff was in a state of paralysis. It was an administration in chaos. And the nation's economy was on the brink of collapse.

Falcon grabbed the *Wall Street Journal*, skimmed it, then did the same with the *New York Times*. They too were full of stories about Penn-Mar, the lawsuit, and the surprising revelations yesterday in Baltimore's federal courtroom; about NASO's insolvency and the cracks forming in the financial system; about how banks other than NASO were experiencing funding problems in the overnight market, particularly those that had joined NASO in lending to Penn-Mar; about long lines at bank doors across the country; and about the Dow's crash. But there were only small stories about the Lodestar raid and no mention of a confidential memorandum linking the President to insider trading. The raid had taken place at two o'clock that morning, much too late for either the *Journal* or the *Times* to include it as a major story. But the *Chronicle* had conveniently waited. Because Bailey Henderson, president and CEO of the *Chronicle*, knew exactly what was going to occur. The Sevens had set up the *Chronicle* as a vehicle of manipulation. No wonder it sold at such a low price. The Sevens didn't care about profits. They wanted market share.

It was one of the primary rules of war for any aggressor: Control the press. Manage the flow of information to the people. Tell them what you want them to hear.

The *Financial Chronicle* had broken the story on the Lodestar raid because the Sevens controlled the paper. They were using the *Chronicle* not only to manipulate its readership of financial types, which as a percentage of the total population was small, but also to control every other newspaper in the country. Senior people at the other publications would see the *Chronicle* breaking story after story and scream for their people to dig deeper and faster. They would devote entire staffs to these stories and encourage their people to rely on fewer independent confirmations just so they could break a piece of this situation, which was becoming the story of the decade. It would be a feeding frenzy, and Buford Warren was the prey.

Falcon flipped on CNN. A reporter stood before the Washington office building that was home to Lodestar. CNN had confirmed the existence of the Lane Memo and that it indeed, according to an anonymous source, appeared to be very damaging to the President. Lane's fingerprints were on the original found at Lodestar, and it was a file on the firm's central computer. And then suddenly the network flashed back to New York, to a scene in front of the NASO headquarters on Park Avenue. Armed guards stood before the doorway to the lobby, allowing no one but badged officials to enter. A huge mob milled around the building. Suddenly, another squad of police officers, dressed in riot gear, began to pour out of a bus that had just pulled up before the building.

Falcon shook his head. President Buford Warren was in trouble. The banking system was crumbling, and he had an insider-trading sign the size of Texas hanging from his neck. Falcon glanced at the bag again. It was a bogus sign, but only he and a few other people knew that.

Falcon stared at the television. Unless something drastic happened, Buford Warren's political career was over. As Falcon lay secluded on the hotel bed, hiding from the men who were perpetrating the heinous scheme, he sensed it slipping away from Warren. The press was going to have a field day with this one. Here was a President the people had finally come to trust, a man of the middle class, an outsider. And now it became suddenly obvious that he was no different from the rest of the politicians, worse in fact, because he had conned everyone into swallowing his down-home act. And now it turned out he was slicker than any of them—making huge profits on inside information with no regard for the fact that the national banking system was being destroyed in the process. The President was going to crash and burn in a huge ball of flames—unless Falcon did something about it. Falcon held the key in that gray bag sitting on the table.

Falcon checked his watch. Ten-fifteen. It was time. He leaned toward the night table, picked up the telephone, and dialed the number.

"Funds Transfer."

"Eddie!"

"Mr. Falcon?" Martinez said the words in a low voice.

"Yes. Have you found anything yet?"

Martinez paused. Falcon could hear his heavy breathing despite the voices yelling in the background.

"Eddie!"

"Yeah, yeah. I . . . I found everything," he whispered.

Falcon's heart began to pump quickly. "What did you find?"

"I found the wires."

Falcon could barely hear Martinez over the din in the background. "You've got to speak up. I can barely hear you. What the hell is going on there?"

"It's crazy. The place is going nuts. Everybody and his mother is trying to get money outta here. I can't stay on too long."

"What did you find?" Falcon asked.

"A thousand wires."

"A thousand?"

"Yeah, it's unbelievable. They came in starting all the way back in January. The last one came in late June. A thousand of them. Can you believe that?"

"But how do you know what you found?"

"I found a billion dollars, just like you said I would. Exactly a billion. Every one of the wires is for some amount of dollars and seven cents. A thousand wires and they all add up to a billion bucks. Remember you said to look for Penn-Mar or sevens or something? That's how I found them. They all ended in seven cents. All the transfers. I added them up, all the transfers that end in seven cents, and they came to a billion even. Remember how you told me?"

"I remember." Falcon was shaking. It was more than he could have imagined Martinez would find. A woman shrieked in the background of the Funds Transfer Group. "Eddie!" Falcon spoke loudly to keep Martinez's attention.

"What?" Martinez's voice was cracking. He was nervous as hell, worried that he had somehow put his entire family in harm's way. Falcon sensed it over the phone.

"It's all right, Eddie, I swear to you it is."

"I hope so, Mr. Falcon. I sure as hell hope so."

"Eddie, did you track the wires?"

"Yeah. They came from lots of different places, but they all originated from one place. Some investment bank named Winthrop, Hawkins."

Falcon almost dropped the phone. "You've done great, Eddie. I need you to print out all that information."

"I already have. It's locked in my drawer."

"Beautiful. I'll pick it up from you tomorrow."

"Where?"

"You tell me."

"Brooklyn Heights. On the Promenade at noon. You gonna have my money, Mr. Falcon?"

"Twenty-five hundred, Eddie. Twenty-five hundred. Go back to work, Eddie. I'll see you tomorrow at noon—sharp."

"Oh, Mr. Falcon."

"Yeah?"

"There's something else."

"What's that, Eddie?"

"I found another wire." Martinez's tone was strange.

"What?"

"Well, there's a wire out of an account of yours. The wire was dated July ninth. It's in the amount of thirty thousand dollars. It goes to some account of yours at Citibank. The notation on the advice says 'for Penn-Mar shares.' "

Falcon caught his breath. July ninth was the day before Veens had announced the initial tender for Penn-Mar. So they were going to try to pin an insider-trading charge on him too. These bastards were unbelievable. They had even found the squirrel account at Citibank. He swore at himself for not closing it. "What's the number of the NASO account?"

Martinez read it.

Falcon laughed to himself. It was not the account he had been given upon coming to work at NASO. It was another account. One he was obviously not supposed to know about, at least not until the trial. "Thanks for the information, Eddie." Falcon hesitated. "It's not what you think, Eddie."

"I don't think, Mr. Falcon. I don't think at all. I just want my twenty-five hundred. I'll see you tomorrow."

The phone clicked in his ear. Falcon hung up, then quickly picked up the phone again and dialed another number. It was time to start getting some answers.

"Hello." The voice was soft.

"It's Andrew."

"My God, where are you?" The woman was suddenly excited.

"It's better if I don't tell you. You'll be safer that way."

"Safer? Tell me what's going on. Please tell me. Tell me where you are. I want to help you. Please!"

"I can't tell you. Meet me tomorrow morning."

"Where?"

"On the New Jersey Transit train."

"I don't understand. Why can't we just meet in New York someplace? Why the train?"

"Please, just do as I ask." Falcon allowed irritation to creep into his voice.

"Fine. I'm sorry. I'm just worried about you. You know that. I just love you so much. I want to help. I want you to tell me what's wrong. My God, the papers are all full of this Penn-Mar thing. Is that what this is all about?"

"Yes."

"Oh, God. Where will I meet you?"

"There will be a northbound train arriving at Linden from Trenton at 8:06 tomorrow morning. Get on that train at Linden. Get on the first car—the car closest to the locomotive. I'll meet you there. Do you understand?"

"Yes, of course. Linden. The northbound New Jersey Transit train. Eight minutes after six. The first car. I'll be there."

"Good, I'll see you then."

"I love you," she said.

"Me too." Falcon replaced the telephone and stared at the television. So Granville was going to take him down with an insider-trading charge. Then there would be a very public trial and then prison, and a little influence money to the judge just before sentencing to ensure a very long and brutal prison sentence. So Granville wanted to play rough. Well, he had no problem with that. Because Granville didn't know what a real street fight was.

"PG, it's Rutherford."

"Yeah." Phoenix Grey stared out the window of his Parker Meridian Hotel room. He needed to act tough. As though nothing was wrong. As though he had not missed Falcon yesterday evening. He had simply told Rutherford this morning that Falcon had not shown up at the boardinghouse last night.

"How did it go today?"

"Went off without a hitch. I stayed until the cops got there. Boreman will be reported dead tomorrow. The car was destroyed. But the cops found the license plate. I made certain of that."

"And the body?"

"Burned well beyond recognition."

"How can you be sure?"

Grey laughed. "I burned it before I even put it in the car."

"Of course you did." Rutherford paused. "We have new information."

Grey peeled a banana. The strong odor reached his nostrils immediately. "What's that?"

"Falcon is going to meet our contact on a New Jersey Transit train from Trenton tomorrow."

"How do we know this?" Phoenix stuffed the banana in his mouth.

"She told me."

"Of course, the woman." He struggled with the words through the banana.

"What's that supposed to mean?"

Phoenix swallowed the last of the fruit. "Her information wasn't very accurate last night."

"My friend says it was very accurate."

Phoenix detected an iciness to Rutherford's tone. "Your friend?"

"Yes. My friend says there was an ugly scene in the 135th Street subway station. Something about a young black man having his trachea removed."

"Your friend said that, huh?" Phoenix Grey's voice dropped to a whisper.

"Yes. Don't miss this time, Phoenix. Or it will be your last miss."

"Yes, sir."

"And don't ever lie to me again."

"Yes, sir."

"Falcon will be on a train that originates in Trenton, New Jersey, and terminates in New York City, though I have no idea where he will actually board the train. He has asked our contact to meet him in Linden. She is to board the first car of the train that arrives in Linden at 8:06. You know what to do."

"Yes, sir." Phoenix Grey sniffed his fingers. They reeked of banana. "Why would he want to meet her? Shouldn't he be a little suspicious of her?"

"He should. But maybe he thinks he can use her against us. Maybe he hasn't had time to be suspicious. I don't know. But we have nothing to lose by showing up tomorrow."

"No, we don't. Nothing at all to lose."

"Phoenix, what did you end up doing with our friend, Mr. Prausch?"

Phoenix smiled as he sipped a Pepsi. "He changed his name to Boreman and drove a car off a cliff."

The President moved quickly past his aides lining the short passageway into the White House press room. He stepped confidently up onto the platform and smiled an authoritative smile at the assembled press corps as he moved behind the podium bearing the Presidential seal. The spotlights were incredibly hot, but he did not show discomfort. That would have been suicide.

"Good evening. I'm sorry we're running a little late, but things have been very hectic today, as you might imagine." He spoke deliberately. "I will read a short statement and then take a few questions." He paused to clear his throat. "Let me first say that the nation's banking system is sound. Officials of the New York Federal Reserve have been meeting all day with senior management of the National Southern Bank. While that institution did experience some liquidity problems, we believe that depositors will be made whole."

"When will it open again?" Someone screamed the question from the back.

The President shielded his eyes from the bright lights to determine who had been so brazen as to interrupt him in the middle of a prepared text. But he could not tell. He made a mental note to find out later from his aides so that he could have the reporter permanently barred from these briefings. It was probably the jerk from the *Chronicle*. "We believe it will reopen by the end of next week."

A murmur raced through the room. Not until the end of next

week—and from the sound of it the President wasn't even certain on that point.

The President heard the murmur and the scribbling on notepads. "Look, NASO is a huge entity. Opening prematurely might be devastating. . . ." Buford Warren tried to swallow the word. It was a stupid mistake.

"Devastating!" the same voice screamed from the back. "What does that mean? Devastating?" Other voices began to chime in, yelling questions at him in rapid fire.

"Hold it!" The President held up his arms and glanced into the television cameras nervously. How could he have been so stupid as to use the word *devastating?* "Just hold it! I will finish my prepared speech or I will take no questions."

The press corps quieted slowly.

"The banking system is strong, and the Federal Reserve is in complete control of the situation. Enough said on that point. Second, I want to say that I am in no way connected to the events, to the raid on Lodestar Investment Management in the early hours of this morning. I have been acquainted with Victor Farinholt for many years, but I am not a close contact of his. My wife and I did invest money with his firm, in a blind trust, as have several Supreme Court justices as well as many Congresspeople, both Democrats and Republicans." Warren smiled after finishing the last sentence, as if it automatically cleared him of any wrongdoing. "It is preposterous to think that I would try to influence anyone illegally or use any information to profit illegally." Warren did not use the phrase "insider trading." His aides had coached him well on this point. "That is all I have to say."

The reporters began to scream, "Mr. President!" immediately.

Buford Warren glanced around the room through the wildly waving arms until he found Cynthia Drewes, White House correspondent for *USA Today.* Never had she written a harsh word in any of her columns about him or his politics. They had an understanding. She would set the tone. He smiled and pointed at her. The rest of the press corps quieted and sat as she rose.

Cynthia wasted no time. "Mr. President, please comment on the existence of the Lane Memo and the fact that it supposedly links you directly to insider trading." Her voice was tough and determined.

The President stared at her and swallowed. The room was suddenly still—and frightening. It had always been a friendly place until today, a place where he could manipulate and charm. Not today. "I have no knowledge of this memo and really can't comment." He scanned the room and pointed immediately at Richard Ellet, columnist for the *Washington Post* and another heretofore friendly face.

Ellet rose slowly. "Mr. President, I'd like to follow up on Ms. Drewes's question. Please tell us what you know about the Lane Memo, which supposedly discussed your call to Peter Lane requesting him to put you into Penn-Mar only days before the takeover." Ellet's voice was confrontational, as if he were irritated at the President for ducking Cynthia Drewes.

"It's a matter under investigation. I can't comment." Buford Warren glanced helplessly at his aides, who were drawing their fingers across their necks and mouthing the words "cut it" over and over.

"Investigation?" Franklin Brenner, a senior staff reporter for the *Wall Street Journal*, exploded from his seat. "What investigation? Has a special prosecutor been named yet?"

"No, no, no!" The President waved his arms frantically across his face.

But it was too late. The room became chaotic as reporters, aides, camera crews, and the President began screaming hysterically. The words *investigation* and *special prosecutor* had cut the body wide open. The feeding frenzy had begun. And the *Financial Chronicle* reporter, sitting in the very back of the room—a position he had been relegated to since the early days of this administration—began to smile broadly. The President had always treated him like garbage because of his tough questions. Now the President was getting his.

Wendell Smith stared at the other members of the FOMC. It was almost midnight, and most of them had arrived in Washington less than an hour ago on hastily arranged charter flights. National Airport had remained open beyond its normal closing time to allow these flights to land. The faces were grim. Except for Harold Butler's. He was smiling. Smith smiled back.

Butler leaned forward. He was going to knock that damn grin off of Smith's face and have a wonderful time doing it. "Well, well. So, Wendell. Wallace Boreman is a prudent man." His tone mocked Smith. "So prudent he drove himself off a cliff this afternoon rather than have to face the music about NASO. Or maybe you didn't catch that on the late news."

The other members of the FOMC stared at Wendell Smith. They had trusted him. They had been burned.

"I saw it," Smith said quietly. "I apologize to each of you. I have made a great mistake."

"Apologies are cheap, Wendell. I want your resignation," Butler hissed. Several of the other members began to nod. "And I want an investigation into your friendship with Wallace Boreman by a Senate committee. I think there's more here than meets the eye." More of the members nodded.

Smith glanced down. "I see. Well, that might be a little premature, Harold."

"I don't think so." Butler's voice reigned supreme.

Smith rose from his seat and walked slowly to the huge fireplace. He stood beneath the mammoth eagle and gazed out at the men and women seated around the table. "Ladies and gentlemen, I believe you are aware that Warner James, chairman and CEO of J. P. Morgan & Company, is a close friend of mine. If you'll recall, I was on the board of Morgan before I joined the Fed. I have been speaking to Warner off and on all day. In principle, he has agreed that Morgan will acquire NASO and that it will pay a very fair price for the shares, given NASO's difficult situation. Investment bankers at Winthrop, Hawkins & Company will handle the transaction. Depositors will be made whole, and Morgan will honor all of NASO's foreign exchange and derivatives contracts. Pending your approval tonight, an announcement will be made early tomorrow morning with respect to this development. The markets will respond very positively. I expect the Dow to regain most of the losses it has sustained in the past two days." Smith smiled confidently at the rest of the FOMC. "Warner would like to know that I will remain in my position. He wants assurances. It is a huge transaction, even for Morgan. He is concerned that I will resign." Smith raised an eyebrow at the other members as a warning. If they took any action against him at all, he would crater the Morgan deal.

The members of the FOMC stared at Wendell Smith as he stood beneath the great eagle, as calm as ever. Because of a high-level friendship, he would be able to calm markets around the globe. With one phone call he had saved the financial system, something Carter Filipelli would never have been able to do. Smith had erred by not being diligent enough with Wallace Boreman, but he had atoned for his mistake by calling in a favor from Warner James, chairman of the most powerful bank in the world. They understood his subtle warning and would not support Butler's call for Smith's resignation.

President Flynn spoke. "I think you should continue to proceed on this track."

The others nodded.

Sheep, Smith thought. Nothing but sheep. He inhaled deeply. It had been as easy as Granville Winthrop had said it would be.

Harold Butler slouched down in his chair. Filipelli had been a fool to think that he and the President could do anything to fight the blue-blooded mafia. They were more powerful than any clan on earth. And they were profiting from all of this somehow. He was sure of that, though Butler didn't know how and didn't have the strength left to find out. He stared at the huge eagle above Wendell Smith's head. It seemed to be mocking him.

31

Phoenix Grey stepped onto the second car of the New Jersey Transit train as it waited at the Jersey Avenue station, four stops south of Linden. He was disguised so that Falcon would not recognize him. He wore shoulder pads beneath the windbreaker to make his upper body appear more developed, and his hair was shoulder length beneath the Los Angeles Dodgers baseball cap. A beard and mustache completed the transformation.

The car was crowded with a group of Trentonians trekking to New York City for the day. Most of the seats were occupied, and those that weren't were filled with rain slickers and umbrellas. The forecast was for rain, but that didn't dampen the mood of the group from Trenton. They were boisterous, ready for a day in the Big Apple.

Phoenix Grey selected one of the few unoccupied seats, a window seat near the middle doors of the car. As he squeezed past a fat woman on the aisle, he pulled the baseball cap down well over his eyes. He wanted no part of this celebration.

A bum sat in the last seat of the car and observed as the lone passenger boarded the train at Jersey Avenue and moved into the window seat next to the fat woman. The bum's hair was longer than Phoenix Grey's, and it was scraggly and stringy. The bum also wore a hat, but it was old and tattered, as was the tan raincoat. The bum's face was so covered with dirt that the whites of his bloodshot eyes stood out strangely. And he smelled, terribly, of the street.

The train pulled away from the Jersey Avenue station, picked up speed briefly, and then slowed as it pulled into the New Brunswick station. The two stations were closer together than most on the Northeast Corridor line. As the train slowed to a stop, the bum picked up his bag of aluminum cans and moved slowly out the end door near where he had been sitting. He was the only passenger to detrain at New Brunswick. As he stood on the platform, he could still hear the revelers from Trenton inside the car.

The bum had not recognized the man initially—the disguise was very good, as he knew it would be. But he had recognized the walk, something the man could not hide. It was the stooped and furtive walk of a man who had lived his life in the shadows, a man who had lived his life trying not to be noticed.

Falcon watched the train pull away from the station, heading on toward Linden, where the woman was supposed to be waiting. She probably wasn't there. She had probably passed the job off to the assassin. The urge to jog alongside the train and bang on the window next to where Phoenix Grey sat was almost overwhelming, but that, Falcon knew, would be stupid. Grey was a desperate and resourceful man. He might find a way to detrain even as it was picking up speed.

The bag of aluminum cans fell open as Falcon threw it against a trash receptacle on the platform. He looked up and gazed at the train as it disappeared into the distance. So it was her. The whole thing had been an act. He should have known.

Jenny walked slowly across the mall's huge parking lot, loaded down with packages. She counted rows of cars as she walked and finally located her aging Toyota Camry. She placed the packages on the car's hood, then removed the keys from her pocketbook and slid the proper one into the lock. As she was about to turn the lock, out of corner of her eye, she noticed the indigent standing on the other side of the Camry, staring at her.

"Oh, my God!" She brought her hands to her face and moved back quickly against the door of the car next to hers. She stared back at the man for several seconds, transfixed by the eyes, which seemed somehow familiar. They bored into her. Her heart raced but she could not move. Finally, she grabbed the keys from the lock and, without bothering to scoop up her packages, turned and ran for the mall.

Falcon walked calmly to the rental car parked just a few feet away. The engine idled as he climbed behind the wheel. He had seen in her eyes what he needed to see.

The view of lower Manhattan was beautiful from the Promenade, despite the ugly weather. But Falcon did not care about views now. He pulled Cassandra Stone's home telephone number from his pants pocket, picked up the pay phone, and dialed.

"Hello."

"Cassandra?"

"Andrew?"

"Yes."

"Did you get the information from Martinez?" she asked.

"Everything. It's all here. He did a good job. I know he thinks he's involved with something terrible."

"He is."

"Well, he's out of it now. I paid him twenty-five hundred dollars." Falcon glanced around. There was still that matter of the dead guard back in Ohio. He had visions of the authorities coming for him at any time—of them throwing him against the wall, shackling him with handcuffs and leg irons, and reading him his rights before ducking him into an unmarked police car. But he saw no one suspicious on the Promenade. "What were you able to find, Cassandra?"

"Pretty much everything. I don't have any favors left from anybody, so I guess I won't be writing too many legislative stories anytime soon. But what the heck."

"Talk to me. Tell me what you got."

"First of all, William Rutherford is former CIA. He lives in Boston. For the last few years he hasn't done anything real. He has a defense-consulting business, which might explain why he flies all over the place. He spent over thirty thousand dollars on airline flights last year alone, according to his credit card. But the business hasn't generated any revenue, according to his tax returns of the last three years. He receives his CIA pension, but it sure as hell isn't enough to support his lifestyle. I'm checking to see if he could have inherited anything big."

"That's great. It makes sense too. The other guys are businesspeople. They wouldn't have the stomach for the dirty work this thing required. And they wouldn't have the time either. Except Chambers. But he wouldn't have the strength."

"I have most of the phone bills too. Not surprisingly, they call each other a lot. They weren't as careful about whatever this thing is as they should have been."

"You are too much, Cassandra. Those phone bills will go a long way to proving conspiracy. It will link them together."

"I also spoke to Jeremy Case's widow," Cassandra continued.

"And . . ."

"And, she didn't want to say a whole lot, at first."

"Understandably."

"Yes. And I didn't really know what to ask her, so I just sort of talked to her for a while. She seemed to like that. It was sad. I felt sorry for her. Finally, I asked her if there was anything odd about her husband's death. Anything that didn't make sense, not that any of it probably made sense to her at the time. Or now for that matter." Cassandra paused. "Anyway, she said the one thing that stuck out in her mind was that her husband had apparently taken out a big life insurance policy just before his death. They never discussed it, even though she was very involved in their finances. She said it was strange for him to take out a policy without telling her. She is convinced that he was murdered, and that what happened wasn't some argument over a woman."

"Of course. Check out the—"

"The insurance policy. I am."

"Anything else?"

"Yes. Peter Lane, the name you asked me about."

"Yes?"

"He works for Lodestar Investment Management in Washington, D.C. That firm was—"

"I know. It was raided by the SEC, the DOJ, and the FBI on Thursday. I read it in the *Financial Chronicle*. Look, I think I know what this whole thing is about now. I think I know what the Sevens are trying to do."

"You do?"

"Yes." Falcon took a deep breath and glanced around the Promenade again. "I think they are trying to take down the President. I think this is an elaborate plot to destroy the administration, an administration that is very unfriendly to the Sevens' way of life."

Cassandra was quiet.

Falcon continued. He sensed the disbelief in her silence. "Did you read about the President being linked to some memo at Lodestar? A memo that outlined how the President had directed Lodestar to invest in Penn-Mar for him because he knew it was going to be taken over."

"Yes." Her voice was nothing more than a whisper.

"A guy from the *Financial Chronicle* broke the story yesterday."

"I know," she said. "He works downstairs."

"Do you think it was coincidental that someone from the *Chronicle* broke the story, Cassandra?"

She said nothing.

"Jesus. Do I have to spell it out for you?"

"No. You think the *Chronicle* was able to break the story about the memo because the Sevens somehow knew about it beforehand, and Henderson leaked that information to the guy downstairs."

"Exactly. Except that the Sevens didn't just know about the memo. They planted it. They have framed the President with it."

"Come on, Andrew! That's too much."

"Why is that so far-fetched?"

"The story in the *Times* this morning says that the authorities actually recovered a copy of the memo from Peter Lane's desk. The article goes on to say that the memo was covered with Lane's fingerprints. The prints on the memo matched exactly the prints he had to give to register for his Series Seven exam—the exam people are required to take before they can sell public securities."

"So . . ."

"So, how could the Sevens have arranged that? How could they have gotten Lane to leave a memo lying around with his fingerprints all over it, basically indicting himself and the President? Lane wouldn't have been that stupid. No one would be that stupid. He's convicted himself."

"Have they found Peter Lane yet? I mean, the authorities must be looking for him."

"They are, and, no, they haven't found him yet. At least according to the papers."

"And I bet they won't find him. At least not alive. The records indicate that Lodestar invested twenty thousand dollars into Penn-Mar on behalf of the President just days before the takeover was announced. Lodestar also bought a large call-option position for him at the same time. They probably got Lane to execute the trades by paying him. But I bet Lane didn't write the memo."

"Then how did his fingerprints get on the memo?"

"I don't know." Falcon couldn't explain that. That was the hole in his theory.

Cassandra sighed. "So you're saying the President is being set up."

"Yes. I know you don't believe me, but answer this. Why would he risk his entire political career, his entire life, just to make a couple of hundred thousand dollars on a stock and option position? It makes no sense. He'll make that amount for a couple of speaking engagements after he's finished at the White House."

"Well, if he's being framed, then he will be able to prove that he's being framed and the Sevens' plan will fall apart."

"An insider-trading charge isn't that easy to shake. Believe me, I know. The public records indicate that Lodestar bought the shares and the options for the President just days before the takeover was announced by Veens, and now the authorities have the Lane memo, but there's no Peter Lane to refute it. How's the President going to prove he's innocent if he can't get hold of Peter Lane? Even if he can get to Lane, it might not matter. In the best of all worlds, it would take at least six months to clear himself. More likely a year, given the evidence. Insider-trading cases drag on forever. He won't be able to shake this thing by the election. The damage is done, Cassandra. The people convict him on what they read in the *Chronicle*, controlled by the Sevens. And you know the American people will think he's as guilty as sin. He's a politician, for Christ's sake. And at the same time the insider-trading fiasco is going on, the financial markets are tanking. By tomorrow the Republicans will be on him like a pack of lions. His approval rating is going to take a nosedive. He'll lose the election by a landslide. It's all too neat, Cassandra. In fact, it's incredible. They're going to accomplish with this conspiracy what no assassination plot could have ever done."

Cassandra went silent. She did not argue. The vision of lions tearing prey apart was vivid in her mind. What Falcon was saying made too much sense.

Barksdale sat on the balcony of his Park Avenue apartment, sixty-two stories above street level, staring through the misty darkness at the lights of the city. It was a beautiful city at night, particularly from this lofty vantage point. He took several more gulps of the highball, then put the glass down on a small wooden table in front of his chair. It was his fourth glass of whiskey in the last two hours.

So tomorrow would be his last day of freedom. His lawyers had been unable to negotiate anything with the government. He wouldn't be booked or charged yet, but it would be the beginning of the end. Tomorrow they would start the investigation. Tomorrow they would begin asking the questions. And they would find the truth. They would find him guilty of something. They almost had to. He would spend time in a penitentiary. The attorneys had assured him of that. It was just a question of how much time. Tomorrow his good name would be splattered all over the *New York Times* for all of his friends to see, his reputation sullied forever.

Barksdale glanced through the glass doors. Vivian, his wife, was babbling on the telephone. That was about all she did anymore. He hated her. He had for years. Didn't all husbands hate their wives? And vice versa. Wasn't that what marriage was all about?

The ice cubes pressed against his upper lip as he emptied the glass of whiskey. He set it down carefully on the table, stood, climbed onto the brick restraining wall of the balcony, and jumped.

32

"What the hell is going on?" the President screamed. He stared blankly down at the quiet streets of Richmond, Virginia, from his suite atop the Omni Hotel. "In fifteen minutes I've got to deliver a speech to the blue bloods at St. James Episcopal Church. This is suicide for me. They hate the tax bills I've passed in the last four years, and they abhor the social programs I've instituted with what they consider 'their' money. Up until this point, there wasn't much the blue bloods could do about it. They had to make the best of it. But now look!" Buford Warren pointed at the new campaign figures, then turned and hurled the newspapers at Dick Walsh, his chief of staff, who sat in a large easy chair of the suite's living room. "They are going to tear me apart out there. We might as well cancel the appearance. We might as well cancel the entire campaign at this point."

Walsh took a deep breath and glanced at the front page headlines of the Sunday *New York Times* and the *Richmond Times-Dispatch*, both spread out over the floor at his feet.

PRESIDENT EMBROILED IN WALL STREET SCANDAL

LANE MEMO TO BE RELEASED TODAY BY FBI

"A week ago everything was fine. We were ahead of Whitman by ten points. Now the markets are in a meltdown, I've been accused of some bogus insider-trading charge, and suddenly I'm in a dead heat with him. If it keeps going at this rate, I'll be ten points behind Whitman by tomorrow. You're my chief of staff, Dick! Do something!" The President slammed a fist against the wall.

Walsh stood and motioned for the three aides to leave. They melted from the room.

"And look at this!" The President pointed at another headline.

PRESIDENT OF NEW YORK FED CALMS GLOBAL MARKETS

"Wendell Smith and the Republicans are coming out of this smelling like roses. They say this Morgan deal that he and another couple of WASP bastards cooked up is going to save the day. And that the American people ought to be damn glad that there are people like Wendell and Granville Winthrop around to save the day when things get really tough. Are they joking? Wendell Smith is the one who is responsible for the NASO mess. And he's going to come out of it looking like a hero. I had nothing to do with it, and I'm going to come out of it looking like day-old shit."

Walsh wanted to tell him that that was Washington, but he didn't. Now was not the time. Walsh stared at his President. Warren was not holding up well in the face of adversity. His face was drawn. Under his bloodshot eyes were great bags, unnatural and grotesque. And he seemed suddenly thinner. "It's tragic." Walsh could find no other words.

"Of course it's tragic. It's me. If it were anyone else, it would be a shame. Since it's me, it's tragic. But do something about it, Dick. Don't just sit there and say, 'It's tragic.' Do something!"

Walsh shrugged. He did not know what he could do. He had tried to find a friendly ear in the press corps, but suddenly people who had been so willing to publish a well-timed op-ed column to help the President in the past were nowhere to be found. The train was already out of control, and it looked as if there would be no way to put it back on track before the election. Maybe the best thing for Walsh's own political career was to jump off the train now, while he still had a chance to survive.

The President ranted on. "And the press. I can't believe those rat bastards. They've jumped on this insider-trading thing as though it's not obvious that I've been set up. Isn't it obvious to you?"

Walsh nodded halfheartedly.

The President stared at Walsh for a moment, and then his shoulders slumped. He could see what Walsh was thinking. "My God, Dick. You don't really believe I influenced Farinholt or anyone else at Lodestar to trade for me on inside information?" His voice shook. "You don't really believe any of that Peter Lane memo crap. Do you?"

"Of course not," Walsh replied slowly.

"You know it's not true. How would I know anything about the Penn-Mar takeover before it happened?"

"You couldn't." Walsh's voice was hollow. "You couldn't." But Walsh could not forget the fact that one of the President's best friends in the world was the current chairman of DuPont. Walsh stared out the window, past the President. It was a gorgeous, cloudless summer morning in central Virginia. And it was definitely time to jump off the Buford Warren train. He had no doubt. Timing was everything in the political game.

"Cassandra?"

"Hello, Andrew."

"Can you talk?"

"Yes."

"Were you able to find out anything else?"

"A few more things. Did you read this morning that Peter Lane's body, or what was left of it, showed up in St. Croix?"

"Yeah, the sharks had a nice time with him. Doesn't surprise me either."

"I'll have to admit, Andrew, you were right on target."

"Now the only person who can refute the memo is the President, and people aren't paying much attention to what he's got to say these days. What else did you find out?"

"The insurance company that paid the death benefit to Jeremy Case's widow is a Swiss company. Guess who owns it?"

"Humor me."

"Winthrop, Hawkins. Guess how much the death benefit was."

"Seven hundred thousand dollars . . ."

". . . And seven cents." Cassandra finished his sentence.

Falcon was quiet for a few moments. It was all coming together. "Cassandra, I need you to send me all of the information you've put together—the information on the insurance company owned by Winthrop, Hawkins, the information about Rutherford, and particularly the telephone records of the Sevens."

"Where do I send it?"

"To Boston. To the Federal Express office in Faneuil Hall. Send it for early delivery. By ten o'clock tomorrow morning."

"Why Boston?"

"I've had to run a little errand here."

Cassandra sighed. She knew why he was there. "Be careful."

"I will." Falcon hesitated. "I need to ask you a huge favor."

"You're running out of favors, Andrew. This is it." But she laughed as she finished the sentence.

"This is very important."

"Okay."

"I'm going to put all of the information I've compiled into a safe-deposit box here in Boston. The information will include the four files I took from Penn-Mar, information regarding wire transfers that implicate the Sevens, what you've gotten for me, and a synopsis I've put together of everything that's happened. The safe-deposit box will be at the Bank of Boston on State Street. There will be only two people with access to that box. You and me."

"What?"

"I can't trust anyone but you, Cassandra. Please."

"Andrew, I—"

"Please. You know I never say *please* twice in a row."

There was a long silence. "What do you want me to do?"

"From now on, you will check every night with an answering service that I have contracted with. I've prepaid for a year's worth of service. That should be enough." Falcon gave her the number of the service. "I'll leave a message for you by eleven o'clock every night. Every night!" He emphasized the words. "The message will always contain a color. If there is no message by eleven or the message doesn't contain a color, you are to come to Boston immediately, take the information from the safe-deposit box, and turn it over to the federal authorities. No questions asked. Just do it! I'll send you a key and the number of the box by overnight mail. I'll send it to the post office in downtown Manhattan near where you work. That's probably safer than for me to send it to your home. And more convenient."

Falcon endured another long pause.

"So, if I don't get a message, then I can assume something's happened to you."

"Yes. And at that point you must go to the authorities. You can do it anonymously. I don't care. But you have to promise me you will go to them with all of the information from the box."

"I will." She hesitated. "But why don't I just keep a second copy of all the stuff here with me?"

"No! More than one set of this stuff, and we run the risk that somebody else gets his hands on it. I can't have that. Besides, it wouldn't be safe for you."

"Okay, okay."

Falcon relaxed his grip on the phone. Things were coming together.

"Andrew, did you see that the chairman and vice chairman of NASO both committed suicide?"

"What?"

"Yes. Barksdale was the vice chairman, right?"

"Yes."

"He jumped off of his apartment balcony in New York City last night."

"Holy—"

"And Boreman blew himself up in his car Friday out in Westchester County. There was a note back at his house. Said he couldn't live with what had happened at NASO. They haven't been able to positively identify the body yet. Apparently, it was pretty badly burned. But the license tag matched Boreman's car."

Falcon stared at the wall in front of him. "You said it was Friday that Boreman killed himself?"

"Yes."

Falcon nodded to himself. There was something he needed to check out.

"Why haven't you been able to get Falcon yet? My God, it's been five days."

"We know where he is." Rutherford used a bored tone. He yawned into the telephone's mouthpiece. He was tired of these constant calls from Prescott.

"How do we know that?" Prescott emphasized "we" sarcastically.

"Our female friend."

"Of course." Prescott snorted through the phone. "Well, if we know where he is, then why in the hell don't we kill him?"

"We know he is here in Boston. We just don't know his exact location in the city yet. But we expect to learn that in short order." Rutherford had told no one of Falcon's escape from Phoenix Grey in Harlem.

"Boston?" Prescott was surprised. "Boston?" Then alarmed. "Christ, he's come right into your backyard."

Immediately Rutherford regretted relaying Falcon's whereabouts to Prescott. "So what?"

"Why do you think he went to Boston? Do you think he's going to try to contact you?"

"He could have done that by phone from New York."

"Then why did he go to Boston?"

"I don't know. And I'm not going to worry about it."

"Sure, it's easy for you not to worry. It's not your career. Hell, if this thing really blows up, if Falcon does go to the authorities, you'll melt into the cracks and the rest of us will face the music alone. With your background, you could disappear and no one would ever find you."

Rutherford hesitated a moment for effect, then exhaled heavily into the phone. His voice was quiet but steady. "Do you really think I would do that? Leave you men after all we've been through?"

Prescott swallowed hard. The pressure was destroying him. "I . . . I'm sorry, Bill. It's just that . . ."

"I am the most loyal person you will ever know." Rutherford's voice rose in intensity at the end of the sentence.

Rutherford knew that Prescott regretted the insult. He knew that it was simply the strain of the situation. He had seen it many times at the CIA. It was a natural reaction to supreme stress. But it could not be excused. It was a reaction that had to be silenced—immediately. Dissension from within was more powerful a force to reckon with than any enemy one could face. It would be dangerous to allow Prescott to continue thinking this way. He might convince the others to abandon the conspiracy. Or worse, cut a deal with the authorities. He had to come down hard on Prescott and teach this sniveling little civilian a lesson. "Apologize to me!"

"I apologize." Prescott's voice was barely audible.

"You're weaker than I ever imagined, Turner. Now is when you must be stronger than you ever thought you could be."

"Right." Prescott cleared his throat. "Yes."

Rutherford softened his voice slightly. "If Falcon were going to go to the authorities, he would have done so by now. I think he wants to cut a deal. You see, he has that little problem in Ohio."

"You mean the dead guard?"

"Yes. He probably knows that we're aware of his involvement in that shooting. He knows that we could contact the authorities, and they would find him. You see, we both have information that could seriously damage the other. It's an interesting dilemma. It's a case of who will blink first."

"But the authorities will figure it out sooner or later. They must be checking the visitor logbook for that day. They'll find Falcon's name, and when they call him at NASO just to ask a few questions and find that he hasn't been at work in a week, they'll track him down."

"Chambers removed both Falcon's and Barksdale's names from the visitor book. And he has kept Landon away from the authorities."

"But Falcon wouldn't know that."

"You're right. Which is why I think he will make contact with us soon." Rutherford glanced out the window of the suburban home. "What's going on with the lawsuit?"

"Penn-Mar's attorneys are trying to settle, but we're having none of that. Meanwhile, I don't know how many different federal and state agencies are crawling all over Penn-Mar. The President is all but dead with the insider-trading charge and what's going on in the markets. Bailey Henderson is killing him at the *Chronicle*. And the other major newspapers are following the *Chronicle*'s lead, just as we knew they would. The whole thing is going perfectly—except for this problem with Falcon."

"Don't worry, Turner. We'll get Falcon."

"I—I know you will. I have faith in you."

"Good. Listen, I've got to make a call. I'll talk to you later."

"Okay."

Rutherford hung up. Prescott was right. If this thing did blow up, he would disappear forever. The others could fend for themselves. Rutherford gazed out the window. What the hell was Falcon up to?

Cassandra stared at Bailey Henderson's file cabinet. She had already procured all of the phone bills from her contact at the telephone company. She had sent the bills and the other information to Falcon in Boston. She had done her job. She didn't have to do any more. But there might be more information. That one more shred of evidence that would tie the whole thing up in a nice, neat package. And it might be right here in Henderson's office.

She had been here five minutes now, in the secretarial space of Henderson's sprawling first-floor office. Five minutes was a long time given the situation, but it was very late and Henderson was away in California. She had checked and rechecked his schedule.

Cassandra moved through the dimly lit room to the other file cabinet and knelt down. She pushed the thick screwdriver into the lock and began to twist.

"What the hell are you doing here?" Suddenly, the overhead lights illuminated the room brilliantly.

Cassandra dropped the screwdriver and rose to her feet slowly. She did not panic but was very calm. She had no reason to panic. Falcon had anticipated this possibility, and he had told her what to say if there ever was a problem.

Bailey Henderson stood between Cassandra and the door. "What are you doing here?" He was becoming agitated. He was breathing hard. He squinted at her. "You're Cassandra Stone, aren't you?"

"Yes," she whispered.

"Why are you rooting through my personal files?" His voice wavered.

They stood twenty feet apart, staring at each other.

"Answer me!"

Cassandra stared at him coldly. "I work for William Rutherford." Then, without another word, she walked calmly past him toward the elevator.

Henderson stared at her as she passed him, and swallowed hard.

33

Falcon walked slowly along Albany Street, the main thoroughfare of Boston's South End warehouse district. Huge eighteen-wheelers crawled down the potholed roadway, searching for the correct loading bay in which to park. The late morning was consumed by revving engines, blasting horns, and diesel exhaust fumes.

The information was securely stored in a safe-deposit box at the Bank of Boston's main branch on State Street: the files from Chambers' office at Penn-Mar; the wire-transfer records Martinez had compiled; the information Cassandra had sent to the Federal Express office; his own "to whom it may concern" memo; and everything else. All of it was safely compacted into the metal box. And the extra key and the number of the box written on a piece of loose-leaf paper had reached Cassandra yesterday morning. Falcon breathed deeply as he moved through the shadows of the huge buildings. There was one more thing in that safe-deposit box, just in case.

Falcon turned off Albany Street and made his way down a side alley toward the Days Inn where he was staying. He walked slowly now. Cautiously. Before leaving his room this morning, he had called to tell her of his exact location, assuring the fact that he would be found. He wanted this confrontation. It had to occur.

There was no choice. But the confrontation had to be on his terms. Otherwise, he might not survive it.

The semi's horn blew so loudly that Falcon almost fell over. The truck was nearly on top of him before it had signalled its approach into the open door of the warehouse. Somehow he managed to stumble to the brick wall, out of harm's way, as the huge tractor trailer bounced noisily by. The driver pulled on the horn twice more as he passed Falcon.

Falcon watched the truck as it rolled into the building. His heart pounded in his chest and perspiration poured from his body. He had not slept in forty-eight hours, and he was losing the edge. As Falcon leaned against the bricks, he allowed his eyelids to shut. It felt so good to rest. The information was safe and the key was with Cassandra. He had done all he could do. There was nothing left now but to wait.

He opened his eyes. The man was running toward him, a look of desperation on his face. The same man who had chased him in Harlem and boarded the New Jersey Transit train at Linden was running straight toward Falcon from the direction of the Days Inn. The waiting was over.

Falcon's vision blurred momentarily. He squinted at the sprinting figure and his eyesight refocused. The man was just fifty yards away and closing quickly. There could be no doubt of his identity. Falcon turned and began to run. Give me strength.

Phoenix Grey pumped his legs as hard as he ever had. He could not fail this time. There would be no third chance. Rutherford had made that clear.

Falcon raced across the empty parking lot, dodging empty beer cans as he ran. Broken bottles crackled under his feet like faraway machine-gun fire. Where the hell was the door? He searched the side of the huge abandoned warehouse as he moved. But his vision was very bad now. There was little strength left in his body.

Grey noticed with satisfaction Falcon's sluggish gait. The prey was weakening, and his own hunger was strong. It would be over soon.

The door, where in the hell was it? There! Falcon moved along the wall of the building to the white wooden door. It would be unlocked. He had made certain. Falcon thrust it open and rushed into the cool, dark structure. It reeked of mildew. He climbed the black metal stairway to the second floor, leaping three steps at a bound. Strength was coming from somewhere, though he knew not where.

Grey took the steps four at a bound. He was closing in. Falcon was done. There would be no escape this time.

Falcon reached the huge open space of the second floor. It was as big as a football field. He sprinted toward the middle of the space. The pursuer was close now. He could feel it.

Grey reached the top of the stairway, pulling the pistol from its holster as he ran.

Falcon stopped suddenly in the middle of the huge room and turned toward Grey. He stood defiantly, arms crossed over his chest.

Phoenix Grey stopped too. He was not more than fifteen yards from the prey. He drew the pistol in front of him. This would be an easy shot. What the hell was wrong with Falcon? Did he want to die?

"If you kill me now, the Sevens will be revealed. The world will know about the conspiracy," Falcon said firmly. His words echoed in the huge space. "You, Rutherford, and the rest will be hunted down like animals until the authorities find you. They won't stop until they find you. The information they will get is detailed. I know everything. And all of that information is stored away. If anything happens to me, there are people who will know to recover it. And they will know if anything happens to me."

Grey stared down the barrel of the pistol at Falcon's chest, still heaving from the chase. He moved slowly toward Falcon.

"I want to talk to Rutherford. If I talk to him, the information is safe. If I don't, the authorities will have it tomorrow."

Grey began circling slowly behind him now. Falcon stared straight ahead. He knew better than to move. "You kill me, and you're as good as dead yourself."

The cold steel of the pistol pressed against the back of his neck.

"Do you understand what I'm saying? Don't make the mistake of thinking that I'm bluffing, pal." For a moment Falcon wondered whether his strategy had been correct.

And then everything went black.

Falcon opened his eyes slowly. The world did not come immediately into focus. God, the back of his head was killing him. He closed his eyes.

"You'll be all right." The voice was military and tough.

Cigarette smoke reached Falcon's nostrils. He opened his eyes again. The room was stark, lit by a single naked bulb hanging from a long, black cord like a man at the end of a noose. Falcon shivered. He could not see beyond the small arc of light.

"You hungry?"

Falcon shook his head slowly and stretched. He leaned back against the cinder-block wall.

"Need to use the latrine?"

Falcon shook his head again. He looked up. The man sat backward in the wooden chair and stared down at him. His elbows rested on the back of the chair.

The man gazed at him for a few moments, then inhaled deeply from the cigarette, dropped it onto the cement floor, and stepped on the burning ash with a large black boot.

Falcon's vision cleared. The man was big. Very big. Arms of a blacksmith bulged beneath the cotton golf shirt. His head was huge, highlighted by a mammoth forehead and a Roman nose. His hair was clipped close to his scalp in a crew cut. Falcon could not tell the color of the hair because the light in the room was too dim. Somehow he was not what Falcon had expected. "William Rutherford?"

"In person," Rutherford said in a commanding voice.

Falcon let his head fall back against the cinder-block wall. "Jesus Christ." He touched the back of his scalp. There was dried blood. "Why the hell did your goon have to hit me so hard?"

"He didn't want you to get away again. He was pissed off. I have to hand it to you, Falcon. I've never known anyone to elude Phoenix Grey the way you have. And I've known Phoenix for a long time."

Falcon continued to rub his head. "What time is it?"

Rutherford checked his watch. "It's six o'clock. It's been about seven hours."

"That's fitting," Falcon said under his breath.

"You're a funny guy, Mr. Falcon." Rutherford reached for a pack of Marlboros from the shirt's top pocket, removed one, and lit it. He took a few more puffs, then pointed a finger at Falcon with the hand that held the cigarette. "What do you want? Why did you come to Boston?"

Falcon sat straighter against the wall. "To get a few answers."

"Okay, the world isn't really round; it's flat. And I'm sorry to be the one to tell you, but there is no heaven, just a living hell here on earth. And it's going to get much worse for you, boy, before it gets any better. That about do you?"

Falcon ignored Rutherford. "I know you killed Jeremy Case. You killed Carter Filipelli and Peter Lane too."

"And a few others." Rutherford didn't bat an eye.

"How did you get Lane to invest the money on behalf of the President?"

"Paid him half a million dollars. He was up to his eyeballs in gambling debts. He took off a little before we had anticipated, but we found him."

"But he wouldn't have been stupid enough to write the memo

the authorities found at Lodestar and put his fingerprints on it. Even for half a million dollars."

"Phoenix Grey, the gentleman who's been bird-dogging you for the last week, tracked Lane down on a lonely beach in St. Croix. Before Phoenix threw him to the sharks, he got Lane's fingerprints all over a memo that I put together on my computer upstairs."

"And of course you used the *Financial Chronicle* to manipulate the public and the other media types."

"Of course. The power of the press. Never underestimate it."

"And you leaked the information about Lodestar and the President to the DOJ."

"Actually, it was the FBI. We were already using the DOJ for something else, so we wanted to use another agency for that one."

"I thought Victor Farinholt, the senior partner at Lodestar, was involved too. The papers said he traded on the information also. Or did you set him up, just as you set me up?"

Rutherford laughed deeply. "No, he wasn't involved. And we didn't set him up either. That was just good luck. Financial types kill me. They'd sell their mother for inside information." Rutherford paused. "So you found out a few things about us?"

"I found out everything. I found the wire transfers into NASO from Winthrop, Hawkins. I also found out about the insurance policy for Jeremy Case's wife. I've got your telephone bills for the last six months. All of your telephone bills. Each Seven. And most importantly, I've got the files from Chambers' office at Penn-Mar, which have some very incriminating handwritten notes in the margins."

Rutherford finished the cigarette, allowed it to fall to the floor, and put it out next to the first one. He smiled wryly. "How did you find out about us? How did you know where to look when you went to Toledo?"

"Things struck me strangely along the way. Taken individually they were nothing, but in the aggregate I could not ignore them.

There was the fact that the headhunter who called me about the NASO job knew about the position two days before the woman whom I replaced was actually fired. The fact that NASO was willing to put so much money into one deal, which was so far overpriced. The timing of Filipelli's death. The fact that senior officials holding the same job at NASO had been murdered. The fact that DuPont pulled out of the bidding for Penn-Mar at the eleventh hour, even though they had plenty of dry powder left." Falcon glanced up at Rutherford. "You influenced that, didn't you?"

"That's what we used the DOJ for. Wendell's got a lot of friends over there."

"To answer your question, I went to Toledo with the intention of going through Chambers' office. I didn't think I'd really find anything. But I did."

"I suppose that's also how you found yourself killing the security guard too, eh?"

"Yes." Falcon stared at Rutherford, grim-faced.

Rutherford shook his head, but said nothing.

Falcon pulled some of the dried blood from his hair. "It isn't just the Sevens, is it? I mean, there are more than seven people involved in this conspiracy, aren't there?"

"Conspiracy is such a nasty word, Mr. Falcon. *Cause.* I like the word *cause* a lot more than I like the word *conspiracy.* Let's use that word. Yes, there are more than seven people involved in the cause. Some of them know they are involved. Some of them don't."

"You all made a lot of money on the Penn-Mar transaction, didn't you? You traded ahead of the announcement, right?"

Rutherford nodded. "Of course. Through various on- and offshore accounts. In total we netted a billion-dollar gain on our investments. We lost a billion in the LBO, but we made two billion buying before the announcement. I'll take a six-month, billion-dollar, one hundred percent profit any day. Of course, that wasn't the primary motivation."

"I know," Falcon said calmly.

Rutherford sat up in the chair. "Look, Falcon, what do you want? Clearly you came here for something."

Falcon made it to his feet. His head throbbed. He rubbed his hands to his eyes. He felt as if he was going to throw up but managed to continue. "Rutherford, it seems to me we both have problems. There ought to be a mutually agreeable way of solving those problems."

"I'm listening." Rutherford lit another cigarette. "Don't expect miracles."

"I've got enough information to put you and your friends away for life. If what I have stored away in a remote safe-deposit box ever became public, the disclosure would destroy you and probably a lot of people in addition to the Sevens."

"Perhaps," Rutherford acknowledged.

"If something happens to me, I've got friends who know where to go to look for everything I've put together. They don't know what's in there, but they know to go for it if they don't hear from me on a regular basis."

"Pretty basic plan, Falcon."

Andrew shrugged. "Maybe so. But I think it works. Your goon could have killed me at the warehouse pretty easily, but he didn't."

Rutherford glanced away.

"But I've got some problems too."

"Yes, you do."

"First of all, it's going to be pretty hard for me to find a job after what happened at NASO. At least in this universe. Second, you could make things pretty bad for me as far as the investigation into the death of that guard at Penn-Mar."

Rutherford's eyes became nothing but slits. Falcon had it all figured out. "So, what's your proposal?"

Falcon's throat was dry. He coughed. "First, I want ten million dollars. You made a billion dollars on Penn-Mar. You can spare a dime. I don't think that's a lot. Second, I want you to buy me this farm up in Vermont too. I mean, I'll have ten million dollars to spend, but it would be such a nice touch for you to get the farm for me. I always did want to live in Vermont. And it will give the authorities one more trail to follow if anything ever happens to me. Third, I want you to take care of that wire transfer at NASO that might make someone believe I was guilty of insider trading. And fourth, I want you to lead the authorities away from my involvement in the guard's death at Penn-Mar. Not that you probably care, but I didn't murder him. It was an accident."

"I'll have to check with the others," Rutherford said.

"Don't pull that pass-the-buck crap on me. The others will do whatever you say. You can do it and you will do it. You are the bottom line."

"No, I'm the bottom line." Granville Winthrop moved smoothly out of the shadows.

Falcon recoiled involuntarily against the cinder-block wall.

Winthrop continued to walk slowly across the cement floor until he was only inches from Falcon's face. "I should have had you killed a long time ago."

Falcon regained his calm quickly. "You tried. You sent a professional assassin after me and he couldn't kill me." His eyes narrowed, then he flashed the crooked smile. "Don't you get it, Granville? You can't beat me. You've tried to kill me. You've tried to hang an insider-trading charge on me. You made it so no one on Wall Street would hire me. You probably even put that bug in the software at MD Link, didn't you? Didn't you, Winthrop?"

Winthrop nodded.

"But here I am." Falcon's voice was dead-sea calm. "And I've got you and your blue-blooded buddies over a barrel. A very big barrel. I could put you away for good if I wanted to. If I wanted to, Winthrop. I'm in control. How do you like that, Granville? It burns you, doesn't it? But there's not a goddamn thing you can do about it."

Winthrop stepped back as though punch-drunk. He stared at Falcon for a few moments through glazed eyes, then reached beneath his long raincoat and withdrew a .44-caliber Magnum. He trained it on Falcon's chest.

"Granville!" Rutherford barked. "Put that down!"

Winthrop ignored Rutherford. "I've always wanted to kill a man, Andrew. Putting a very big bullet through your chest seems like a pretty good way to satisfy that urge."

Falcon stared into Winthrop's eyes. He had seen that look before, in Reid Bernstein's eyes. Winthrop wanted to pull the trigger badly. Unlike the guard in Toledo, Granville wanted to kill.

"You pull that trigger, and it's all over, Granville," Rutherford whispered. "Everything. You've told me you admire my dedication to mission. The fact that I am perfectly rational. It would be completely irrational to kill Falcon. He could destroy us in death. He would not have come to Boston unless he was certain he could take us down. He arranged this meeting. He allowed us to find and catch him."

The gun began to shake violently in Winthrop's hands. He cocked it and turned his head slightly to one side.

Falcon stared down the gun barrel into the old man's eyes and didn't like what he saw.

Suddenly Winthrop pulled the trigger. The bullet smashed into the cinder block next to Falcon's head and ricocheted around the room.

Falcon dropped to the floor and covered his head instinctively. Rutherford dove at Winthrop, knocking the older man to the floor and taking control of the weapon quickly.

"Get off me, Rutherford! I wasn't trying to kill him! If I was trying to kill him, he'd be dead!" Winthrop yelled.

"You could have killed all of us, you idiot!" Rutherford yelled back.

All three men staggered to their feet. Falcon and Winthrop stared at each other. The hatred in their eyes surprised even themselves.

"You will meet my demands," Falcon said icily.

"What makes you so sure?" Winthrop hissed.

"Rutherford said it. I arranged this meeting. I allowed you to catch me. Why would you blow everything you've worked for just to kill me? I'm chicken shit in your grand scheme of things. I'm giving you life, and you're giving me life."

"I'm giving you a pretty damn good life, I'd say."

"My silence is worth ten million dollars."

"You keep forgetting, Mr. Falcon," Rutherford interjected. "I've got you here in my custody. I've spent the better part of my life prying information out of people. And prying is the operative word. You see, I know just how much pain the human body can withstand before it expires." He brandished the .44. "I could very easily find out where that information is."

"Do you really want to gamble that you can get the information out of me? If my friends don't hear from me by eleven o'clock tonight, they will be at the location to retrieve the information at nine o'clock tomorrow morning. I can hold out until the morning." He shivered again. This place was cold.

Rutherford stared at Falcon. "Yes, I suppose you could."

"Then we have a deal?"

Rutherford stood in silence for several moments and then glanced at Winthrop, who, after several moments, nodded.

"In principle we do," Winthrop whispered. There was no choice. He turned to go.

"There's one more thing. One more condition to my silence."

Winthrop turned back to face Falcon. "What now?"

"I want to be a Seven."

Winthrop and Rutherford looked at him in disbelief.

"And just to show you that it will be worthwhile to have me as a Seven, chew on this, Granville. Boreman's supposed to be dead, right? Burned up in a fiery automobile crash?"

"Yes, God rest his soul."

"Happened Friday?"

"Yes."

"Then why didn't the Harvard chapel bell ring seven times at seven minutes before midnight on Friday night? And why isn't Wallace Boreman's name on the plaque? That's supposed to happen within forty-eight hours of a Seven's death. His name isn't up there. I checked. And his name isn't there for a reason. He isn't dead."

The two men said nothing. They just stared at Falcon.

34

The couple walked hand in hand through the darkness. They were both graduate students, he in anthropology and she in law. They were returning from a small dinner party on the other side of the campus. The woman pressed close to her lover for warmth. The air was crisp, and the smell of chimney smoke wafted through the fall evening.

They hesitated for a moment before the dark gothic chapel of Harvard University. It was bathed in subtle spotlights, and they stopped to admire its beauty.

As the couple stood before the impressive structure in the stillness of the late hour, both were startled by the sudden clanging of the steeple's bell. The woman glanced at her watch. Exactly seven minutes before midnight.

The bell rang seven times and then was still. The couple exchanged nods, then turned and hurried for the heat of his apartment. They would check the plaque in the next few days.

Suddenly the lights bathing the front of the chapel went out. A gentle breeze moved through the boxwoods in front of the stone structure; then it faded to nothing and the bushes were still. Devon Chambers had lost his long bout with cancer.

Bob Whitman moved confidently across the stage erected in the Grand Ballroom of Washington, D.C.'s Marriott Hotel. He waved as he walked. A tumultuous roar arose from the Republican throng. They were delirious.

A voice boomed over the loudspeakers. "Ladies and gentlemen, Bob Whitman, your next President!"

The crowd burst into another round of chaotic applause as Whitman reached the podium in the middle of the stage. He held both arms aloft, signalling for order. Finally, the audience yielded.

"My fellow Americans!" The crowd began cheering again at the sound of Whitman's voice, then became silent so he could continue. "President Warren has just called me from his campaign headquarters to concede the election. . . ."

Falcon switched off the television from the couch with the remote control. He didn't need to see any more. The race was over. And it was late and he was tired. He nudged Alexis' shoulder and whispered in her ear, "Come on, let's go to bed." She moaned and pulled her head up from his chest. She had fallen asleep hours ago. Falcon ran his fingers through her hair, and as he did, he noticed that the brand on his inner right forearm, the brand of the Sevens, was just beginning to heal.

Phoenix Grey stared at the Vermont farmhouse through the darkness and the falling snow. This was it. Something that should have been taken care of long ago. Now it was finally going to be over. He hated Falcon because the man had ruined his credibility with Rutherford. Now he was going to restore that credibility.

Phoenix breathed in the cold damp air. The new snow was good. It would cover his tracks. He felt for the .22-caliber pistol hanging inside the down jacket. The silencer was already attached.

Alexis watched Falcon's face closely. His breathing was slow and measured. It was three o'clock in the morning. He was fast asleep.

She hadn't wanted to come to Vermont. It was cold and dark

seven months of the year. But Andrew had asked nicely enough, and Winthrop had ordered her to do so.

Alexis rose from the bed as gently as possible. Springs squeaked and slats groaned as her weight shifted. She held her breath as Falcon moved slightly. She stood on the cold wooden floor for a full five minutes, barely breathing, too afraid to inhale normally as he settled down. Finally, his breathing became slow again. Alexis moved quietly from the bedroom.

Despite the cold, she did not bother to don her robe or slippers. She did not notice the chilly air of the bedroom. She could think only of the wonderful times they had enjoyed over the past months and how she had come to truly love him. Vermont had turned out to be a very nice place.

He had never once asked if she was involved with the Sevens nor about how she had relayed information to Rutherford that had put him in mortal danger. She realized he must have known, but he had never mentioned it. Now this. The damn call from Rutherford yesterday.

To ignore the call would have been stupid. No, suicidal. She still worked for Winthrop. She always would. He pointed that out at every opportunity. He had saved her from the orphanage. He alone had rescued her from what probably would have been a life of whorehouses, pimps, and drugs in Italy. And he could send her back if he so chose. He never missed an opportunity to impress that upon her either. God, she hated him.

Many times during the day, Alexis had considered conveying to Falcon what had transpired: Winthrop had finally located the safe-deposit box at the main office of the Bank of Boston on State Street after a long and arduous search. Winthrop had been searching for the information since the day Falcon had cut the deal sitting in Rutherford's basement. Allowing Falcon to become a Seven was simply Winthrop's way of buying time and his confidence. Winthrop had used just about every favor he had left in the world to locate the information. And now Phoenix Grey had come to kill him.

Many times during the day, she had considered telling Falcon to run, to withdraw as much money as he could from the Rutledge branch of the First National Bank of Vermont and go, to melt into the landscape and never be heard from or seen again. But it would be useless. They would find him sooner or later. And she would be signing her own death warrant.

Alexis reached the first floor. It was even colder down here. Now she began to feel it. That was one thing she would not miss. The cold. There was always a bright side to everything. She wondered what would happen to her now. Would she become Winthrop's mistress? Her lip curled involuntarily. She could not think on that possibility now.

The entire house was locked tighter than a drum. It was so secure it reminded her of an army base. Falcon had made certain of the home's security before they had moved in. He was fanatic about it, and she knew exactly why. But learning the security system had not been a problem, since Falcon had been only too happy to teach her about it. It would not present an impediment to what she had to do tonight.

Alexis moved into the pantry off the kitchen, disengaged the electronic surveillance system, and then moved to the back door. She peered out the glass into the snow and darkness beyond but saw nothing—as she knew she wouldn't.

A burst of ice-cold air blew into the kitchen as Alexis unlocked the two dead bolts, then opened the back door. The wind sliced through her flowered flannel nightgown, forcing it against her skin. Instinctively, she crossed her arms over her breasts. Where was he?

From out of nowhere Phoenix Grey, dressed completely in black, moved into the doorway of the kitchen, taking her by surprise. In one smooth motion he drew the pistol directly to Alexis's forehead and fired. She did not have time to react, so quick was his aim. Not even to bring her arms up from her breasts.

The force of the hollow-point shell exploding out of the back of her head actually thrust her body forward. Phoenix caught her, then allowed the corpse to fall gently to the cold gray slats of the back porch. He gazed at her face for a moment. Blood oozed from the tiny hole in the exact middle of her forehead, contrasting with the gaping wound at the back of her skull.

The back door squeaked slightly as Phoenix closed it behind him. From a vest pocket he withdrew a pair of night-vision goggles and pulled the strap down over the back of his head. Instantly, the world became different shades of green, gray, and white. The goggles were effective. He could see everything.

Phoenix Grey reached the top of the stairs quickly. He knew the layout of the house intimately. In fact, he had walked these steps and hallways several weeks ago—when Falcon had travelled to New York for a day—in preparation for this night. He had committed the route to memory for this mission.

Phoenix hurried down the hallway toward the bedroom. There was no need to be cautious now. It was all over. There was nothing Falcon could do. So he wasn't as invincible as he thought.

Phoenix burst through the door, gun drawn. He squeezed the trigger and pumped the clip into the bed. They would clean up the mess later. No one would ever know what had happened here.

35

"Gentlemen, please join me in a toast." Winthrop glanced about the Racquet Club's small private dining room at the other five tuxedo-clad men.

They rose in unison, holding their champagne glasses aloft. They wore the smiles of men who had accomplished a great feat against insurmountable odds, men who knew that if in fact they never accomplished anything again in their lives, it would not matter. This was the ultimate. They had changed the course of history.

"First, on behalf of all of us, I want to thank myself for arranging this delicious dinner here in New York at a most appropriate venue." Winthrop looked around with an impish smile.

The other men laughed and sipped the Dom Pérignon. Their smiles grew more obnoxious. They were gods. They had derailed a socialist devil and restored capitalism. They had a right to their victory smiles. They had a right to anything they wanted.

"Second"—Winthrop lowered his voice out of respect—"since this is the first time we have been able to convene as one since the death of our dear friend and comrade, Devon Chambers, I ask for a moment of silence in his honor."

As one, the men bowed their heads and set their jaws. For a moment anyway, the victory smiles faded.

"Third, I want to inform you that at exactly three-seventeen yesterday morning Phoenix Grey put an end to the life of one Andrew Falcon. He did so because, after some time, we were able to recover the information Mr. Falcon appropriated from us in Ohio."

The victory smiles returned. They were safe. They were untouchable. They truly were gods.

Winthrop glanced around the room. He was beaming. "Finally, gentlemen"—Winthrop paused and made eye contact with each man at the table—"here is to us!"

"Here, here!" The men cheered one another and shook hands. The victory smiles could no longer be contained. Normally reserved, the men allowed themselves this moment of uncontrolled joy.

And then, slowly, the door to the private room swung open. Wallace Boreman, still wearing the disguise he had used to travel from the ranch in Wyoming to New York, noticed him standing in the doorway first. He motioned to the other men. One by one they turned to stare, and slowly the room became as quiet as a tomb.

Andrew Falcon was also dressed in a black tuxedo. He smiled. "Good evening, gentlemen." His voice was hushed. "I didn't get my invitation, but I decided to come anyway. I hope you don't mind."

Turner Prescott sank into his chair and brought his hands to his face.

"What's the matter, Turner?" Falcon asked. "You look as if you've seen a ghost. Or maybe that's what you're hoping. But I hate to tell you I'm very much alive."

"What are you . . . how are you . . . ?" Rutherford stammered. He was incredulous.

"It's impossible," Granville Winthrop murmured.

Falcon walked slowly across the room until he stood directly before Winthrop. "I knew that you would never stop looking for those files. And I knew the moment you found them you would hunt me down and kill me, that the initiation as a Seven was a complete sham. I knew that. I set you up, Winthrop. I set you all up." Falcon glanced at each of them. "Because all of you set me up." He laughed. "And it took you long enough to find the files. I had to keep dropping hints to Alexis. I must tell you, Granville, what you recovered were not the original files. I still have those in my possession. But you couldn't know that because Chambers was dead. He was the only one that could have told you if they were the originals."

It was Wendell Smith's turn to join Prescott as he dropped to his chair. The other men continued to stand and gape, unable to speak.

"But I spoke to Phoenix this morning. He said he killed you. He shot you in your bed." Rutherford was pleading with himself, unable to believe what he was seeing.

"When he burst into the room, old Phoenix started blazing away immediately. Gave me plenty of time to aim carefully. I got him in the shoulder and the back of the knee from the closet where I was standing. Forty-four-caliber bullets are pretty effective. He spoke to you from the hospital. The Feds had him pumped up on some pretty potent drugs. He was willing to say whatever we wanted him to say."

"But how did you know Phoenix was coming?" Winthrop put the champagne glass down on the linen tablecloth. "Alexis turned on me! I knew she would!"

Falcon shook his head. "No, Granville, she was true to you right up until Phoenix put the bullet through her head. I knew you had discovered the safe-deposit box because I had left an alarm device in the box. A tiny chip. My end went off at eleven o'clock Thursday morning. Alexis started getting all kinds of phone calls right after that. I have to admit, I didn't sleep much Thursday or Friday night. I was awake when she got out of bed. But even if I hadn't been, the security system of the house would have awakened me. She had to turn it off to let Phoenix in. She knew how to turn it off because I showed her. But she didn't know how to turn it off *and* disengage the small alarm to the bedroom. I never told her about the bedroom alarm. And she never asked, God rest her soul." Falcon glanced around. "I knew why she was getting out of bed."

Falcon stared into Granville's eyes. Winthrop's expression was one of stone-faced defiance. "Why did you do it to me, Granville? Why did you put the bug in the software at MD Link? Why did you keep me away from any other jobs on the Street? Why did you make certain I got the job at NASO? Why did you want to see me go down so badly?"

Winthrop's face did not change and he did not speak.

Falcon stared at the older man. There was much more he wanted to say, much more he wanted to know. This man had been a father to him. But Winthrop's silence would not be broken. Finally, Falcon turned slowly away. "I'm finished!" He yelled the words at the door.

And the authorities began to pour into the room.

As they did, Falcon turned back toward Winthrop. "It's the final sanction, Granville. The final sanction . . ."

36

Cassandra Stone gazed out over San Francisco Bay. The sun was low in the evening sky over the Pacific, and the fading light cast eerie shadows on the water. A frigid gust of wind kicked up from the waves below, lapping at the base of the pier. Cassandra pulled the wool coat tightly around her neck and shivered. She took a deep breath. She had been in hiding here with her aunt since talking her way out of Bailey Henderson's office with the Rutherford story. She had been able to make it out of the office and into the street as he tried to call Winthrop. She had escaped. But she could never go back to the *Chronicle.* That would have been suicide.

Falcon had sent her a million dollars as payment for help in bringing the Sevens to justice. And now that they were behind bars, she could relax and begin to look for a job.

The silver safe-deposit box key lay in the palm of her right hand. Cassandra pondered its significance for several minutes. It was the only tangible memory that remained. Slowly, she leaned over the wrought-iron fence and allowed the key to slip from her hand. It splashed lightly into the icy harbor waters, hung near the surface for a second, then disappeared from sight as it tumbled to the murky bottom.

* * *

They walked slowly across the white sands of Grand Cayman. More than once Jenny attempted to take Falcon's hand. He would allow it for a few moments and then pull it away to brush back the hair from his eyes or adjust his bathing suit. And he would not give it back to her when he had finished the chore. It wasn't that he didn't love her. It was simply his personality, and she accepted that.

The surf swirled gently about their ankles as they splashed through the water. Falcon stretched. The sun felt incredibly good on his body, and the hangover was beginning to wear off. They would stay here for a while. Six months, maybe more. It would be his rehabilitation. And then he would put the nine million to work. He glanced at Jenny's body through his sunglasses. She was naked except for the thong. Well, maybe they'd stay here for a year. Then he would start working.

Jenny ran ahead and bent down to pick up a particularly beautiful shell. She had been true to him throughout. She had given Rutherford little bites of information. Bites of disinformation. It was Alexis who had been setting him up the entire time.

Jenny ran back to him and tugged at his hand. "Andrew, I have one question I've been wanting to ask you."

"Mmm."

"What if they hadn't come for you in Vermont?"

"What are you talking about?" Falcon kicked at a shell with his toe.

"What if Winthrop hadn't looked for the files? What if he had let you be a Seven for the rest of your life? What would you have done? Would you have lived that way?"

"It's a moot point. I knew he would come after me as soon as he could."

"But what if?"

"I don't like 'what if' games."

"Come on, Andrew. For me. Just for me . . ."

Falcon stopped, turned toward Jenny, and put his hands on her shoulders. He kissed her gently on the forehead, then pulled her against his chest. "Someday, when we're old and gray, I'll talk to you about it." He stared down at her face for a long time. Finally, he spoke again. "Did I ever tell you that my mother died when I was very young too? As your mother did. It's one more thing we've got in common."

Jenny smiled at him. She did not answer his question directly. "You've got lots you want to tell me, don't you, Andrew?"

"And just how do you know that, Jennifer?" He smiled back at her.

"I can see it in those beautiful eyes of yours."

Falcon's gaze moved to the turquoise water, which stretched to the horizon. It was over. Somehow he wished it didn't have to be.

ACKNOWLEDGMENTS

As with most projects in life, *The Takeover* was a team effort. So—special thanks are due to . . .

My literary agent and good friend, Cynthia Manson. Her commitment to the book and guidance during the entire process were invaluable. I am very fortunate that she chose to take on this project.

My editor at Dutton, Peter Borland, who is nothing short of a manuscript surgeon. I don't mind saying that you are reading many of his words too. I hope we have many more of these together.

My partner in crime and the chairman of my pre-submission editing committee, Stephen Watson. His suggestions and support were extremely important.

My film agents, Richard Green and Howard Sanders at Pleshette, Green & Sanders. The Paramount deal still amazes me.

Mace Neufeld, Bob Rehme, and Albert Beveridge at Neufeld/Rehme Productions.

Horst Fuellenkemper, John Paul Garber, Roland Chalons-Browne, and August Kumbier for their support.

Others I want to thank: At Dutton—Elaine Koster, Peter Schneider, Lisa Johnson, John Paine, Sara Bixler, and Jane Leet. Elsewhere—Gerry Barton, Giff Breed, Gordon Eadon, Kevin

Erdman, Barbara Fertig, Walter Frey, Jim and Anmarie Galowski, Susan Hancock, Judy Hansen, David Jones, and Jim O'Connor at Aubrey Lanston; Mike Lynch, Patrick Lynch, Kheil McIntyre, and Ray Murray at Paramount Pictures; Rick Slocum, the Sonnhalters, Rick Stoddard, Bob Sroka, Stewart Whitman, and Bob Wieczorek.

READ MORE IN PENGUIN

In every corner of the world, on every subject under the sun, Penguin represents quality and variety – the very best in publishing today.

For complete information about books available from Penguin – including Puffins, Penguin Classics and Arkana – and how to order them, write to us at the appropriate address below. Please note that for copyright reasons the selection of books varies from country to country.

In the United Kingdom: Please write to *Dept. EP, Penguin Books Ltd, Bath Road, Harmondsworth, West Drayton, Middlesex UB7 ODA*

In the United States: Please write to *Consumer Sales, Penguin USA, P.O. Box 999, Dept. 17109, Bergenfield, New Jersey 07621-0120.* VISA and MasterCard holders call 1-800-253-6476 to order Penguin titles

In Canada: Please write to *Penguin Books Canada Ltd, 10 Alcorn Avenue, Suite 300, Toronto, Ontario M4V 3B2*

In Australia: Please write to *Penguin Books Australia Ltd, P.O. Box 257, Ringwood, Victoria 3134*

In New Zealand: Please write to *Penguin Books (NZ) Ltd, Private Bag 102902, North Shore Mail Centre, Auckland 10*

In India: Please write to *Penguin Books India Pvt Ltd, 706 Eros Apartments, 56 Nehru Place, New Delhi 110 019*

In the Netherlands: Please write to *Penguin Books Netherlands bv, Postbus 3507, NL-1001 AH Amsterdam*

In Germany: Please write to *Penguin Books Deutschland GmbH, Metzlerstrasse 26, 60594 Frankfurt am Main*

In Spain: Please write to *Penguin Books S. A., Bravo Murillo 19, 1° B, 28015 Madrid*

In Italy: Please write to *Penguin Italia s.r.l., Via Felice Casati 20, I–20124 Milano*

In France: Please write to *Penguin France S. A., 17 rue Lejeune, F–31000 Toulouse*

In Japan: Please write to *Penguin Books Japan, Ishikiribashi Building, 2–5–4, Suido, Bunkyo-ku, Tokyo 112*

In Greece: Please write to *Penguin Hellas Ltd, Dimocritou 3, GR–106 71 Athens*

In South Africa: Please write to *Longman Penguin Southern Africa (Pty) Ltd, Private Bag X08, Bertsham 2013*

READ MORE IN PENGUIN

A CHOICE OF BESTSELLERS

Therapy David Lodge

A successful sitcom writer with plenty of money, a stable marriage, a platonic mistress and a flash car, Laurence 'Tubby' Passmore has more reason than most to be happy. Why is it, then, that nothing can cure his puzzling knee pain or his inexplicable mid-life angst? 'A real treat. It's a Bumper Book or Hit Parade of all his comic devices' – *Observer*

Riding the Rap Elmore Leonard

'The low-life portraiture remains unimpeachable. Bobby Deo, one-time bounty hunter, part-time gardener, full-time psycho, is as nasty as anything Leonard has dreamed up' – *Daily Telegraph.* 'A great read ... his underworld remains a bizarre but strangely accurate funhouse-mirror of America-at-large' – *Sunday Times*

No Night is Too Long Barbara Vine

Tim Cornish, a creative-writing student, sits composing a confession: an admission of a crime committed two years ago that has yet to be discovered. 'Storytelling of the highest order, with a narrative that grips like the *Ancient Mariner*' – *Literary Review*

The Paperboy Pete Dexter

'Dexter's characters come and go like phantoms from a Hitchcock movie ... he writes about huge themes and hardly misses a beat ... his characters all come complete with pasts and futures – fully realized, almost touchable creations' – *Time Out*

Pig Andrew Cowan
Winner of the *Sunday Times* Young Writer of the Year Award

'A first novel of extraordinary poise and accomplishment, treating a boy's coming of age amid the squalid realities of the new British underclass with a delicacy and lyricism which is both gripping and moving' – Michael Dibdin. 'A wholly satisfying book, quietly beautiful and inescapably ominous' – *Observer*

READ MORE IN PENGUIN

A CHOICE OF BESTSELLERS

The Secret History Donna Tartt

'*The Secret History* tells the story of a group of classics students at an élite American college, who are cerebral, obsessive and finally murderous . . . it is a haunting, compelling and brilliant piece of fiction' – *The Times*

What a Carve Up! Jonathan Coe

'Coe's novel arraigns a whole gaggle of gargoyles, and delivers a comeuppance with pungent brio . . . he has written a book that counts the human cost of the self-help, screw-you philosophy currently at large, but the sound it makes is not of tubs being thumped or hands being wrung – it's the raucous and far more apposite sound of horrid laughter' – *Independent*

Virtual Light William Gibson

'In an alert and often graceful prose, Gibson charts a nightmare landscape with surprising flashes of humour and beauty . . . Cyberpunk doesn't come any more stylish than this' – *Sunday Telegraph*. 'Sheer inventive zest' – *Independent on Sunday*

All Our Yesterdays Robert B. Parker

In the 1920s Conn Sheridan was betrayed. He never forgot – and he was never able to forgive. Years later, in another country, he was able to exact his revenge: a revenge that would affect two families, their children, their grandchildren, and the entire political health of the city of Boston. And now, in the 1990s, those sins of yesterday are about to be paid for . . .

The Destiny of Nathalie 'X' William Boyd

'In the title story of his bracing and sometimes stunning collection Boyd writes, exquisitely, the most quixotic exposé of Tinseltown I have read since Scott Fitzgerald's *The Last Tycoon*. It is a fairytale infused with the brimstone of truth' – *Scotland on Sunday*. 'A master of fantasy, farce and irony' – *Sunday Express*

READ MORE IN PENGUIN

A CHOICE OF BESTSELLERS

Brightness Falls Jay McInerney

'The story of a disintegrating marriage set in New York in the frenzied few months leading up to the Wall Street crash of 1987. It is his biggest, most ambitious novel yet – a sort of *Bonfire of the Vanities* with the added advantage of believable, likeable characters' – *Independent on Sunday*

The Burden of Proof Scott Turow

One afternoon in late March Sandy Stern, the brilliant, quixotic defence lawyer in *Presumed Innocent*, returns home to find his wife Clara dead in the garage. 'Rarely has a plot as political, as sexual, as criminal, as moral, so lip-smackingly thickened ... A wonderful read from tight start to taut end' – *Mail on Sunday*

The Russian Girl Kingsley Amis

'Dazzling skill with dialogue and ... no less dazzling ability to conjure up minor characters – policemen, academics, businessmen, Russian émigrés – who, for all their hilarious oddity, somehow remain believable' – *Evening Standard*

The Children of Men P. D. James

The year is 2021. For twenty-five years no child has been born. Nor will there be any more children for infertility has spread like a plague and the human race faces extinction. 'The central images haunt the mind terrifyingly ... It has extraordinary power and visionary passion' – *Observer*

Pronto Elmore Leonard

'The American crime master moves to Italy and stays on top of his form in a cracking tale of small-time criminals' – *Independent*. 'Elmore Leonard keeps you holding your breath as usual, and your heart pounding' – Alec Guinness